NUMEROLOGY FOR THE NEW AGE

PREVIOUSLY BY THE AUTHOR

The Tarot and Transformation

Written as his Master's Thesis for a degree in psychology, this stimulating book has opened a whole new approach to the Tarot and its symbolical guidelines on the Path toward Cosmic Consciousness. A popular companion to the sincere student searching for esoteric direction to his or her life. The author has blended current psychological systems with time-honored traditional esoteric teachings. Guidelines are given to upright and reversed interpretations for both exoteric and esoteric guidance.

FORTHCOMING BY THE AUTHOR

Synergy Session©

Now in preparation and scheduled for completion in late 1979 or 1980. The author has developed a new holistic system of counseling/healing by blending his academic expertise and vast experience in various phases of metaphysical and natural healing.

This intense session synthesizes skills from various systems of psychology, along with metaphysical concepts of self-healing. Work is conducted on all levels using facets of kinesiology, acupressure, meridian therapy, aura cleansing, alignment of the etheric meridians, and chakra attunement, to effectively harmonize the physical anatomy with the esoteric anatomy. These techniques, along with the application of the laws of self-forgiveness and the acceptance of Grace, exorcism (when appropriate), and a non-hypnotic prenatal regression (if needed), have created an intense healing session that allows participants to recognize and begin to eliminate deep-seated blocks on all levels throughout the physical, etheric, emotional (astral), and mental consciousness.

NOTE: This volume is not expected to be complete until late 1979 or early 1980.

Numerology
for the
New Age

by Lynn M. Buess

Cover Design by David Stoddard
Illustrations by David & Shari Stoddard

DeVorss & Company
P.O. Box 550
Marina del Rey, Calif. 90291

ISBN: 0-87516-265-7
Library of Congress Catalog Card Number: 78-067442

Printed in the United States of America
by Book Graphics, Inc.

TABLE OF CONTENTS

Dedicated to Students and Teachers
of the LIGHT.

ACKNOWLEDGMENTS

Primary appreciation must be given to my wife, Louise, who has spent countless hours typing, editing, and critiquing the early rough drafts for this volume. I am also most appreciative toward a friend and academic colleague, Gregory B. Simmons, Instructor of English and Communications at Green River College, Auburn, Washington. His structural, technical, and grammatical editing has been crucial in allowing the author's original ideas and views to be clearly expressed. Many thanks to David and Shari Stoddard of Atlanta for their excellent professional illustrations and Dave's cover design. Thanks to Sydna Terman of Atlanta for her finishing touch with the proofreading of the final drafts. I must also give special thanks to my mother for her final typing and personal encouragement. Finally, to my son, Kwynn, whose untimely interruptions during my writing brought humorous moments and relief of tension despite the minor irritations a four-year-old can create.

PREFACE

Early in the 70's, my interest in Tarot study led me to seek out the esoteric and spiritual facets of its symbolism. It was then nearly impossible to find literature which gave adequate attention, in today's language, to the deeper wisdom.

Realization of that gap prompted my first book, *The Tarot and Transformation*. Its focus is upon the path toward higher consciousness as revealed by the Tarot symbolism, written in modern style for today's reader. *The Tarot and Transformation* was accepted as my Master's Thesis for a psychology degree at West Georgia College. The thesis was then published in paperback, and it has since been circulated and recognized nationally in its field.

A perusal of numerology literature in early 1977 was strikingly similar to my earlier experience with Tarot literature. I found an almost total lack of contemporary attention to the experiential facets of mankind's unfoldment as revealed by numbers. The available flood of literature on numerology virtually ignores the cosmological, metaphysical, and experiential attributes of numerology in daily life. I am speaking of numerical symbology as it concentrates on the flow of consciousness—human and divine. This volume is written in an effort to fill that gap. The value of my effort, in strength and durability, is for each of you to judge for yourself. Each reader stands also as a critic, saying how well this work serves his need.

I am indebted to the excellent work of Florence Campbell. Her book, *Your Days are Numbered*—still both important and useful—initiated and inspired my own studies in numerology. Much of what is currently available is no more than reworded or diluted phrasings of her insights and system.

Another significant book is Juno Jordan's *Numerology: The Romance In Your Name.* Certainly there are many new and old numerology texts, and I do not intend to diminish the contribution of any. However, these two stand above the rest as basic sources. Each author offers original material in unique style. Readers are encouraged to seek out the value in each system; mere differences in style should not present confusion. It is by blending insights from the diverse sources that you will build your own style of interpretation.

The intent in this volume is to avoid the blandly repetitious descriptions and interpretations for the numbers in so much of the current literature. Instead, I write from my years of experience and the thousands of readings I have conducted, working within a self-evolving framework.

Humanity is experiencing a very rapid awakening in this transition from the Piscean Age to the New Age of Aquarius. Part of this awakening involves our preparation, or adjustment, for living in the consciousness of the New Age.

Millions of incarnate human beings on this Earth are working, consciously or subconsciously, on their Self, anticipating the coming events in evolution. Many are working to master and integrate personality. Others are awakening to soul awareness; they strive to bring soul and personality into full, cooperative expression. This book is written specifically to assist those rapidly awakening seekers of light.

This admittedly personal perspective interweaves ideas from various esoteric scholars and teachings. In that we are all in constant evolution and self-growth, some of this material may have immediate application and some may not. Hopefully, there will be much new information for your integration and insight. Use that which your heart and soul recognize as useful; set aside that which may not apply at the moment.

This book is a reflection of my perspective in July of 1977. I foresee the need to constantly revise and expand my viewpoint and realize, therefore, that some of the material will become outdated even in my own consciousness. I also realize that material which is of the Truth will speak through all time.

All of what is written here is given in sincere anticipation of assisting you on your voyage of consciousness. May the Light be with you in your study of this work, and may Truth touch and inspire your Soul in the quest for Self-discovery through numbers.

I

CONDENSED HISTORY

Numerology is a science of symbol, cycle, and vibration. Today's scientists and technologists are paying ever increasing attention to the use of vibrations and frequencies. The advent of electricity introduced whole new applications of working with natural cycles. Radio, television, x-rays, and sub-atomic cycles, are some facets of modern technology which have opened the door to greater study and application of the principles of cyclical oscillations. Physicists have learned that materials previously defined as inert, also have their own identity, which is established by their rate of vibration or frequency. New knowledge of the bio-rhythm cycles has made the public more knowledgeable about just how important it is to be aware of the cyclical patterns in our daily life.

Numerology provides a means of understanding cyclical patterns or qualities related specifically to each of us in our personal life. By understanding one's own particular rhythm, it becomes easier to flow with life and become the master of fate, rather than a victim of destiny's circumstances. The application of numerology is valuable right now in our life even though its historical roots originate in remote antiquity.

The history of numerology is discreetly secreted among the annals of time. Modern historians suggest our system is derived basically from the ancient Hindu teachings. The author's belief is that numerology dates for certain back to the Atlantean era, and most likely back to the Lemurian civilization as well.

1

For purposes of identification with recorded history, let us recognize its first known application in the ancient Hindu culture. Modern numerology, in its evolution, was also influenced by the Arabic system. Yet another important branch is in the tradition and symbolism of the Kabbalah. It is known that the Egyptians, Sumerians, Chinese, and Phoenicians used written numbers. Within the esoteric traditions of these cultures is a wealth of yet unrecovered wisdom based upon the arcane teachings of their numerical traditions. The Bible is richly laden with symbolism based upon pure numerological structure.

The individual most responsible for influencing the method of numbers in use today was Pythagoras, a Greek philosopher born between approximately 600 and 590 BC. Pythagoras founded a school where the instruction of mathematics, music, astronomy, and philosophy was conducted along with the esoteric wisdoms. He taught the law of relationship between man and the divine laws reflected in the mathematics of numbers. Upon his philosophical strength, the science of numbers as it is today, has been established.

This volume is written with emphasis upon the Pythagorean method. In the ever expanding field of numerology, there is a select group of students with backgrounds in higher mathematics, who are developing theories using the most advanced academic knowledge and mathematical techniques. Future advances in the field will come from these researchers. The numerology herein is based upon simple addition and works with the single digit numbers (except in the case of master numbers). Many new descriptive methods are included.

Our own vibration or cyclical patterns are numerologically determined by our date of birth and given name. By understanding these cycles we can learn to more effectively express our potential, human and divine. This volume concentrates more upon the experiential value of numerology, than the historical. Hence, there has been a relatively brief history presented. If you are interested in the details of its history, other authors have given more attention to developments and personalities in the field. The focus throughout this volume is using numbers to benefit your life right now.

As mankind approaches the awakening of the Aquarian Age consciousness, with its revelation of our Divine origin and relation to the Cosmos, it becomes increasingly important for teachers of the symbolical sciences to emphasize man's relationship to his Creator and to the Divine Laws of Manifestation. Keeping this in mind, the author will present first the cosmology of numbers, followed by the descent and ascent of the Divine Self portrayed through the symbolism of numbers. Finally we will examine the application of numerical guidance for your current lifetime on this physical plane of material existence.

II

THE COSMOLOGY OF NUMEROLOGY*

Let us start at that point in pre-existence which is often described metaphysically as the "unmanifest." The unmanifest represents a state of being wherein all of consciousness is in a state of equilibrium, and we might say homeostasis. Within this condition is the potential for all duality and manifestation (or creation); yet, since it is pure balance, there is no interplay of dualism or sentience as in the manifest state.

Because we, as living beings, are of the manifest it is impossible to completely fathom the essence of the unmanifest. We are able to intuit this essence to some extent. However, being a part of the manifest phase, men refer to the unmanifest as a void, or silence. Perhaps an approximate analogy to this comes from the concept in physics called "ground state," a sort of void or vacuum in atomic interplay.

As part of manifestation, we can at best limit the nature of the unmanifest through attempts at description. The safest statement perhaps is to say that IT IS.

As mentioned, there is within the unmanifest, the potential for duality, expression, or creation. We might describe this potential in terms of an abstract movement. We might also describe this abstract movement as a desire.

*The contents of this chapter are heavily influenced by the writings of Dion Fortune, *The Cosmic Doctrine*. It is highly recommended that students intrigued by this chapter, further study her material which she channeled from the inner planes in 1923 and 1924.

This desire for movement within the existence of the un-manifest eventually topples the homeostasis, and we have the beginning of creation or manifestation.

At this point the symbolism of numerology begins to share its depth of meaning, serving as a guidepost to cosmic event. The primal number, ONE, is inclusive of the all and all. Within the prime ONE is potential, yet unexpressed, of all that is to become. It is timeless, yet all of time exists within. It undergoes no change, yet it is not changeless. It simply IS.

With first movement comes sentience and the primal duality, the number TWO. TWO brings creation or manifestation, and this primal duality is the understructure to all later dualisms we experience in life—such as day/night, man/woman, good/evil, for example.

At this point ONE is unmanifest; TWO is the manifestation. Even though potential is now exercised, the events of the manifest existence resonate upon the homeostatic foundation of the unmanifest. Therefore, experience never occurs totally detached from the inclusiveness of the ONE.

Let us now pursue the progression of unfoldment in the creation. We spoke of the first movement, described metaphorically as thrusting forth from the center of being. The term given to this activity is the Ring Cosmos. A second desire—namely, for return to the unmanifest, acts as a check upon the first movement, thus creating curvature in the movement and underscoring the absence of straight lines in the Cosmos. So the Ring Cosmos returns, after eons, to a point whence it started, to form a spinning ring.

The flow of the spinning ring (of the Ring Cosmos) forms a secondary spinning current forming in opposition and at a right angle to the Ring Cosmos. This new secondary current is known as the Ring Chaos. The two rings interact and interplay over eons. The attraction and repulsion between the positive and negative polarities gives rise to a third spinning ring, which is called the Ring Pass-Not. (See Figure I).

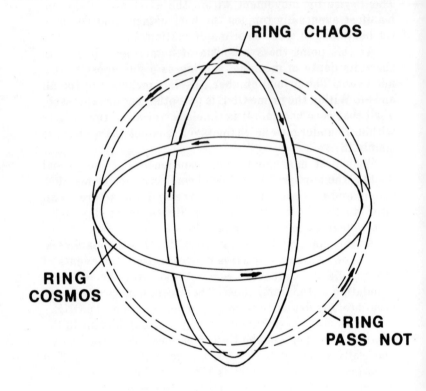

Figure 1

The Ring Cosmos carries the first impulse of manifest expression; its movement is evolutionary; and its force tends toward the center of emerging awareness. The Ring Chaos acts as resistance to evolution, thereby assisting in the building of consciousness. Its tendency is to return toward outer space (the unmanifest). The Ring Pass-Not acts as a stabilizer between these two divergent forces and defines the outer limit of creation, which is infinity.

By producing a thrust-block or an opposition to the Ring Cosmos, the Ring Chaos helps create a stability. This stability allows a raising of pressure which enables concentration to be established. The environment of concentrated, or focused, attention provides a foundation for awareness and evolution. If this tension did not exist, the cycles of the Ring Cosmos would repeat endlessly, and there would be no opportunity for elaboration or originality in manifestation.

The triune dynamics of the three primary rings represent an attempt (metaphorically and symbolically) to convey the primal attributes of the Absolute or Supreme Being. The three facets of the Supreme Being constitutes a Primal Trinity, the three in one and the one in three. We see a partial reflection of this primal trinity in the symbolic structure of major religions. In the Egyptian lore there was Isis, Osiris, and Horus; in the Hindu faith, Brahma, Shiva, and Vishnu; and in the Judeo-Christian tradition, the Father, Son, and Holy Spirit.

Another way of conveying the dynamics of the Rings Cosmos, Chaos, and Pass-Not (attributes of the Supreme Being) is to display them in a trinity as diagrammed below:

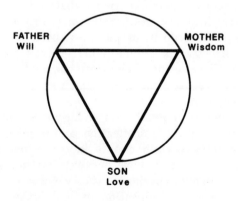

Figure 2

The circle represents the infinite domain of the Absolute. The triangle represents the threefold nature of this one creator. The Father or male polarity (yang) is expressed through the dynamics of Divine Will. The Mother or female polarity (yin) is the factor seeking wisdom. And, finally, the third is the Son (son-daughter) which is the balancing (tao) and cooperation of the two dualistic energies in the harmony and unity of Love.

The Will factor emerges from the center of Being; as an expression of Divine Will, or desire, it reaches out to initiate elaboration of consciousness. The receptive or Wisdom quality seeks to absorb the benefit of experience in the manifest existence. The condition of reciprocation and oscillation between the facets of Divinity allows for a point of reflection or awareness to emerge. The two energies reunite and resonate in harmony, through the third quality of Love, having the added perspective of insight received through experience. In a sense, even the Creator is constantly adding to and improving upon the Creation.

This concept becomes more easily comprehensible if we step out of the realm of cosmic events to consider these three patterns in our daily experience as human beings. The human will seeks to gain experience that adds to our evolving understanding of ourself. Sometimes in the pursuit of experience we overdo it, or pursue experience which opposes the directive of Divine Will received through our Higher Self. The overindulgence into one particular experiential pattern creates imbalance which we might describe as "sins of commission."

At the other extreme, the search for wisdom puts us into many situations of study, reflection, and intellectual indulgence concerning certain events in our experience. Too much emphasis upon analysis prevents further growth of will from additional experience. Thus we create a condition of limitation and crystallization in consciousness, or are caught in "sins of omission" (that which has not been experienced).

When we learn to balance in the synergic love consciousness, there is established a flow of moving into each
experience — absorbing the needed lesson into the soul —
then letting go of that experience in order for yet others
to unfold. Throughout the book, we will recognize this simple dynamics in numerical study and life experience — too
much, too little, and balance.

Now — back to the cosmos where the three rings: Cosmos, Chaos, and Pass-Not, continue in a path — each operates
in rhythmic pattern on a flat plane; each rotates something
like the earth on its axis. Note that the dual motions of the
rings create a spherical appearance.

At that point in the center of the sphere where the three
become synthesized, their movements give rise to a series
of revolving radii — the Rays. The Rays move outward in
revolving spirals to the Ring-Pass-Not and return along the
unmanifest opposite Ray quality. The twelve Ray energies
reflect qualities of the Absolute in a new format.

We might think of these as a Primal or Archetypal
Zodiac, a reflection of which we see in our own night sky.
The point where the Rays converge is known metaphysical-
ly as the Central Sun.

The converging activity of the Ray gives rise to a secondary movement which expands into concentric circles.
These circles settle into the seven cosmic planes. The activity of the cosmic planes and Rays constitutes the Cosmos.
The Cosmos is generated from, but remains outside the
Absolute. The Absolute, with its cycles, becomes the subconscious of the Cosmos. Relative to the Cosmos, it is unmanifest.

The Rays are revolving spirals traversing the cosmic
planes. As previously mentioned, they work in pairs, moving out on the manifest aspect and returning along the unmanifest portion. The first and twelfth work together; as do
2-11, 3-10, 4-9, 5-8, and 6-7; if we could stretch that
spiral out, we would see that the Ray energy fluctuates
in the mode of a sine wave, $\sim$. The unmanifest portion

THE COSMIC PLANES AND RAYS

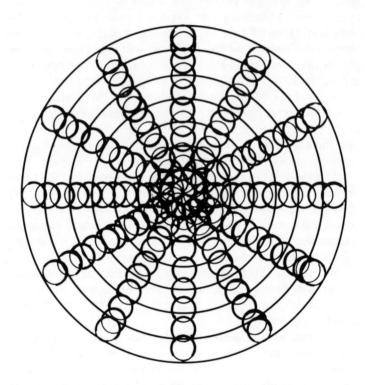

Figure 3

on its return completes a circuit and gives us a cosmic clue to the structural nature of the number four. Within this matrix, the beginning of form takes place (see Figures 4 and 5).

The attraction and tension between the two Ray paths breaks the Cosmos into segments; and within these infinite segments, lines of force originate. The term given to these lines of stress is "tangentials." As the paths of divergent

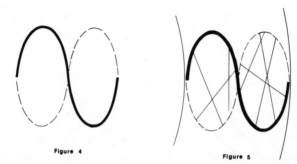

Figure 4

Figure 5

tangentials cross, a vortex is set up by the opposing influences which modifies the action of each. Therefore, a relatively stable composite unit is set up which is influenced by the two factors of itself and to a lesser extent by the greater forces of the Cosmos. This new force is called a "primal atom," a vortex of forces gyrating in tight units rather than circling the limits of the cosmos.

The same laws are at work in the primal atom that started the Ring Cosmos and the Ring Chaos in its building of the Cosmos. The axiom "as above so below, but in another manner" is totally appropriate in this case. With the primal atom, yet another phase in cosmogenesis is initiated: the evolution of individualized consciousness within the Cosmos.

Recognizing that a primal atom consists of two opposing movements which gyrate around one another, it is also important to realize that the vortices formed induce a secondary motion. This secondary motion is the angular path. Some atoms remain in simple form to constitute matter of each cosmic plane. *The reader should note this point as being crucial to an understanding of the simple atoms.* Other atoms, moving in like paths, begin to attract each other in near orbits, similar to the bonding of valences in chemical bonds. These organized structures form composite atoms.

The number of facets or angular paths is related to the nature of primal rhythms upon the cosmic plane formed. On the first cosmic plane the rhythms are reflected from the subconscious and are closest in nature to the Absolute;

Figure 6

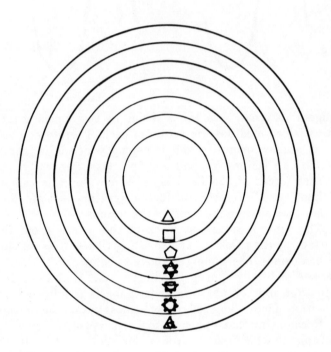

hence, three faceted. On the second cosmic plane, the spinning atoms are four faceted; on the third, they are five sided;
fourth, six sided, and so on.

(The reader is encouraged to underscore and meditate
upon this significance). This is another cosmic clue to the
whole pattern of numerological evolution. One to nine represents the phases of evolution toward attainment of perfection, and then with 10 we start another spiral of evolution
with 1 (one) plus the zero (0) which suggests the embarking
upon another stratum or cycle of vibration. Later we will
more completely realize that through our structure of seven
levels of consciousness, we as humans resonate to each level

and the laws of that level. The study of numbers assists us in recognizing more completely the unseen vibrations in our environment and the application of vibration to master our destiny. (Later in the volume, we will work with the numerological cycles and lessons chosen by the soul for the life cycle).

By understanding, mastering, and balancing the lessons of this lifetime, one is freer to direct attention to the vibrational pattern of the Higher Self. Then he becomes divinely guided and cosmically attuned. These early pages are meant to assist your ascent and attunement to the higher frequencies. It is hoped that this study will make it one step easier to learn the art of pure attunement, so that we may some day drop the symbol as reference, and just EXPERIENCE our complete COSMIC BEING on all levels. One way to reach that attunement is by conscious study and contemplation of symbols which attempt to convey the pure process of Being.

With our goal in mind, we return to the cosmic events of atomic evolution. As the composite atoms attract like atoms, a congregate atom with cosmic weight and mass is formed. Eventually this congregate atom responds to the centrifugal force of the cosmos and embarks upon a journey along the cosmic highways (the Rays) toward the outer reaches of the Cosmos. In its travels the atom attracts simple atoms of the other cosmic planes which create the different levels or bodies of the globe. After circling the various planes (following the spiral Ray paths), it reaches the Ring-Pass-Not and returns along the unmanifest portion while contemplating the experience derived from its traversing of the cosmos. This travelling atom returns to the central stillness for contemplation and alignment to the cosmic design; then it once more responds to centrifugal force and moves out along yet another Ray. This pattern is repeated until each of the Ray paths has been pilgrimaged and the travelling atom returns to rest.

Once all of an infinite number of atoms in this great cycle have completed the circuit of twelve Rays and come to rest, the Cosmos reaches "cosmic night." During the cosmic days the cycles of inhalation and exhalation of the grand breath set the pulse. On the outer breath the Ring Chaos predominates, and movement of the atoms and Ray energies speeds the progression of awareness outward to expand experience. Then the Ring Cosmos predominates and the tide turns inward, bringing the atoms back toward the center on their evolutionary journey. At the close of the Cosmic day—after the exact cosmic cycle is completed—all of the cosmic systems are drawn back into the central stillness and come to rest. The experiencing atoms and Ray energies are realigned to the homeostatic equilibrium of the Absolute. All factors are absorbed into the Being of the Absolute and stamped with Divine alignment: "and God saw that it was good." So the unmanifest harmony of the cosmic night prevails.

The potential for manifestation of another cosmic day is within this state of rest. The potential comes from the abstract movement left over from the atomic dance of the cosmic day. Even though the matter of the atomic structure was shed, returning into the central stillness, the abstract movement of the atomic pattern continues. Eventually this desire for movement overcomes the balance and the cosmos awakens into another day. The same cosmic cycles of the Rays, circles, and atoms, repeat their prior activities as the new day proceeds.

One significant alteration emerges in this second cycle. The travelling atoms from the first cycle which completed the entire circuit of Rays once again begin to respond to the centrifugal pulses and move outward. This time, however, the Ray pathways are cluttered, obstructed by the newly developing atoms of the second grand cycle. Therefore, these previous cycle atoms advance along the Ray paths to the appropriate cosmic plane, depending upon the facets of the primal atom and mass thereof. Upon reaching the appropriate plane, these atoms gravitate into orbit around the central sun. The name given to these newly orbiting globes is "great organisms."

The great organisms are like lesser deities whose fundamental structure reproduces, in lesser degree, that of the Absolute. Their very nature is derived from, but now of another order from, the Circles and Rays of the cosmos. With a capacity to reproduce, the great organisms deliver progeny which do likewise, in their turn. This stellar evolution inhabits the cosmos with an infinite number of organisms.

The great organisms generate their own cyclical pattern of expansion and contraction; this self-generated rhythm eventually vibrates and interacts with the cosmic rhythms which are congruent with the subtle cycles of the Absolute. The tension and interaction of these intermingling forces activate Self-awareness or Self-consciousness of the great organisms.

The term used to describe the awakened Being is "great entity." Another term, perhaps more familiar to readers and becoming synonymous with great entity, is solar logos. We are discussing the origin of stars in the cosmos; not just seventh plane physical globes as we perceive through our eyes, but a deific solar being with primal atom and attendant vehicles of the cosmic planes.

Having attained self-consciousness, the Great entity then projects a thought form of itself into a portion of the cosmos. In doing so, the great entity becomes a lesser creator in its own right. Remember that the consciousness of the great entity is derived from cosmic law, which is subconsciously reflective of Absolute Law. Because the great entity possesses the memory and capacity of creation, it commences a building program of its own. The great entity taps the various Ray qualities and acts like a transformer, by reducing the Rays into sub-rays and projecting them forth to establish a lesser zodiac, like unto the Greater Zodiac of the Cosmos. The converging sub-rays spin off a secondary motion, giving rise to sub-planes of being which are reflections of the cosmic planes.

The term given to the organized portion of Cosmos over which the great entity has influence is a universe. This is to distinguish it from the cosmos, although it is still a part of that greater body of creation. We might associate it more readily as a solar system. The great entity is the Creator and sustainer of its universe. It is omnipotent and infinite to everything of the universe because without its sustaining thought form nothing in the universe would exist.

Great entities exist on all of the cosmic planes. We will concern ourselves with one on the seventh cosmic plane; specifically, our sun or solar logos.

The atomic evolution in the universe closely resembles evolution in the cosmos — with some distinct differences. Travelling atoms of the universe experience all the twelve sub-rays and finally return to the center. Here it is important to remember an abstract movement exists along with the moving object (the atom). The atom is a product of the universe, but the abstract movement is stimulated by the latent cosmic cycles and events. As the traveling atom of the universe returns to the center, it encounters a circumstance where the unmanifest (in this case cosmic cycles) wells up and leaves an imprint upon the atom and the abstract movement which is the track it leaves in space.

Thereafter the travelling atom still responds to the laws of the solar logos of which it is a part; the abstract track is left with an imprint of the cosmos and a distinct impression of a greater destiny. The imprinted track is divine spark. There will be more about the role of the divine sparks later.

This is an excellent point for another insight into the cosmic and universal panorama that has been quickly reviewed. When we study human consciousness, three levels are distinguished for clarification. These three levels are the Higher Self, Soul, and Lower Self or personality. We see an analogy in celestial design. The great entity is equated to the soul. It is a being in a phase of self-growth and evolution; it receives guidance through its Higher Self, the cosmos. The great entity works to organize its personality (the universe) into an orderly environment reflecting the original concept of self.

The Higher Self represents a stratum or portion of a being which has become settled in its harmony with Divine Law. The personality is a stratum of potential reactions generated with the addition of consciousness (in this case the universe). The central self (soul or great entity) is the trainee guided from one stratum that knows and recognizes Truth; then it applies higher principle through growing self-awareness until the inner self is mastered and brought into harmonious phasing with All of Being.

The inhabitants of the universe that the solar logos works with in its evolution include the planets and the populations that develop thereupon. Also included in the universal populace is the member of the angelic or Devic Kingdom. The author does not intend to describe this kingdom. A study of Kabbalistic symbolism by esoteric cosmologists such as Heindel, Steiner, or Blavatsky should be of assistance to those desiring detailed examination of the Devic realm.

Briefly, there are cosmic, systemic, and planetary hierarchies of the angelic kingdom which serve primarily as the servants and executors of the Law.

The divine sparks are responsible for the preparation and expression of life forms in the universe. There are three primary waves of divine sparks that manifest as part of the threefold nature of the Solar Logos. The first wave expresses the Fohatic energy from the will of the solar logos. They move down through the universal planes and set up an archetypal galvanic stress pattern of globes that will serve as molds to the planetary bodies. The second wave expresses the pranic energy and builds the planetary form or body on each plane. The third wave carries the creative potential of the kundalini energy. They have some spare time while waiting for the previous waves of sparks to complete their chores. The extra time allows for some individualization of these third wave sparks to grow.

This individualization process is often referred to as epigenesis, and it is a factor that allows for self-creativity and varied processes of life forms and families to arise. The epigenic factor is later a basis for "free will" in human culture. This free will has allowed for the condition known as evil to unfold on our planet.

During planetary formation, however, even this individualized behavior is completely in compliance with the laws of the solar deity. The three waves working together build the planetary structure and the fourth brings the tide of sparks of humanity. The latter waves of sparks (fifth to seventh) help to build the lower bodies of man's personality (mental — not mind, emotional, physical). The latter waves also help build the differing levels in the lower kingdoms of minerals, plants, and animals.

The fourth waves or sparks of humanity will be discussed extensively in the section on the anthropogeny of numbers.

At first we spoke of prime duality — unmanifest and manifest. Within the scheme of manifestation, we must again review numerical definition. Number one in the manifest represents the Absolute; number two is the cosmos, that is, rays and planes; three is evolution, which starts with the primal atom and later becomes a great entity; four is form, in our case the planet earth; and five is life, in our case the number of man. Learn and know these well.

Admittedly this chapter has been a whirlwind tour through complex and completely transcendental domains. Hopefully, some meaningful questions have been answered for you. If, hopefully, there is merit to this material, many more questions have arisen within your mind and soul. (I certainly do not have all the answers). It is recommended that the study of this book, and particularly this chapter, be accompanied by time spent in meditation. By turning over the deeper probing to your own soul and Higher Self, the door that will take you into the *experience* of these processes, is further opened. If this chapter helps give focus to that probe, my goal is partially attained. As the reader becomes increasingly comfortable with cosmic metaphors and analogies, he or she will appreciate more readily why numbers mean what they do in the day-to-day work of personal interpretation.

ANTHROPOGENY AND NUMBERS
THE HUMAN CYCLE

Earlier in this chapter, we covered cosmic, systemic, and planetary events with clues to numerical significance. We are all responsive, consciously or subconsciously, to the cycles of the cosmos, solar logos, and planetary logos in particular. The earlier discussion was designed to help us to comprehend our relation to these rhythms more clearly.

In this portion, we will examine how numbers symbolically outline the path of human involution and evolution. We are going to shift gears in consciousness and re-examine the meaning and symbology of numbers, with slightly new guidelines and perspectives. The following key interpretations shed light upon some archetypal meaning inherent in the structure of numbers:

> When zero, or the *full circle* is used, it represents the Higher Self or superconscious. It is the capacity to move awareness to a higher plane for perception.
> The *straight line* represents conscious awareness. The vertical line is masculine and assertive in its action. The horizontal is feminine and receptive.
> The *crescent* represents the soul or in some cases the subconscious. It is receptive to information or subtle energies and rebroadcasts them on the conscious level.

With these fundamental keys in mind, we can pursue the anthropogeny of numbers. The fourth wave of divine sparks represents three-faceted atoms poured forth from the body of the solar logos and periodically inspired by cosmic stimulus. They are like virgin spirits with the threefold nature of deity incorporated as their essential dynamics. Yet, despite the simplicity of deity they possess, the sparks lack awakening to full awareness of their divine attributes. To gain this, they start on a voyage of the universe—plunging into the various strata and planes of matter to educate themselves and become masters of their universe. This voyage eventually includes passage through the planes of each of the planets in the solar system. For purposes of this volume, we will concern ourselves with their earthly sojourn.

The sparks descend through the highest spiritual planes, and the Monad or Higher Self becomes self conscious on the third plane down. The sparks then attach themselves to the personality which includes substance from the three lower planes. With the mind as a link between the higher levels and lower levels, the human being begins to build the soul consciousness. Through rebirth and reincarnation into many personalities over time, the soul consciousness evolves under the tutelage of the Higher Self. It employs the vehicles of personality for opportunity to grow in mastery. The soul develops with accumulation of the experiences garnered through embodiment. Through guidance from the divine spark (Higher Self), the soul endeavors to balance excesses and avoidance in experience and bring all events into mastery. This has been a brief outline of the chain; how this chain of events is revealed through numbers follows.

The number one in the human cycle represents the divine spark still at ONE within the embracing realm of the solar logos. Total consciousness prevails and life is in harmony with all beings in the body of god (solar logos—not Absolute).

With the number two, we have the fall of man. Soul awareness begins to awaken, and the consciousness of lower self is in a receptive phase of development. The lower planes here receive the archetypal format that molds the vehicles for use by the soul and higher self.

With three, we see the soul adjusting to awareness of both spirit realm and material realm. Here it seeks a balance to bring spirit and matter together. This phase also is indicative of the division of consciousness into male and female forms. It inspires the seeking of unity and balance by working consciously with a mate to bring forth life and creative expression.

Four reminds us of the threefold consciousness taking on the form of body. Man stands upright now with the germ of his divine self awaiting the trials of earth for unfoldment. The cross epitomizes those trials and sacrifices to come. It is the number of form and earth.

In number five the consciousness of senses and mind reigns over the soul. Five is the number of experience, free will, and lessons to be learned through indulgence in the lower vehicles. It leads to awakening. It is the number of man.

Having encountered multitudes of lifetimes and experiences, the realization grows that maybe there is purpose to life. Man begins to take responsibility for his action; he vaguely seeks higher self (still at the bottom or dormant state). The thrust is now upward.

The number seven represents mastery and balance over the lower levels. The male-female (yang-yin) energies are in a harmonious flow of intuitive receptivity and assertive action. Wisdom is attained and the aspirant now begins to direct attention to higher law.

Counterpoint to seven showing mastery and balance of the earth plane, eight shows the rhythm and balance of eternity. The aspirant here attunes to the law of spirit and executes all the way through his, or her life. Higher law prevails in heaven, and on earth. Eight is authority and brings leadership and divine administration.

Nine is the number of the New Age. It is the Divine man on Earth. The superconscious is now predominant, and its directives flow to Earth. It is attainment and fulfillment of perfection in the earth sojourn.

These are certainly only capsule summaries of the potential in the numbers. The reader is encouraged to spend additional time on inner study and in meditation upon these ideas to best deepen his understanding of these stages in unfoldment.

Another brief sketch may provide more clarity to the searching mind. The flow of the numbers reveals the descent of the divine spark into involvement with matter; with its awakening and ascent or evolution, we move to divine consciousness.

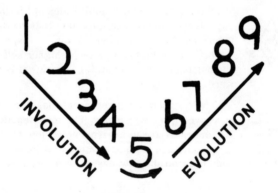

Figure 7

Students have often raised a very significant question at this point in the study. Why move from pure spiritual existence into material existence simply to return to spirit? This crucial question plagued my early years of study. This answer represents the best of my understanding at this point in consciousness — subject to change upon ILLUMINATION!

Our true identity is that of a divine spark. The divine spark issues forth from the body of god and is a three-faceted replica of its creator. The divine spark has awareness of a divine simplicity, but none yet of the universe. It attracts atoms from each level to form an awareness in all seven levels. Through eons and sequential spirals of lives, the personality and soul are finally mastered; the experiences from these attributes of self are impressed upon the divine spark. At the end of the evolutionary spiral on the planet, the divine spark emerges with *divine* consciousness PLUS *self*-consciousness. The divine spark is intimately linked to the travelling atom, so we are a part of that consciousness.

Once the entire circumstances of this planet have been mastered, the cycle is repeated on the other planets until the whole systemic circumstance is completed. Then the developing deity may work with the solar logos for its internship of divine preparation. Perhaps it works with the will activity, then the wisdom, then the love action.

Having graduated from systemic mastery, the lesser deity may work for yet another great entity in another galaxy. Finally, the mission is complete. The travelling atom, having completed all the planes and rays, begins to orbit a greater sun and projects its own thought form into space to become a creator (great entity) in its own right! "Know ye not, that Ye Are Gods"?

My feeling at this time is that the wave of divine sparks today involves millions of the Earth's human population still living in unawakened mass consciousness. Many are on the verge of self-awakening into individualized consciousness of personality, and a few of soul. Other awakened souls

serving as teachers and advanced students of Light are—
in most cases—beings who have come to the Earth from
another planet to contribute certain teachings and complete specific karmic lessons.

By studying the name and birthdate chosen in this lifetime, each of us has a guideline to certain potentials, pitfalls, and opportunities we will encounter. By wise application of this knowledge, growth can be accelerated and
destiny attained with greater ease.

I intend the following chapters to shed more light upon
your search for Self. Our focus will be on numerology to
reach mastery of this particular Earth spiral in your environment.

III

THE VIBRATIONAL ASPECTS OF ONE TO NINE

Our whole world of living is one of responding to vibrational patterns or creating them. These patterns can be discordant or harmonious. Each of the bodies in our seven levels of consciousness works in a specific range of vibration.

Each of the planets, the sun, our Earth, and all its life has its own vibration. Through the interaction, stress, and reconciliation of these various patterns, we evolve.

Each number has its own particular aspects or vibrational characteristics. There are three principal tendencies inherent in each number—the assertive (yang-masculine), the passive (yin-feminine), and the harmonious (equilibrium). An examination of these principal tendencies in numbers follows.

INDIVIDUALITY (Will)

1

Assertive—willful, domineering, selfish, arrogant; puts own needs before others regardless of personal consequences; boastful, impulsive.

Passive—dependency, submissive, fearful of making decisions or taking initiative, stubborn, procrastinating.

Harmonious—strong willed and ambitious with consideration for others, courageous, organizer-leader-pioneer, individual, original thinker.

For the one to find a point of balance between its own extremes, it must learn to resonate with the number two, whose primary lesson is:

COOPERATION (Peace)

2

Assertive — meddling, arbitrary, careless, strident, tactless, extremist, dishonest; overlooks detail, creates divisiveness.

Passive — vacillating, sullen, devious, faultfinding; too much attention to detail with delay in accomplishment; inability to take a stand.

Harmonious — diplomatic, adaptable, able to fuse divergent opinions or groups, rhythmic, gentle; gathers information from both sides of a position before taking a stand.

The two can get caught between other viewpoints and needs, and therefore, to establish balance, must learn to resonate with the number three, whose primary lesson is:

SELF-EXPRESSION (Creativity)

3

Assertive — superficial, extravagent; likes to gossip, has false vanity, wasteful ego attachment to creative gifts, gaudy taste; dislikes the practical.

Passive — lacks concentration; failure to fully develop creative potential; asexual, gloomy, lacks imagination.

Harmonious — gift of speech, creative and artistic, intuitive, joyful, sociable, enthusiastic, tasteful in dress and decorum.

The creative expression of number three may go undeveloped or can take on such an exaggerated spontaneous execution that it is too out of the ordinary for the acceptance of the intended recipients. To balance and properly express the talents, the three needs to resonate with the number four, whose primary quality is:

DISCIPLINE (Work)

4

Assertive — stubborn, sees one way of doing things, intolerant, too serious, brusque, lacks emotional sensitivity, overworks.

Passive — lazy, resists new methods, narrow, must see practicality before accepting ideas, fights intellectualism.

Harmonious — loyal, consistent, patient; fulfills a given task well, sticks to facts; organized, economical, has integrity.

The tendency of four is laziness or too much repetitive activity in one's method of approaching life tasks. "All work and no play makes Johnny dull," so fours need to resonate with the number five, whose primary lesson is:

FREEDOM (Change)

5

Assertive — restless, disregards values, irresponsible, nervous, over-indulgent (particularly with senses); has too many interests, ignores rules and laws.

Passive — fears the new or change, wants a rule for every behavior; sexual confusion, failure to learn from experience, uncertain.

Harmonious — progressive, has diverse talents and friends, is curious, seeks freedom; quick, flexible, adventurous, energetic; enjoys travel.

Fives tend to overindulge in experience, or fear experience and move along too quickly without learning the meaning of the experience. Fives seek perspective and balance from the six:

RESPONSIBILITY (Service)

6

Assertive — over-involvement with others' problems, self-righteousness; is worrisome, domestically dictatorial, prone to arguing, overly coventional, easily upset.

Passive—martyrs himself, resents service, lacks concern for family and home; constant complainer, anxious, carries too many burdens (real or not) on shoulders.

Harmonious—has harmonious home, serves humanity, is unselfish, artistic in taste, conscientious, fair; seeks emotional equilibrium in self and others.

Sixes either take responsibility too seriously or avoid it like a plague. They are often victims of their own emotional imbalance who can best find an antidote to their flaws by seeking the qualities of the seven, primarily:

WISDOM (Detachment)

7

Assertive—severely critical, too analytical, has intellectual conceit and vanity; deceptive, aloof, eccentric, faultfinding.

Passive—skeptical, has inferiority complex, cynical, suppressive, cold; thinks rather than acts; crafty, prone to emotional withdrawal, secretive.

Harmonious—excellent analyst, seeks deeper truths, has technical ability, reaches, has faith; mystical and intuitive if higher mind is tapped; has stoic temperament, is discerning, has poise.

Sevens have a tendency to become overly attached to intellectual viewpoints, or they may fear mind development and new ideas. They must learn to put ideas to practical use through administration and execution with proper use of the eight vibration:

AUTHORITY (Power)

8

Assertive—over-ambitious in order to attain leadership or power; has callous disregard for others, is crassly materialistic, demands recognition, loves display; abusive.

Passive—fears failure, unable to take a leader's role, has poor judgment; scheming, disrespects authority, dishonest in business, has careless regard for money.

Harmonious—has executive ability, respects wealth; successful, good judge of character, confident, administrates with personal consideration for others.

Eights fear or misuse power and money. An unenlightened eight uses others to gain selfish ends and can create much suffering for others. Eights work best to balance their extremes by learning particularly from the nine:

ALTRUISM (Compassion)

9

Assertive—impractical, fickle, over-idealistic, lacks tolerance for others' views, too generous, indiscreet, anarchists at extremes.

Passive—aimless, gullible, easily used by others, depressed, indifferent, pessimistic about the world and the future.

Harmonious—inspired, attuned to New Age concepts, compassionate, generous, gifted artistically; seeks world brotherhood and harmony, is a perfectionist, works to build group consciousness.

Nines can lose themselves in broad ideals and group or universal causes. Their desire is great to let go of self to serve the selfless calls of the New Age. They need to balance the potential loss of self identity through attunement to the vibration of number one—INDIVIDUALITY.

A WORD ABOUT MASTER NUMBERS

Some authors of numerology identify the numbers 11, 22, and 33 as master numbers. From my research and personal experience, I feel that there is a definite added potential and vibration to these numbers.

A frequent mis-association with master numbers is that they are an indication that the person is a master from the planetary leadership of ascended souls (hierarchy) who has incarnated. Or there is a tendency to think of a person with a master number as some awesome leader who holds in consciousness some magical powers and metaphysical mystique. But this is seldom fully true.

It is possible that one or more of the hierarchical souls may choose to incarnate for a special purpose, and their name or date of birth possesses master numbers. By no means can we expect everyone born with these numbers to be such souls.

In most cases, however, the presence of master numbers does suggest an older soul coming into this lifetime to make an important contribution for mankind in a field of a spiritual, scientific, medical, religious, educational, governmental, or technological nature.

Often master numbers indicate an older soul trained in the ancient esoteric schools many lifetimes previous who now returns to manifest or teach particular New Age methods of healing, psychic development, or invention.

In rare instances the presence of master numbers may indicate a dynamic soul who is incarnating this time from another planet or system to fulfill some specific destiny or mission.

Many old, important, and masterful souls have names and birth dates with no master numbers, so we must be careful to keep this whole matter in perspective.

My studies have brought me to the tentative conclusion that no matter where the master number may appear, the higher vibration does not fully unfold until the soul has awakened. In many instances certain gifts manifest through grace; in fact, the individual possessing the gift may not have initiated conscious discipline and study of spiritual law in this lifetime.

Those who have master numbers appearing in their name or birthdate generally are endowed with special tendencies toward leadership and inspiration that set them apart from mass consciousness. Because the numbers are of intensified vibration and potency, those who possess them have a heightened obligation in life, such as greater requirements of self-discipline and purification of consciousness.

Until the needed purification and awakening of soul awareness takes place, the individual operates in the vibrational influence of the two rather than 11; four rather than 22; and six rather than 33.

Tendencies and qualities exhibited by the master numbers follow:

REVELATION

11

Assertive — fanatical, cultic, overzealous, lacks practical realities, attacks dissimilar viewpoints, uses psychic or divine gift for self purpose.

Passive — fails to apply inspiration, over-reacts to criticism, apathetic, fears higher energies and gifts, sensitive to public reaction.

Harmonious — gifted channel or clairvoyant, seeks to express higher consciousness, unites spiritual Truth to material plane; inventive, visionary leader.

Elevens fly high in the clouds and must strive to plant their dreams on terra firma. To effectively convince others and stimulate change in the world, elevens need to study and absorb the quality of the twenty-two:

SACRED STRUCTURALIZATION

22

Assertive — tendency to over-evaluate self importance; exaggerates information, promotes hasty causes, resents lack of recognition, misuses wisdom or power.

Passive — apathetic toward human needs; in extremes, uses heightened awareness for criminal goals or black magic; unable to adapt self to group needs.

Harmonious — integrates higher wisdom into organizational administration, is in control of self and environment, puts universal goal ahead of self pride; a practical mystic.

Twenty-twos become so engrossed in the work of their destiny and mission that they fail to recognize the subtle emotional needs of co-workers. In their labors, they often forget the humane quotient, so they benefit from learning the lesson of the thirty-threes:

UNIVERSAL SERVICE

33

Assertive—forceful in attempts to serve others, intolerant of differing mores and opinions, over-emotional, unable to adjust to needs of others.

Passive—overprotective, rebellious, hides from positions of responsibility, seeks praise, backs down from own position to have harmony.

Harmonious—sympathetic, is a good counselor (often psychic or spiritual), has concern for welfare of masses; a kind of cosmic parent or guardian, creates harmony at home and work.

Thirty-threes in many instances have an ego need to demonstrate just how hard they are working (see 33 life number) to serve others. It creates a grandiose martyr complex when unchecked. They benefit from the idealism of 11, and intellectual practicality of 22, to keep the magnitude of their work in perspective.

IV

WHAT YOU CHOOSE TO RECEIVE FROM LIFE

The most significant interpretations in the natal chart are the birth-date and the breakdown of the name as it was at birth. From the name comes insight into one's character, potentials, weakness of person, and numerous shades of self-evaluation. All of these will be covered in the next chapter. First we will consider the significance of the birth date.

The date of birth is determined by the soul and higher self of the incoming child. Every mother has the experience of knowing that when the child is ready, birth occurs. It is right and proper that the soul does the choosing because the life number indicates the type of circumstance, opportunities, challenges, and destiny that life experience will bring to you for experiential evolution. The life number provides a clue as to what fate has in store. How we will react to life depends upon the numbers in our name, our own free will, and the attitude from our encounters with life events. Proper utilization of numerological guidelines can provide each individual with tools of consciousness. If the tools are handled with skill, each person can better understand himself and life. With understanding comes the foundation upon which effective actions are based; and right action releases us from the wheel of karma and rebirth, furthering the evolution of soul onto higher spirals and planes.

THE LIFE NUMBER

Now it is time to see exactly how the life number is ascertained. The life number is derived from the sum total of the number in the month, the day, and the year of birth which is reduced to a single digit (except when dealing with master numbers).

For example the birth date of July 21, 1931, is calculated as follows:

$$7 \quad 21 \quad 1931 \quad = \quad 7+2+1+1+9+3+1 \quad = \quad 24$$
$$= \quad 2+4 \quad = \quad 6$$

or:
$$\begin{array}{ccc} (7) & (3) & (5) \\ 7 & 21 & 1931 \end{array} \quad = \quad (15) \quad = \quad 1+5 \quad = \quad 6$$

or:
$$7$$
$$21$$
$$\underline{1931}$$
$$1959 \quad = \quad 24 \quad = \quad 6$$

Another example is: November 12, 1934

$$11 \quad 12 \quad 1934 \quad = \quad 1+1+1+2+1+9+3+4$$
$$= \quad 22$$

or:
$$\begin{array}{ccc} (11) & (3) & (8) \\ 11 & 12 & 1934 \end{array} \quad = \quad 22$$

or:
$$11$$
$$12$$
$$\underline{1934}$$
$$1957 \quad = \quad 22$$

In the above instance, the sum is 22 and—being a master number—is not reduced to four. When 11's, or 22's appear in the month, day, or year, they are generally left in that form, for purposes of calculation.

One more example: January 10, 1908

$$1 \quad 10 \quad 1908 \quad = \quad 1+1+0+1+9+0+8 \quad = \quad 20$$
$$= \quad 2+0 \quad = \quad 2$$

$$\text{(1)} \quad \text{(1)} \quad \text{(9)}$$
or: $\quad 1 \quad 10 \quad 1908 \quad = \quad \text{(11)} = 11$

or: $\quad 1$
$\quad\quad 10$
$\quad\quad \underline{1908}$
$\quad\quad 1919 \quad = \quad 20 \quad = \quad 2+0 \quad = \quad 2$

In this example, the number 11 does not result in two of the three examples given. Since it is there in one, the 11 vibration has to be considered as a possible influence. The strength of influence must be weighed from an examination of the entire chart.

1 LIFE NUMBER

A person choosing the one life number has come into this lifetime to learn individuality, self-reliance, and proper expression of will—human, and Divine. Very often he is born into a family with a very domineering, interfering, or unyielding parent(s). This creates early tension and conflict of wills between parent and child. The resentment reaches a boiling point in the late teens or the twenties and once the child leaves the home environment, a period of rebellion transpires. Ones need to learn that pure rebellion, a lifestyle of pure opposite reaction, does not necessarily establish independence and self-direction.

By the thirties, the one life path individual usually starts to outgrow and release the rebellion and overcome it with self-awakening independence. Having grown into an appreciation of self-identity, the one starts to more fully value individuality in others. Only now can he cooperate and grow.

With other ones (1's) the parent(s) may simply express indifference towards the child's growth and personal interests. This leaves an inadequate feeling with the child. So much so, that he may have difficulty taking initiative in later years.

A lengthy discussion will be given to karmic trends in numerology, during a following chapter. It needs to be said here that every number in the name and birthdate has a karmic overtone or implication. If there had not been some imbalance in previous lifetimes, it is unlikely we would be here now—but would have progressed into discarnate planes of existence.

People with a one life number may encounter supervisors, ministers, school teachers, relatives, spouses, with whom they experience intense conflict of wills. (Ones, remember that the tension and anger in these conflicts is a closer look at yourself). As you have sown, so also will you reap! The karmic implication of this cliché applies to all the following life numbers. Qualities seen in others represent qualities that you have likely expressed in an earlier life, or lives. Now is the time to balance obstinacy and self with cooperation and harmony.

Ones who have not worked out the subconscious conflict of will often marry a person of extreme obstinance or willfulness. The one is finally berated, intimidated, or ignored so long, he sets out to "do his own thing." Sadly, it often takes the death or divorce of the spouse to awaken a one into self-reliance and acceptance of the fact that he can go it alone.

As mankind and the New Age become closer, with the heightened awareness the union will afford, the esoteric and deeper interpretations of numerology become more important. A very consequential nuance of number one has become more in evidence in recent years; it is the adjustment from human will to Divine Will.

Many advanced seekers of Light have come to a conscious turning point in their growth where they have made the decision to put their lives into harmony with Divine Plan and Divine Will; "thy Will, not mine, oh Lord my God." The higher frequency of the number one symbolizes Divine Will or the Father's Will. We all go through the challenging transition of wills eventually, but those with the number one (not necessarily just in the life number) usually have a genuine struggle.

On many occasions, a person may reach his forties, fifties, or later years and really overcome for the first time the resentment and resistance from a life with a domineering parent, particularly the father (even when the domineering parent may have been the mother, the manifestation of will is an archetypal male energy and conflict arises with the big Man in the sky) and perhaps the spouse. Age makes little difference other than that the pattern may be more ingrained with added years. The seeker is joyous and confident at having truly found a greater awareness of self-reliance and strength.

Perhaps the seeking party has been studying metaphysical philosophy for some time and has made an effort to know and follow the Father's Will. Consciously this may all be well and good; however, subconsciously the mind is saying, here I am just starting to find my own will and become free, and now I have to become subservient to another's (Father) Will. Thus, a subconscious battle rages and the balancing of will continues. Each time we expand higher in awareness, we go deeper into the subconscious to rework conflicts and karmic blocks. And the battle for balance continues.

In the case of a well-balanced chart, the one may grow up in a very supportive and congenial atmosphere that fosters self-esteem. Because of having reached balance in early life or a previous lifetime, the individual is securely self-aware and free to live productively.

Ones have come to be leaders and pioneers in their calling. As such they are independent and are best left alone to complete a task. They become the owners, supervisors, and managers. There is a tendency to become fixed and set in habits and attitudes. They have difficulty taking orders and can become bossy and opinionated, not their sweetest attribute.

Originality, invention, and courage are native to ones, but they can sour to varying degrees of overconfidence and egocentricity. Once a goal is sighted, it is easy for you to concentrate your attention. Paradoxically, ones must be wary of the tendency to start a new project and become bored and go on to something new before completing the first. Blame this simply on rampant ambition.

Ambition is a significant driving force to you and you are determined to succeed and be productive. Overcoming obstacles and limitations is an exhilarating challenge to you, and once you learn to cooperate without losing your identity, the sky is the limit to your productivity.

When one occurs in numerology, there is likelihood of Aries and Leo being prominent somewhere in the person's natal astrological horoscope.

2 Life Number

Those choosing two as the life number very often come into a family environment where a parent or parents are prone to pettiness, contrary opinions, and criticism. The child is seldom complimented or given reinforcement for personal accomplishments. Such a child is more often reminded that he could have done better—gotten an A instead of a B, come in first instead of third. This environment can undermine self-confidence and heighten inability to cope with criticism in later years. At the very least, two will find it hard to make a decision for fear of being wrong.

Very often those with a two life number are the brunt of seemingly unjustified or unwarranted gossip or criticism, especially in the school and early adult years. Worse, these uncomfortable accusations may occur in any aspect of social exposure. Often the accusations are untrue, and the victim asks, "why are they saying this about me"? They may be caught in the very sort of pettiness that they themselves created in a previous life or lives.

If the two responds with anger, hurt, or revengeful behavior, he perpetuates the karmic pattern. It is important to remember the criticism comes from the other party, and is *their* problem. When you react with negativity, it becomes your karma also, and you link yourself to the instigator. Learn to release judgmental, self-righteous, and critical attitudes in self.

At their best, twos are natural diplomats who bring change through persuasion rather than force. Twos are more often found in the middle ranks of business, lacking the drive of ones. When a two does achieve the highest position, it is by influence, diplomacy, and finesse. You do well helping others reach their goal, and are best at team effort rather than solitary endeavors.

Twos work well when bringing groups or people with divergent attitudes into a unity of understanding. Twos' talents emerge when carrying out an idea which originated elsewhere. It is important that twos pay attention to details in all endeavors. A two may often be the person doing the real work for those who capture the headlines. Such patient service pays off, and all proper effort is someday rewarded on the wheel of destiny.

The esoteric side of two is opening the door between heaven and earth. Twos can be excellent integrators of intuitive guidance into day-to-day experience. Twos are happiest when the door to the soul has been opened and the Higher Light pours into their lives.

When two appears in the chart, Virgo, Libra, or Scorpio usually is prominent in the natal horoscope.

3 Life Number

One is an aggressive male energy, while two is intuitive and feminine. Progressively, threes work to enhance the male-female matrix and from the union bring forth creativity and self-expression.

They are often found in entertainment, the creative arts, public media, sales, crafts, writing, and related endeavors. Threes have come into this life to create, radiate beauty and harmony, and express self. The unfoldment of the creative ability and the opportunity to express it in life come naturally for many. This is especially true when indicators in the whole chart show balance and flow. More often the person with the three life path is born into a family where he encounters considerable inhibition, resistance, or indifference to artistic or creative skills he possesses.

The suggestion is that in a previous life or lives, the three very likely had developed pronounced abilities and failed to discipline them to highest virtuosity, or became superficial about the gift. Once again, the three may have the potential, but this time life has thrown obstacles in the way of development. So the gift is truly respected, appreciated, and expressed with dedication. Examine these hypothetical situations.

A young lady may strongly desire to play the piano and has shown ability at a school tryout. She lives in a family where money is scarce, and the parents are unable to afford the instrument.

Another example might be a young man who has shown outstanding proclivities toward acting and singing. He may have a father from the old puritan work-ethic culture. The thought of having an effeminate Milquetoast artist as a son is overwhelming to his male ego, so the son is intimidated and forced to pursue "manly" occupations.

In another instance a three-year-old child may create a particularly colorful, symbolic, and aesthetically pleasing finger painting. Unfortunately it is done on the new kitchen cabinets, so the child is severely punished for his/her creativity. Hence, the spontaneity of creation becomes associated with chastisement and pain. It may not surface again for many years.

All creative acts result from releasing the creative force, or kundalini. The same creative energy expressed in the physical act of creativity (sexual intercourse), is channeled into other levels of expression, be it job creativity, artistic creativity, intellectual creativity, or soul creativity. Very often early childhood awakening to sexual curiosity or outlet is associated with feelings of guilt, shame, embarrassment, chastisement, or confusion. Such incidents as self-exploration, childhood sex games, being molested, stimulation from a family member, petting and foreplay, or guilt-ridden early sexual relations leave a scar of guilt, fear, shame, or confusion in the subconscious attitude toward creativity on the sexual level.

When that adult commences a new creative endeavor later in life on another level (work, art, soul), the subconscious conflicts become activated, and the individual will react to the subconscious stimulus by terminating the project prematurely. A three with this conflict may become involved in a multitude of creative diversions, but he will fail to truly excel in any of them. He may have several incomplete paintings, poems, stained glass fixtures, projects of every creative nature, underfoot in his home. Each time we expand our consciousness higher and outward, we go deeper into the subconscious to release deeply hidden blocks. This conflict with creativity may also apply when three appears elsewhere in the chart, i.e. personality, letters in the name, day or month, etc. The principle applies when manifesting creative components of any number.

You must learn to investigate the laws of the creative energy and work to release it sensibly in harmony with all other factors in consciousness. On the esoteric level, three is

The Word spoken, the Christ Consciousness manifest (see
No. 3 of Actualized Self). Threes are the heralds and spokes-
men preparing man for the dawn by the illuminating inspiration of their works, despite the subconscious conflicts they
must outgrow. But when the struggle is won, life is glori-
ous for a three. They are naturals as hosts and benefit from
socializing with other seekers and creative folks. At their
best, they are imaginative, inspired, and able to tap deep
emotions. They are gifted with the ability to use words but
must be careful not to slip into pettiness and superficiality.
Misguided or, perhaps should I say "unguided" threes are
very capable of speaking endlessly and having very little to
say. They need to discipline energies and avoid spreading
their talents too thinly. Threes often run with the "in"
crowd and jet set and when out of harmony can squander
away talent in self-indulgence, luxury, and pseudo-sophisti-
cation.

When three appears in the chart, Sagittarius or Libra is
usually promient in the natal horoscope.

4 Life Number

Fours are workers of the world. They must strive diligently and dedicatedly to achieve their goals. In most instances, things will not come easily, but only through effort.
The suggestion is that they bring in a tendency toward laziness or avoidance of work from a previous life or lives.
When that is true, fours may begrudge the work at hand and
become irritated in their labors.

When you resist the lesson of learning the four vibration, you tend toward the unconventional and refuse to
honor custom or social norms. They decidedly dislike routine and system and will want to pass detail and monotonous
requirements to someone else. The result is a constant seeking of shortcuts and ways out of duties. When this attitude
prevails, a four may get to a point of success, but eventually

his whole world collapses. He will have to start again step-by-step, brick-by-brick, from the solid foundation to the well-earned heights.

On the more positive side, fours are loyal, intense, and dedicated workers. Once given an assignment it will be carried out to the nth degree by a four. However, a four may lack imagination or originality when it comes to making any needed adjustment to a job.

Fours may experience several diverse occupations or professional fields before settling into one in which they are content. They handle money well and tend to keep a small reserve for fear of not having any resources. When a four attains a position of wealth, it is from hard work and persistence.

A four needs facts and must be shown the practical side before starting a new project. Fours gravitate toward administration, engineering, and mechanical and technological pursuits. A four's inclination toward life is conservative and protective; he has to know the whys and wherefores before taking any risk.

Fours nurture a strong sense of dignity and worthiness about their life. They tend to help all who are in need, but their conservative nature limits their friends and associates — admittedly an odd combination of traits. In a supervisory position, they expect equal dedication and effort from their employees and are inclined to become overbearing, and bossy to the point of personal severity.

They are not prone to superficial interests and must work on developing a lighter side in their attitude toward life. You may see this manifest in their conern for financial stability.

On the esoteric side, awakened fours have come into this life to build the form for establishment of the divine blueprint on Earth. Once they have recognized the inner work of the soul, fours are truly inspired workers toward the Light. Then they must be patient and tolerant of the awakening masses. When four is in the numerology chart, very often Taurus and/or Capricorn are prominent in the person's natal astrological horoscope.

5 LIFE NUMBER

Fives have come into this lifetime to experience the Earth opportunities more thoroughly. They profit most from contact with other people; therefore, they should seek every opportunity to mingle with all of humanity.

Five brings change, movement, travel, and opportunities. Very often a child with the five life number is born into a family where the father moves often in his career. An excellent example would be a military family where reassignment is the way of life. If not in childhood, sooner or later, there will be a chance to move, travel, and get out to explore the world around them.

A five learns best from contact with other people, and he has much to learn. The karmic suggestion here is that in a previous life or lives there has likely been some prejudice and intolerance of certain nationalities, ethnic groups, religious sect, or political persuasion. Most likely, previous life patterns are heavily intellectual, and very lofty rigid intellectual biases were formed toward select human classifications. This time they have chosen from soul and higher self to be born in a situation that somewhat coerces them to work with people, some of whom they distinctly dislike! They will have the chance to deal with all types of humanity, including rich, poor, those of different races, creeds, religions, colors, and varying political, philosophical, moral, ethical and economic persuasions. This powerful dichotomy cannot *help* but provide a learning experience.

Let us say, for example — a five has come into this life with an intense prejudice against Icelanders. It is likely that as a child or later he will move next door to an Icelandic family. It may turn out that they are the only family on the block with a child who is his peer. Over a period of time, a friendship develops on the day-to-day human level. The five eats Icelandic food, plays with Icelandic toys, learns Icelandic history and family tradition. Sooner or later he realizes that Icelandic people are the same as all people: some are good, some perhaps not. The whole point to learn is to accept people for what they are. Experience is the best teacher; it shouldn't be avoided.

At their shallowest, fives have a tendency to try a little of everything but learn from nothing. They become superficial and are unable to create a sustained or responsible relationship. On the other hand, fives are inclined to become involved in an experience to such an overwhelming extent that they are unable to break loose to try a new opportunity. They are definitely extremists in this respect.

There is a tendency toward self-indulgence. A five strives to learn the balance of knowing when he has learned from a life experience and needs to move on to something else. When out of balance, a five will seek excitement and stimulation in sexuality, drink, drugs, or other sensual indulgence. Life, again, for a five has a strong tendency to fluctuate between extremes.

Many a seeker in the New Age studies has previously been in a life of asceticism, abstinence, and impoverishment, quite possibly as a nun or a monk in earlier religions or esoteric sects. In such lifetimes, contact was avoided with mundane human desires and frailties. Now as a five, he has chosen to come back to make up for experience previously avoided; and he finds himself caught between strong pent-up physical urges and the dictates of religion, society, or family morals and mores.

Fives have come in this time to find a proper balance within self as to the correct expression of their sensual and sexual needs. The tendency is to disregard and flout the social norms or frightfully cling to the law (religious, social, or civic) as a means of dealing with desire. They are certainly fascinating people to observe.

Once a harmonious lifestyle has been achieved, the five knows how to respect the norms of society, yet independently and unobtrusively pursue what is the right lifestyle for himself.

Five is the number of man and free will; as the dualistic counterpoint to freedom, five is also symbolic of Divine Law. Those seeking the esoteric wisdom of five realize that eventually the course of proper action comes from within, and they learn to follow the voice of dharma.

Dharma is a complex eastern concept. Very roughly translated, it means the performance of an action which is precisely proper for the participant at his/her moment of evolution. To react any other way at the moment would create imbalance (too much—too little) and more karma. As we heed the voice of Dharma, it will direct us in a manner which most efficiently balances out karma. To consistently tap the Dharmic Directive, we must learn to bring our life, personality, and soul into balance and under the direct tutelage of the Higher Self.

Where five occurs in numerology, Gemini or Leo is often prominent in the natal horoscope.

6 LIFE NUMBER

Sixes have come into a lifetime of domesticity, responsibility, and service. One of the greatest challenges for them to deal with is that of establishing emotional balance and security. They are often born into a family where dissension and disharmony exist between the mother and father, in many cases leading to separation and divorce. The strain leaves a strong emotional insecurity in the child's subconscious memory.

Persons with the six life number experience difficulty adjusting to the responsibility of home and family. There is often more than one marriage in their life. The karmic implication in the six life number is that in a previous life, or lives, there was difficulty adapting to home, family, and the personal relation in marriage. The person may have been irresponsible or unyielding and caused grief for those nearby. In this lifetime, the six experiences emotional suffering, just as he/she generated it in earlier patterns.

On the other hand, the six life number may bring one harmonious lifelong marriage. Consideration must always be given to the entire chart when considering the analysis of each segment. Sixes have usually come into this life to be of service to others. They are at their best when what they do directly benefits the lives of those they serve. Ministers, doctors, nurses, teachers, counselors and social workers often have the six prominent in their charts. In business a six tends toward assisting others rather than excelling in completely competitive professions.

The karmic suggestion is that there has been a tendency developed in an earlier existence to disregard or interfere with the lives of others. A six may have intimidated intellectually or used power to keep other people insecure and under control. A six is here now to balance the scale by assisting and caring for others.

A six's idealism and desire to serve creates some very strong opinions as to what is best for others, and you should be careful about others taking advantage of your generosity and imposing upon you for assistance. They work upon your karmic subconscious memories of having neglected others sometime in a past existence, perhaps even in current life. By working upon the guilt, they make you feel obligated to give.

You will have to work hard to find tranquility in the home but—once content—your surroundings will be tasteful and harmonious.

The six can succeed at anything when truly helping and serving others. Sixes are excellent at counseling, as an advising neighbor or in the lofty status of an uptown psychiatrist. They are excellent when helping to mend the body, emotions, mind, and soul. They are often self-made martyrs. But sixes can be instruments of a greater cause and sacrifice self for humanity. Truly martyrs in the best sense, they give of themselves nobly.

When six appears in numerology, Cancer or Pisces often is prominent in the natal horoscope.

7 Life Number

Those with the seven life path are constantly searching for a deeper understanding of themselves and the world around them. They analyze, investigate, and probe for hidden information no matter what their calling.

They have accumulated a vast storehouse of wisdom from previous lives and lean toward a cerebral and intellectual life. For some, higher education or specialized professional training is not available, or it is difficult to attain. It is likely that sevens have many times pursued the intellectual route, and life this time, is directing them to use their knowledge in a practical expression, rather than to emphasize another cerebral endeavor. Or a seven may have to struggle to derive perspective and appreciation for the role of intellect in growth of consciousness.

Those with the seven life number tend toward a lonely life of introspection and aloofness. They find strength in self and are reluctant to open up to others for aid or guidance. Because of their tendency for specialization, they often lose perspective on simple personal needs and an ability to enjoy lightheartedly the trivial events of social living. They prefer to wear a mask and play a role rather than be caught up in the pettiness at hand.

The dedication and scientific attitude often enables sevens to accomplish much and attain considerable success. Most importantly, sevens need to balance compassion and human sensitivity with knowledge. This combination inspires wisdom and a deeper search through the occult mysteries and metaphysical studies.

When awakened to inner realities, the seven investigates intricately the deepest mysteries of man and cosmos. As we advance closer to the New Age awareness, many with the seven life path are coming into this period to bring a special spiritual gift or teaching.

When conversely expressed, the seven can become skeptical and cynical toward life. They then enjoy playing with rhetoric and games of subterfuge.

The karmic suggestion is that there has been too much attention given to intellectuality in past life patterns. The need this time is to integrate heart and and feelings into your being. When these become united, your opportunity for spiritual growth is enormous. Seven is the number of meditation, introspection, and self-examination. Through these avenues, your mystical side is awakened.

Sevens tend to value their intellectual ability as a tool for power and control. They can intimidate others with their intense reasoning capacity and cool recitation of the facts. When ego and pride get in the way, they are cunning and deceptive in nature.

As a seven, pride and dignity are natural to your reserved attitude, and the conservative trend makes you selective of friends. Your natural inclination is to trust your own ideas and judgment. When linked to your intuition, this combination leads to decisions of impact and strength that enable you to reach goals.

When seven appears in numerology, Scorpio and/or Aquarius are often prominent in the natal horoscope.

8 LIFE NUMBER

Eights have come into this lifetime to deal with power, authority, and money. Eight is a highly organized executive vibration. In the life number it usually leads to success and leadership.

Those with the eight life number often choose a family where a parent or both parents enforce their authority severely. Or the child may be born into a family heavily burdened by religious, ethnic, or intellectual dogma. Therefore, the tendency of eights is to struggle for their own direction and authority.

In the early years, eights become very resentful of incompetent supervisors but do it their way, because they are boss! Your inclination as an eight is to say, "I could run things better", and you probably could. The karmic implication is that in a previous life or lives, you misused authority because of money, ego, or pride. So in your youth you will feel the discomfort of being at the lower end of the totem pole, carrying the brunt of abuse where leadership is misdirected. At their best eights have an uncanny knack of sizing up another's potential accurately and quickly. They may manipulate this talent for selfish purpose or to attain purely self-centered objectives. They are excellent executives and can handle personnel effectively with this ability.

Eights seek the symbolic trappings that suggest success, i.e. large home, big car, expensive decor, club membership, or whatever the symbols are in their culture. They need to *appear* successful.

In a woman's chart, the eight life path usually suggests a tendency toward a business career, or professional pursuits. This is not to say that she disdains being a wife and mother, but that her need is to prove herself in the outer world. In most instances there is an early childhood or parental circumstance where the child has denied the feminine identity, and built a strong masculine subconscious focus. This enables her to compete and excel in her chosen field.

As we enter New Age realization, the eight vibration is taking on a new significance. Eights in the New Age will be leaders, but must tap their Divine Guidance and execute authority which is based upon universal law. Instead of manipulating and being fearful of helping others develop authority, the New Age eights will manipulate to draw out authority and skills in others to help administrate the raising of divinely ordained cities, governments, and cultures.

The unawakened eight keeps others dependent in order to hold control and domain. The enlightened eight is never fearful of someone taking his position, for he knows that as he enables others to find confidence and self-authority, so also will he expand in greater unfoldment.

Eights are here to learn the proper value and utilization of money. They can attract money more easily than any other number. When wealth or esteem is the only ambition, they may find it slipping away until the proper balance toward money is learned.

If you are an eight, expect to be put into positions of leadership and control. Industry, large institutions, and government are attractive to eights. You are at your best executing others' dreams, in sound managerial fashion.

When eight appears in the numerology chart, Capricorn is usually prominent in the natal horoscope.

9 LIFE NUMBER

Nines are the dreamers and the planners of the New Age. They bring an innate sense of idealism, tolerance, and compassion to humanity. Nines dream of a perfection in society, marriage, and self. At times they are almost naive in their enthusiastic anticipation of the good they know is coming.

This childlike idealism is dissipated by the realities of the less than perfect world, and as nines reach their late teens and early adult years, the enthusiasm may turn to bitter cynicism and at the extreme to anarchy. Nines are often exploited by someone using their blind idealism as a lure to get something done, and then dropping them flat afterwards. It will not be easy, but you are here now to hold this ideal of the perfect world. In time, others will come to your aid and help establish the true kingdom on Earth.

Nine is the finishing number, and you have come to a very significant turning point in consciousness. It is time to finish one major cycle of evolvement to prepare for another loop on the spiral. Consequently, nines have come to let go of the things of this world. When a nine clings to anything less than the eternal, it will eventually weigh like an anchor upon the ship of growth. There is a metaphysical saying, "Let Go and Let God," and this could hardly be more appropriate than to a nine life number.

If you attach yourself to things of this world for your security, it is likely they will eventually be removed by fate until security is sought within the inner self.

Let's say you need lots of wealth for security. All of a sudden, the stock market may plunge, or your property becomes valueless. Or if one is dependent upon the marriage partner, death or divorce can result. The more tenaciously and fearfully one clings, the more intense the life suffering becomes. Stubborn, clinging nines may experience death of loved ones, major illnesses, financial losses, accidents, divorce, etc. Finally their anguish becomes so deep they reach out to Soul and Higher Self, and reach equanimity and balance.

That does not mean life must hold suffering for nines. For those who have learned to let go, the life is often rich in all ways with Divine supply. Because it is a finishing number, the life will often be full of adventure, bizarre and wonderful people and events, inexplicable happenings, invention, artistic achievement, and creativity. Once the *need* no longer exists, the supply comes in abundantly. Nines, because of the outreach of your consciousness, there is a strong tendency to fluctuate between emotional highs of ecstasy, and lows of depression. As the Inner Light is established within, this roller coaster syndrome dissipates, and you then enjoy an enriched and full life.

When nine appears in numerology, the signs Aquarius and Pisces are often prominent in the natal horoscope.

11 LIFE NUMBER

The eleven life pattern unfolds similarly to the two, which should be read in conjunction with the eleven. There are some distinctions. Elevens tend to be drawn to movements and organizations with idealistic aims. In a balanced chart with other power factors they are likely to gain public attention and influence. Many elevens work in the psychic, healing, and metaphysical work and can be excellent channels for the Light. They are often attracted to theatrical, religious, communications, sociological, political, ecological, or metaphysical organizations. When their zealousness overrides discretion, they become caught up in fanatical cults and fringe movements.

In the pursuit of an ideal, elevens are prone to overlook the delicate personal considerations and sensitivity. When this occurs, they may alienate the very people they wish to inspire. It is very important to be a living example of Truth. They must trust and follow the inspiration of intuition, yet maintain contact with the other planes of consciousness.

Elevens need to concentrate on getting their domestic and material lifestyle arranged and controlled in order to blend revelation with constructive organization and a solid foothold.

22 Life Number

The twenty-two life pattern unfolds similarly to the four, and it would be beneficial to review the four pattern. There *are* some differences between the two. You twenty-twos have tremendous power for organization and establishment of institutions which are part of Hierarchical governing. Although you may not lead the work, your contribution will be vital to success, even if the role appears insignificant by worldly standards.

As the New Age approaches, mankind is on the verge of producing cities, governments, spiritual institutions, art centers, and educational facilities which re-establish conscious cooperation between mankind, the Hierarchy, Solar Logos, and the Devic (Angelic) evolution. Twenty-twos of awakened spiritual consciousness are working (often as yet unwittingly) to prepare the foundation for those institutions of the New Age. Twenty-twos must use their mental strength in harmony with body, emotion, and soul. When all levels become spiritually directed and disciplined, they become the supreme master masons and directors of the world.

33 LIFE NUMBER

The thirty-three life pattern is similar to the six, which should be reviewed at this time. Thirty-threes have come to serve mankind in a grand fashion and affiliate with groups or institutions whose primary aim is to relieve the suffering of humanity on Earth.

In many instances, those with the thirty-three have been part of a group in an earlier life who created frustration, confusion, or pain for others on the planet. Consequently, they come back laden with a compulsion to help. At their worst, the compulsion is grating, even obnoxious to those who see them as self-righteous to a fault.

Thirty-threes frequently have very complex and deeply rooted emotional conflicts to resolve, before they are best able to serve. Of course first of all they must see their own self-righteousness. Once the heart center is functioning harmoniously, they become excellent healers, counselors, and instructors. Then they truly are able to alleviate the woes engulfing so many on the planet in this era.

THE TRIUNE CYCLES AND PINNACLES

Most popular numerology texts quite adequately discuss these two delineative tools in the numerology chart. I do not intend to say a great deal about them—other than to share some techniques of interpretation from personal experience which, hopefully, you will find of value in your own studies. Florence Campbell has given much important insight to these in *Your Days Are Numbered;* I recommend it highly.

Using the birthday given earlier in this chapter, we will examine the manner of deriving the cycles and pinnacles:

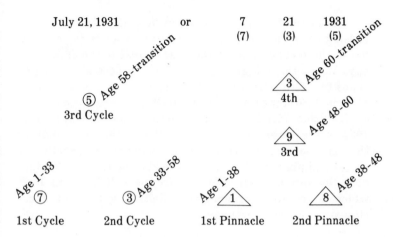

July 21, 1931   or   7   21   1931

The first cycle is derived from the single digit value of the month of birth. The second cycle is from the single digit value of the day of birth, and the third cycle is derived from the single digit value of the year of birth.

To obtain the numerical value for the pinnacles, combinations of the above are added as follows: The first pinnacle is derived by adding the number of the month to the number of birth day. To obtain the second pinnacle, add the day of birth to the number of the year of birth. The third pinnacle is derived by adding the first pinnacle and the second pinnacle together. Finally, the fourth pinnacle is ascertained by adding the number of the month of birth to the number of the year of birth.

Different authors present varying opinions as to when these cycles and pinnacles change, and this author has yet another suggestion. Florence Campbell relates the changes to the 28 year lunar cycle. Juno Jordan changes around the 27th year (3 x 9). Each works in its own system.

My experience is that the primary changes in human consciousness are linked to the 29 year Saturn cycle, and I have developed my approach to the life cycle to reflect this.

The beginning of the second cycle is determined by the passing of the personal year (that corresponds to the number of the second cycle) in the year closest to the 29th birthday. When the triggering year for the second cycle precedes the 29th year, the cycle is initiated, but will not fully blossom into significance until the 29th year has passed.

By using 7/21/1931 as an example, one ascertains that 1964 is the three personal year (the method of obtaining the personal year is presented following the sub-section on cycles and pinnacles) closest to the 29th birthday. This triggers the second cycle. The third cycle will begin in 1989, which is the five personal year (initiating the five cycle) closest to the 58th birthday.

Pinnacles

The change in pinnacles relates to the time of awakening of the soul which should occur during the fifth etheric cycle (ages 28-35). The 35th year is the key to changes in pinnacles.

The first pinnacle covers approximately ages one to thirty-five. The second pinnacle becomes influential when the personal year (coinciding with the number of the second pinnacle) closest to age 35 occurs. In our previous example, using the date of birth 7/21/1931 — 1969 would be the year initiating the second pinnacle because that is when the eight year closest to the 35th (age 38) birthday occurs. The second pinnacle lasts approximately nine years. The third pinnacle starts with the personal year coincidental to the number of the third pinnacle (nine, in this case) which is closest to nine years from the beginning of the second pinnacle. In this chart it would be 1979, the year of the 48th birthday. The fourth pinnacle starts with the personal year of same number with the number of the fourth pinnacle (3 in this chart) which is closest to being nine years from the beginning of the third pinnacle. In this chart the fourth pinnacle starts in 1991, the 60th year.

A method of making a "guess-timate" on the pinnacles is to figure roughly age 1-35 (1st), 35-44 (2nd), 44-53 (3rd), and 53 to transition (4th).

INTERPRETING CYCLES AND PINNACLES

Now that we have set up the triune cycles and pinnacles, what do they mean? The cycles tend to reflect how the person feels within, about life and how he faces life. The first cycle is the more restrictive and inhibitive, bringing out the negative tendencies of the number. If lessons have been learned well during the first Saturn cycle (ages 1 to 29), the second cycle tends to be one of expansion and unfoldment — enhancing the positive qualities of the number. The third is a review and summation period wherein reflection and integration of life experiences take precedence.

The triune cycles interact with the life number and have impact upon the manner in which one relates to life. They also interact with the personality and influence how each individual expresses himself in life. Since they break the life pattern into three phases, one should give notice to their presence.

Whereas the triune cycles reflect inner reactions to life experience, the pinnacles are more nearly indicative of the opportunities life presents to the individual. The first pinnacle inclines toward a cycle of trial and learning with the thrust of the lesson indicated by the number governing the pinnacle. The second pinnacle occurs approximately concurrent with awakening of soul consciousness. Note that this pinnacle period is one rich with accelerated growth and attainment.

It is time to acquire the moral, personal, and spiritual foundations which will govern the prime years of life. Life will provide key moments for education of the personality and soul. In past ages very few of the planet's humanity really awakened to soul awareness, but in our times millions of the population are reaching this awakening. For some it may come a little sooner in life, for most later. When awakened, the second pinnacle brings tremendous opportunity, but when unawakened the second pinnacle can be more trial and error characteristic of the first Saturn cycle (ages one to 29).

The third pinnacle is one of accomplishment and fulfillment. The fourth follows with the reflection and sharing fruits of previous efforts. Detailed interpretations of the triune cycles and pinnacles are not presented herein because it is felt that sufficient understanding as to their significance can be gleaned by taking the number of the particular cycle or pinnacle and turning to the descriptions given earlier — in this chapter — for the life number. Perhaps if you do not feel comfortable following the above suggestion, you might want to seek insight from either Campbell, or Jordan, both of whom have covered these phases in their volumes mentioned earlier in the preface.

THE PERSONAL YEAR, MONTH, DAY, WEEK

The personal years repeat in nine year cycles. Each time the cycle is renewed, it provides the individual with circumstances to elevate the spiral loop of his consciousness. At first, a difficult concept to grasp. Each nine year cycle is replete with innumerable chances for added self-understanding and wisdom. If the challenges of the cycle are faced and overcome, new opportunities enter into the life path. When one fights, ignores, or overreacts to circumstances, the same situations or very similar ones will reoccur. So the concept is well worth holding in mind. Knowledge of the personal year can be invaluable for accelerating development in consciousness.

To determine your personal year number, the month and day of birth are added to the universal year. Employing the birthdate from previous examples, we derive the personal year as follows:

```
7    3    5
7   21   1931    =   6 Life Number (the personal year)

     3    6
7   21  (1932)   =   7 Personal Year

          7
7   21  (1933)   =   8 Personal Year

          3
7   21  (1956)   =   4 Personal Year

          6
7   21  (1977)   =   7 Personal Year

          7
7   21  (1978)   =   8 Personal Year
```

To determine the personal month, add the month in question to the personal year. For example: May, 1977 is a 3 personal month in the above chart—7 (personal year 1977) + 5 (May is the fifth month of the year) = 12 = 1 + 2 = 3. As with any new skill, familiarity and practice come with time.

The personal day is readily obtained by adding the number of the day to the personal month. For example: 5/17/1977 would be a 2 day because we add 7 (personal year) with 5 (universal month) and 8 (1 + 7, the universal day). The total is 7 + 5 + 8 = 20 = 2.

Master numbers are obtained following the method outlined earlier in the chapter for computing the life number.

For perspective in deciphering the meaning of the personal month and personal day, use the following guidelines for the personal year, and just tone down the interpretation to make it appropriate for a month or day.

The personal years should be scrutinized carefully as this is one of the most significant cycles affecting consciousness. It is particularly important to watch those years that correspond to the life number personality, soul, karmic indicators, and stress patterns. How one reacts to the annual vibrations is very indicative of the progress he/she is making in evolution of self-awareness. Read the entire description of the one personal year for more ideas about recognizing the subconscious origin of blocks and defenses.

1 Personal Year

The one year begins the phase of nine years in the entire personal years cycle. It is a time to convert ideas, aspirations, and dreams to physical action. The one year often opens new opportunities in the job or business. There may be a move to a new residence. Because the one year is the starting cycle, it is very important to put things in motion now! If you delay changes in the one year or ignore the chance to expand, there is a tendency to take the steam out of the whole phase of nine years. It is very difficult to break an apathetic or listless habit that is established during the one year.

This is the year to formulate your desired accomplishments for the years ahead and start working toward these goals. It is a time to add to your business or expand into wholly new facets of your profession. If you see no future in your present employment, it is a time to investigate the market for other possibilities.

The one year intensifies the masculine energy patterns. Emphasis is upon individuality, aggressiveness, courage, and self-reliance. In a man's chart, the one year activates subconscious memories and conflicts related to early childhood, particularly those relating to the formation of his masculinity. Conflicts with his father, brothers, male schoolteachers, ministers, or his own masculinity that have their origin in very early years (or prenatal time) are triggered. Once set loose, they flow into the stream of daily consciousness.

For instance, a boy may have had a father who did not want children and was unable to provide his son with confidence and support at key points in the building of his male identity, i.e. the first year in school, at puberty, when turning out for football and playing in a key game, at his first job, and so forth.

Later in his adult life, that boy (having become a businessman) is faced with an excellent opportunity to start a new business venture. Consciously he may be professionally and intellectually equipped to succeed. However, subconsciously he may want to get back at his father's lack of concern by not wanting to give his father the satisfaction of seeing his son become a success. Therefore, the son subconsciously finds reasons to delay the venture and creates critical mistakes which prevent a sure-fire business from developing. An awakened consciousness is needed to counter such an aversion to growth.

The one year attracts activities and situations which put pressure upon an individual to face the yang (masculine) conflicts within self. When these exist, the attitude can become hostile, overly assertive, and defensive. On the other hand, the passive traits of the one may come out as indifference, lethargy, and stubborn resistance to opportunities. Now we step aside from specifics of the one year for the moment.

Let this year be a goad to investigate subconscious origins of conflicts in your life. A tool of assistance in investigation is the progressed chart (provided in a following chapter). When a particularly traumatic year occurs, which greatly upsets the personality and puts unbearable strain upon one's psychological cohesiveness, check the progressed chart for progressed factors involved: personality, soul, personal year, and essence. Trace back through the progressed chart, particularly the formative years, to similar patterns or to the number most indicative of the nature of the struggle: marriage, financial freedom, confusion in male or female energy. The chart should reveal certain years as more relevant than others. Using that guideline, the conscious mind can begin to zero in on memories that will reveal clues to the origin and development of subconscious blocks and defenses.

Let us return to our discussion of the one personal year. In a woman's chart the one year awakens the animus — masculine portion — of her total being. If her life up to the one year has been more passive than assertive, she is likely to exert a more independent attitude. A woman who has reached the five etheric cycle (ages 28 to 35) or after, and who has not yet fully established self-identity, will often begin to break free in a one year. She may decide to start to work, become involved in self-awareness studies previously denied by her family, study for a business license such as real estate, or she just may stop thinking the way social and family norm dictate, and become more confident of her own intellectual strength. But all of these possibilities represent positive growth and should not be thwarted or restrained out of guilt.

This can create some friction in a marriage because her increasing yang (masculine) energy may seem a threat to the husband, especially if he is in a situation where his masculine self-image is weakened, for example by a stalemated position at work, or by a setback in earning capacity. Upon examining the husband's personal year and other chart indicators, it should be clear how both parties can learn to benefit from the experience and work more effectively as a team.

Sometimes, as a woman asserts her new self-confidence and independence, she realizes as the yearly cycles progress that she no longer has much in common with her marriage partner. Her interests have changed, and she will be faced with a major life-course decision. The point that I wish to convey here is the enormity of impact a one year can have. The subconscious and soul know it is time for change, but in many instances the personality may not be ready to face completely the habits and psychological needs that have been established for so long.

Take note of the personal month vibrations during each year. January through March (2, 3, and 4, personal months) are emotional and times for building relationship — integrating consciousness and establishing a new foundation. In

April (5 personal month) expansion and an opportunity for breakthroughs in your life present themselves. May can be emotional, including demands from friends and from the home. The combination of a 1 year, and 6 personal month (May) can erupt underlying tension in marriage or intense personal involvements. The summer months (7, 8, and 9, personal months) are for introspection, assessment and implementation of new goals, and releasing fixed habits and attitudes from the past which no longer belong in your consciousness. September on to the end of the year should provide opportunities to try out new-found experiences and free you to pursue newly established goals.

2 PERSONAL YEAR

The two personal year is a time to nurture that which has been sown in the first year. If new ideas and opportunities were generated in the first year, this year should bring added developments and elaboration. If stony resistance occurred in your attitude last year, be ready for difficult emotional trials that force you deeper into your emotional roots to release blocks and complexes. Cooperation within self and with associates is the keyword to this year. Include helpful people in your life where necessary to accomplish the utmost. It is a year to receive and share rather than push too aggressively for your own way.

The two vibration is strongly yin (feminine) which enhances intuition, receptivity, and emotions. In a woman's chart the passing of this year will stimulate subconscious conflicts related to the feminine polarity—her mother, sister, aunts, female supervisors, female role playing, or her own feminity. Emotional occurrences are heightened during this year and when underlying emotional dissension is present the personality will attract relationships which make it necessary to face and to deal with the problems. She may meet a man who touches her heart more deeply than any in the past. This provides a moment of deep feelings and emotional probing. Suddenly she may realize she is unable to fathom or express the depth of emotion felt; she searches into the past for clues to events that have caused the hardening or repression of heartfelt feelings. Perhaps she is married, or he is, and she isn't. Then a whole array of social, religious, soul and emotional conflicts arises. In solving the crisis, she relates to feelings and matures rapidly her emotional countenance. Two year emotional encounters can reach near overwhelming proportions of suffering and discomfort.

A woman may have been born into a family where a male child was preferred. Subconsciously, as a child she will attempt to fill the parental desire by identifying strongly with the male polarity and in the course of growing up she will at key moments deny her own femininity, perhaps unwittingly.

As the young lady reaches puberty, she begins to mature emotionally as well as physically. Part of the maturation process is the acceptance and adjustment of the astral body or emotional feelings. This is often a volatile and antagonistic period with the parents, school, boyfriends, and social adjustment. The disruption and emotional trauma can become so strong she will repress, deny, or reject the feeling nature and, in doing so deny a part of being what she is: a woman. It is, in other words, a partial denial of the feminine polarity.

Two year emotional relations, especially after the 29th birthday, attract the conditions into one's life that assist the individual in consciously recognizing the emotional block, release some of the steam if willing, and open the door to techniques or individuals who will assist in recognizing and releasing the subconscious roots.

The two year, in a man's chart also activates the anima or feminine energy in consciousness. This can be disconcerting to men who have been trained to control emotions and are uncomfortable with these feminine urges, commonly called "woman's intuition". It is particularly beneficial during this year for a man to remember that accepting his own feminine side does not exclude any of his masculinity. As a man learns to accommodate and integrate the feminine intuition and feeling nature, he in fact often becomes more of a man. It is a time to trust and to follow the higher intuition to success and accomplishment.

The two year is a time to pay attention to details and follow up on the fine print. Things are in motion now from the impetus of the one year, and this is the time to review, and revise the blueprint where necessary.

During the two year, a lot of criticism and gossip may be directed toward you. There is no telling how justified this furor is. It is a time to face the temptation for retaliation and your own proclivity for judgment of others. If you have sown criticism in this or other lives, the same condition returns now. Remember, when others unjustly gossip or rumor, it is their karma. If you allow it to have effect upon yourself, you are involving yourself in the karma. Work to avoid misunderstandings, and build a cooperative spirit.

January to March (3, 4, and 5, personal months) bring new people and occasions to assist in your desired ends. Late spring and into July things may become touchy and personal relationships need attention. July is particularly a time to be discreet, and learn, not push. From August to the end of the year, your deeper hopes and wishes should start to bear fruit if you have applied the knowledge and wisdom of the two year vibration.

3 PERSONAL YEAR

The three year is one of creativity, new ideas and self-expression. The young energy of the number one merges into the year of the number two, and brings forth the product of their unity.

It is an excellent year in the male and female chart to establish a complementary interaction between the yin and the yang, on all levels. Be willing to let out subconscious attitudes that create interference between the two energies, and watch your life unfold!

The three year is creatively rich for the job, home, skills, or inner growth. This year raises hidden fears and guilts associated with early sexual experiences. Review the three life number for further detail.

This is your year to overcome the tendency toward procrastination and pursue the development of that talent and creative skill.

This can be a burgeoning year for new friends and social contacts. For single persons the likelihood of being active with the opposite sex is greatly heightened at this time. Your natural charm is at its best when you are content within self. Avoid superficial attitudes and small chatter in order to let your deeper proclivities reveal themselves. The tendency is to scatter your energy too thinly, so you'll want to be aware of self-discipline. Be careful to review what you write and say; make sure that you have done your best. This can be a year for writing, public speaking, media work; and now is the time to seek a market for your ideas.

One who is in a three year needs to be appreciated, and enjoys admiring friends around. The loss of friendships, especially the most intimate, in a three year can be damaging to the emotional nature and turn the three to self-indulgent luxury, comfort, and superficial associations.

This year starts off very businesslike in January (a 4 personal month). It is a good time to write down inspired thoughts or ideas that could very well pay off, at a later date. The next two months should activate social interests and bring intriguing people into your life. April to June is a good time to spend a little time alone, to organize things. These months could produce very rewarding meditation for those working in the Light. From July on, put your best foot forward. This could very well be one of the best times in years for merriment, friendship, creative breakthroughs, attracting a potential marriage partner. Fertility for hopeful parents is also prevalent now.

4 PERSONAL YEAR

This is the year to roll up the sleeves and concentrate on the work at hand.

Business, career, and life work are important now. This is the time to build a solid foundation preparing for the next move in your life plan. You also need job security, so work to improve both present and future. Put your best foot forward, and try to avoid complaining at work—for it may be that you are being carefully scrutinized by someone in a position to help your future. If you determine objectively that you are at a dead end, it is an excellent year to consider a new vocational direction. This is not a time to be lazy.

The number four year offers many opportunities to enhance the working sector of our life. It may bring the chance to do the one thing you've wished to do in life. In these times the role of breadwinner is more commonly female than in earlier times, so the above information has a feminine side.

With many families, especially in depression times, where income was a struggle, the birth of a child could have been a burden and a worry, particularly in cases where the family unit was already considered complete, when along came a late child. The impact upon the subconscious attitude of such a child can be profound. He or she will feel a strong sense of being a burden on the family. There is a sense of guilt about putting added pressure upon the father to work harder in order to feed and clothe this unexpected addition. Or, subconsciously the child may feel guilty because his father may have missed a chance to find better work (or the work of his desire) choosing, rather, to hold a position of job security in order to provide for this offspring.

As the child reaches adulthood and is progressing along in his job or career, there are times when a chance occurs to really excel or move ahead. Subconsciously, he may also blow this chance, as a means of chastising himself for the time he interfered with his own father's progress.

In many homes the father or mother works exceedingly long hours to provide an income maintaining a comfortable living standard. The child may resent the parent not giving more attention and affection to him during the early years of life. Years later when he/she has a chance to advance in a job by working harder, the subconscious memory associated with hard work triggers other associations of rejection. If the underlying conflict is not released, emotional discomfort may grow out of hand. When this occurs, there is a good chance that one of the supervisors involved has behavior patterns very similar to the parent.

These are two forms of subconscious conflict likely to be confronted during a four personal year (also at times in an eight personal year). The same subconscious dynamics can apply during the following transition in transformation of awareness.

The passage of the four personal year (especially after the 29th birthday) can awaken an inspiration from within which stimulates the search to discover and fulfill the work of the soul. The personality shares a joyful, yet anxious, anticipation of breakthrough. The subconscious guilt pattern creates resistance to discovery. The individual experiences a definite pressure from need to discover, and yet the soul pattern does not crystallize. As the subconscious resistance is recognized, forgiven, and released, the guidance of the soul in a four year can pour through with definite purpose and guidance to the personality. The destiny of the soul becomes more clear, and the work that needs to be accomplished is spelled out with increasing lucidity. The work might lead to a public life in the occult, metaphysical, or mystical studies.

In most cases, the inspired recipient of insight will take his higher wisdom and be directed back to very obscure mundane duties. The greatest test is not congregating with other seekers at New Age centers and activities discussing how profound and evolved each is, because they happened to have read an Edgar Cayce book and performed a psychic and/or healing feat. The genuine test is to take Truth right into your own mundane sphere and continue to live Light amongst ignorance, fear, resentment, and skepticism which runs so deep in the heart and mind of the mass consciousness. This is the year to follow incentives from within the soul, and your inner work can progress with greater ease.

The year may start off in January with such a flourish of activity it looks like you will be in the top job or seventh heaven by the end of the year. Then the next four months fall apart at the seams on the personal/emotional level. Be careful not to let your performance slip, because favorable circumstances may be brewing behind the scenes. From June on, decisions are crucial and things are impending which can open important doors in your career. If you have not improved your working environment this year and are dissatisfied, it is time to do a little self-evaluating and scrutiny. Be willing to see what is in *you* that caused you to miss the boat.

5 PERSONAL YEAR

Five is the number of free will, man, the mind, and five senses. As a counterpoise to free will, five is also symbolic of Divine Law. You can ignore the Law, defy the Law, or work with the Law. Find the Law in you this year; let it start to grow now. Let the flow of Dharma become stronger (see the five life number for brief insight into Dharma).

This is a year for change, growth, fun, and freedom. A lively time! Travel prospects are enhanced this year, so take advantage of this opportunity to meet and mingle with people in far away places. New thoughts enter the mind and you'll benefit from reading new philosophies and diverse subjects. Many people are attracted to the occult and to psychic phenomena in this year.

The employment changes you earned as a four are arriving. Do not be surprised if you move into a new residence at this time. New friends enter your path. Allow intuition and curiosity to roam freely. You can learn many new lessons this year.

Restlessness, impulsiveness, and impatience are a part of this year also; tap this nervous energy and put it to constructive use. If the timing is right, your chance to move ahead is superb.

The acceleration of activity and experience brings trials and temptations along with the good times. The five year accentuates the sensual and sexual, making escapism through indulgences a tempting alternative to responsibility.

During the five year, the need to break from the past gains strength. Moral, ethical, religious, or social situations arise that demand participation in activity or beliefs contrary to those which the child learned from his early environment and parents. The mature adult is torn between participating in a newly discovered stimulating activity and adhering to conscious or subconscious rules programmed during childhood. For instance—a woman whose parents were known for conservative political views might become very much involved with a man of liberal persuasion. The crosscurrents of her admiration for him, conservative upbringing, parental interference, political conscience, and all the other subtleties of the relationship put her into a predicament. Initially, the liberal philosophy is enticing and appealing. Yet she may subconsciously fear parental rejection in the form of less affection, cutting off of funds, or social embarrassment. Thus, she is put into a position of choosing for herself what political viewpoint she really does accept.

Situations of sexual and moral indecision are very likely to be encountered this year. You may find yourself caught between intriguing desire and the consternation of conscience. Whatever the challenge, it is a time to shed the shackles of dogma, iconoclastic intimidation, indoctrination hang-ups, and social dictates in order to let your own inner guidance take command.

Five is the number of experience to its fullest, so this year should be active. It is possible to become overindulgent or perhaps go too lightly through the year and miss the lessons it offers. Use experience wisely, and you'll be free to soar to yet more intense life encounters.

The year starts out with a restless urge for change. This may cause you to feel trapped or bound in your marriage or a personal relationship. This could be tense through April. It is hard to determine when it is best to leave a relationship. Are you fleeing karma, creating karma, or have you worked it out? The summer should be exciting and adventurous in all avenues of life. Doors can open now. Try not to be too pushy or impatient. Overconfidence can create needless errors in decision making. The last three months are an excellent time to incorporate the experiences of the year into an emerging structure of Self-directed and Self-chosen life direction.

6 PERSONAL YEAR

The focus this year is upon home, marriage, responsibility, service, sacrifice, and resolution of personal antagonisms. The six year seems to offer little time to satisfy personal desires. Friends and neighbors come over or call for advice; the job seems bogged down; the children have more sickness and arguments which need attention. Bills get out of hand, relatives seem particularly troublesome, unexpected repairs arise, and the spouse is less than cooperative. Don't be glum, it isn't *all* bad.

This phase in consciousness acts as a test of altruism. You accomplish most by putting others first at this time and resolving the immediate crisis. It is an easy time for false martyrdom. "Oh, look at all I've done for others with no appreciation", is the oft-spoken plea of the six year. Forget the drama and face the demands. It is time to serve unselfishly. Be careful, however, lest others take advantage of your desire to be of assistance.

You may very well encounter a person in need you ignored or rejected in an earlier lifetime. Now is the time to balance your books.

If there is underlying tension in the marriage, the six year is going to aggravate that tension. This may not be comfortable, but now is the time to resolve the causes. The six year will often bring the marriage to an end, either in divorce or separation; or it could be reborn on a greater level of love and mutual cooperation. Old family skeletons from the closets of your childhood start to rattle and make a clatter. Look very closely at your childhood conflicts with your parents, and you will most likely recognize little traits and irritating attitudes in your spouse or yourself as similar to those of your parents. This year can be emotionally wrenching as painful childhood memories are released. Do not be afraid to shed tears; catharsis is one of the greatest methods of cleansing.

It is a time to seek harmony in the home and enjoy pleasant interests with family. If single, the six year stimulates the desire for companionship, family, and marriage. It can be a lonesome year—thinking about old times and old romances. Moodiness and depression can get to you if you dwell too long without attempting to seek the causes. Very possibly one of those admirers you met during the frantic five year will emerge as someone special, and you begin to make arrangements for a more permanent union. This may be a year to remodel or rearrange your dwelling to reflect your awakening being. If so inclined, pursue an artistic or creative talent at this time.

Many will turn to you for counsel; use your insight to bring greater harmony to these seekers. The six year often brings awakening among those with psychic and spiritual sensitivity. Many excellent channels have six prominent in the chart and find their accuracy and range of receptivity increasing in the six year. Hold only your idealism and try to refrain from becoming too critical of injustices around you. Balance your own inequities first, always a difficult task. This is a somewhat tedious year after the rambunctious surges of the five, but each year has its rewards, and by working with the cycles, you can realize the benefits of each cycle.

The first three months of this year may bring delays in your external affairs. Look within to find the keys to progress. Reexamine emotional ties at this time. This is also a time to reconsider your motives and intent. Activity should increase from April to August, with personal responsibilities coming to a peak through the fall and early winter months. A troubled relationship could flounder between September and the end of the year. Solid relationships should deepen and tenderly mature.

7 PERSONAL YEAR

The seven year is a time for meditation, introspection, self-examination and getting it all together. The year promotes philosophical searching and intellectual delving into the nature of worlds, man and self. Your search for self-discovery can lead to deeper religious studies, psychology, scientific research, or metaphysical investigation. Whatever your methodology, you naturally seek access to life's great mysteries. It is a time of personal calm after the activity and seething turmoil of five and six.

This is a lonely year in many respects, and as long as it is lonely, you might as well learn to be comfortable with yourself. You seek quiet, tending to shun noise and raucous social gatherings. To others, you can appear detached, aloof, and indifferent. Misunderstandings are likely to occur if you are not careful to consider others.

You have time now to elevate your consciousness. Those who have been working many years in growth activity may be blessed this year with illumination from within, which puts destiny into perspective and provides cosmic clues

as to the purpose of existence. The revelation and unfoldment of your inner gifts of spirit could happen now if you
can be still and listen to the whispers of guidance.

Each time we expand upward in awareness, we also
delve deeper into the recesses of our subconscious motivation. Some of the residue and debris stirred up the last few
years may surface at this time. Do not let repression or confusion disturb your ability to find inner peace. A tempes-
tuous sea may rage around you; however, your keel is set,
and the inner rudder should be firm enough to conquer the
threatening currents of mass skepticism, doubt, and discouragement.

Use the first two months of this year to completely
release the emotional residue carried over from the six
year just completed. The remainder of the year should be
spent becoming attuned to Self and environment. Enjoy the
awakening of Light abundant.

8 PERSONAL YEAR

This year is one of advancement, social status, finances,
executive ability, power, authority, and business interests.
If you spent time as a seven getting consciously organized
then you should be ready to reenter the social environment
with greater confidence and inner strength. It is time to
live fully the new found Truth and Light unveiled.

This year the world will recognize your potential and
skills. It brings promotions, advancement, and recognition
for your contribution. Go slowly, though, and cautiously,
with this newly acquired power and authority. Very often
an eight feels he has deserved attention or promotion for a
long time. The inner hostility and resentment from injured
pride has been simmering. Finally, when the recognition
comes, the pride and ego needs dictate some vengeful, or
rash behavior. Avoid the evils of false pride in this year,
and enhance your natural ability to inspire and lead.

On the dark side of the same vein, the year can also bring frustration with authority. You may find yourself constantly thwarted by coworkers, spouse, friends, or relatives. They will challenge your word on everything from how to fry an egg, to celestial Cosmology. Watch your reaction to confrontation. Herein is the clue to your growth opportunity: If you attempt to win every argument, refuse to listen, nod politely, and later criticize or quote endless sources as support to your thesis, something is awry. It is time to flex a little and be willing to learn from others. It is time to let go of institutional domination, social pressure, family dictates, and subconscious tyranny. See them for what they are, and relax.

This is the year to recognize and live by the dictates of higher authority. Power should be balanced with compassion and consideration of others. This does not justify breaking the laws of society. It may require an active participation in restoring Divine Law to man's affairs.

You may become critical of church, political, or civil authority. Supervisors or leaders in your department or business will receive the wrath of your opinions. This year is a reminder that the misuse of power and authority you see in others that troubles you so much, is simply seeing yourself. It is very likely that in a previous life or lives you have committed those very transgressions.

There is inclination to rebel against early authority from your childhood such as rigid religious taboos, the way you were forced to eat, dress codes, parents with strong moral-political-ethical-social bias, practicing some lesson. (See the eight life number).

Dealing with money is particularly important this year. A proper perspective should be encouraged that recognizes the rightful energy exchange involved with monetary transactions. You can increase your earnings and cash flow this year. So concentrate on your sense of dollar worth.

Many students of the Light have an aversion to earning money, especially when associated with spiritual work.

Study the laws of prosperity consciousness and work through the hang-ups. It will take money to build the New Age as long as we live in a money society. Money pursued for power, greed, or love of riches may slip through your fingers as rapidly as it is earned. Money earned through productive intuitive guidance can grow and bring yet greater dividends in your pursuit of New Age business laws. The keyword is "perspective"; know what your effort should be worth.

9 PERSONAL YEAR

This year brings a nine year cycle to its finale and closes one way of living while offering prospect of a renewed and revised style of living ahead. Nine is all-inclusive of all the previous vibrations, so this year will bring a variety of life events. This is a finishing cycle, and, with few exceptions, is not the time to enter new business, marriage, new jobs, or partnerships. These changes are more likely to prove successful after September of a nine year if you feel the time is now.

This is an excellent time to sort through the psychological framework and shed remnants of your growth and breakthroughs of earlier years in this cycle. By this I mean recognize immature emotions, negative thinking, and other restrictive behavior patterns. This can be one of the easiest times for release of the negative if you cooperate with the cycle.

Those who tenaciously cling to the past may have some heavy going this year. It is time to let go. That which should be eliminated now becomes burden, if carried over into the new cycle next year.

The nine year is full of mood swings and unexpected happenings. Friendships, marriages, and partnerships which have been floundering will face a point of reckoning during this cycle. Loss of a loved one can open old wounds and inner searching. Be willing to let go of relationships that are no longer in touch with the changes taking place in your life. Let new contacts and acquaintances enter your life to infuse new vigor into the life stream.

This year is one of letting selfishness be freed (See the nine life number) and giving birth to the altruistic inspiration of your intuitive mind. The year can bring greatly increased intuition and artistic inspiration. Psychic sensitivity grows stronger. Balance the ledger and be ready for the new cycle ahead.

The restrictive purging influence of the nine year predominates until about the end of September. If you have been willing to acknowledge and liberate the repository of unbecoming hang-ups by September, the latter three months can bring fantastic times of freedom, unrestricted awakening, and enjoyment.

11 PERSONAL YEAR

The eleven personal year is very similar to the two personal year. A heightened religious, mystical, and psychic awareness can bring one into limelight or a position of influence. It is a time to develop latent spiritual gifts. This year brings inspired thinking, originality, invention, and breakthroughs of awareness. Be careful of fanaticism and overzealousness.

22 PERSONAL YEAR

The twenty two personal year is quite similar to the four personal year. It opens the door to a greater understanding of your soul purpose. It presents an opportunity to serve on a greater scale. Use this time to structure in form the directives of your soul.

33 PERSONAL YEAR

The thirty three personal year is much like the six year. It may bring about a very difficult sacrifice for your inner

cause. This is a time to meet the needs of others wherever
you are placed.

Personal Month And Day

The method for determining the number for the personal month and day was given earlier in this chapter. I
give no detailed descriptions for the month and day, because Campbell and Jordan have covered them well in their
books which are suggested for your further study, and the
details are not needed here. By now you are able to discern the general trend of the month and day by reading the
life number and then, personal year. After that—just use
these themes on a somewhat reduced scale to obtain the
general trend. You saw brief clues to the months at the
end of the description of each personal year.

Personal Week

A cyclical pattern other authors have not mentioned,
but which this writer has found to be very useful, is the
weekly cycle. The personal week is determined independently from the personal month and day, although it is very
intimately related to the personal year. To determine the
personal week, start with the number of the personal year
and add it to the weekly number. For example, the week of
June 26th to July 2nd 1977, is the 26th week of the calendar
year. Add the two and six $(2 + 6 = 8)$ which gives eight.
You then add the eight to your own personal year. Following the personal week cycles is important, and I have found
it rewarding when helping people make decisions.

V

THE WISDOM IN YOUR NAME

Every author of numerology has his own terminology and procedure for interpreting the meaning of the name. All of them work with the vowels separately, the consonants separately, and the two combined. That is where the similarity ends. Sometimes new students become confused by these differences; however, try to remember each system has its place and works within itself. Just take the best of each for your edification.

In this chapter, I will present yet another approach to interpretation for the full name at birth. This concept has emerged as the result of insight received from a lecture in 1974 given by a dear friend and long-time metaphysical teacher, Dr. Neva Dell Hunter. Since that time, I've conducted research, meditated, and received intuitive guidance resulting in the delineations of each number through the personality, soul, and integrated self.

When the term "personality" is mentioned in this volume, I am referring to the little self which each of us uses for manifesting in this life sojourn. The personality is composed from the synthesis of activity expressed through the four vehicles of the lower self: physical, etheric, astral (emotional), and mental (intellectual).

The soul represents our inner Self of ageless wisdom, the repository of all our past life sojourns. It is the soul which seeks further evolution through the vehicles of the personality. The soul strives for balance and completion of Earth experience, so that it may be free to continue into yet higher realms and other planets or systems.

The integrated self represents an ideal or highest state attainable in this lifetime. It is not the Higher Self. Yet, one who is functioning through the integrated self will be very much in tune with the guidance of the Higher Self. When the personality has integrated the soul energy fully and harmoniously, the two forces emerge into an enlightened state of functioning.

The consciousness of all humanity on the planet is quickening in preparation for the Aquarian Age. Advanced humanity is working to eliminate blocks and hang-ups in the personality. Somewhat fewer of the advanced beings are starting to bring about the integration of soul expression into the personality. When that does occur, then increasing numbers of us will be functioning as an integrated self, Divine humans on Earth.

The personality number is a focal point through which you express yourself. Always remember it is derived from the totaling of numbers from consonants in the full name at birth. Each of those separate numbers is present and influences the total. It is just like your astrology chart; your sun sign may be one sign and the moon sign another. These are quite important. However, all the energies of the solar system (planetary and zodiacal) are present. The energy flows through focal points, such as sun sign, rising sign, or where other planets are placed.

Sometimes in life we work with every numerical vibration whether it comes from ourselves, the universal cycles, or another person. Despite our encompassing experiences, we still focus our energy through key numbers. The focal numbers then substantially color the way our personality, soul, and integrated self communicate themselves to others.

The soul number reveals the particular vibration the soul stresses through the personality in this lifetime. It is the energy pattern that the soul, in conjunction with Higher Self, foresees as most appropriate for gaining the appropriate growth at this time. The soul possesses knowledge of all the vibrations, yet focuses its fund of wisdom to utilize this vibrational pattern.

The number for the integrated self indicates an ideal state of expression. Very few of us living have reached this potential for enlightened exaltation. It is the individualized expression of Self resulting when soul and personality synchronize energies into synergic Self integration. The influence of the number is somewhat dormant until the integration, although it comes out rather distorted prior to unity of soul and personality. Their activities and personal proclivities would then appear closer to the personality characteristics and somewhat less exalted.

When interpreting, always remember there is much more than just reading different sections of the book for each numerical description. The full chart should be intuitively linked before rushing to examine the parts. In working with this chapter particularly, remember that the soul number comes through the personality as does the integrated self.

A number one soul working through a five personality, for instance, would be perceived differently than if working through a seven personality. That energy behind the personality (soul) adds tints and hues of subtlety to the outward mannerisms of the personality. Let the higher intuition assist in your own style of synthesizing and delineating the chart.

The procedure for deriving the numerological values for the names starts with a breakdown of the letters in the alphabet into numerical equivalents.

1	2	3	4	5	6	7	8	9
A	B	C	D	E	F	G	H	I
J	K	L	M	N	O	P	Q	R
S	T	U	V	W	X	Y	Z	

Start by totaling the numerical values of the full name at birth (first, middle, last). Add each name separately to attain the single digit value (retaining master numbers). Now combine the single digit number of the three names and reduce to a single digit. This total is the number for the integrated self.

Follow the procedure above working with just the vowels. A, E, I, O, and U are, of course, always treated as vowels. Y is treated as a vowel when it is the only vowel in the syllable or when sounded as a vowel, such as in Jay, Roy, Joany, Roney, et cetera. W is treated as a vowel when placed with another vowel and sounded as one, as in Sow. The sum of the vowels from the three names, reduced to a single digit, provides the soul number.

Do the same with the consonants to derive the personality number.

Two names are provided to demonstrate the breakdown of vowels, consonants, and the total letters.

J A M E S	E A R L	C A R T E R	J U N I O R
1 1 4 5 1	5 1 9 3	3 1 9 2 5 9	1 3 5 9 6 9
12 = 3	18 = 9	29 = 11	33 = 33
6 = 6	6 = 6	6 = 6	18 = 9
6 = 6	12 = 3	23 = 5	15 = 6
10	1	1924	
(1)	(1)	(7)	

Integrated Self = 56 = 11 (3 + 9 + 11 + 33)

Soul = 27 = 9 (6 + 6 + 6 + 9)

Personality = 20 = 2 (6 + 3 + 5 + 6)

Life Number = 9 = 9 (1 + 1 + 7)

You may wish to browse through the book to see if you feel these numbers are descriptive of our current President. Just an interesting side-light, you will notice the life number is the same as the soul number in his natal chart. The election day, on November 2, 1976, was a 9 universal day. Inauguration day, January 20, 1977, was a 9 universal day. The year of re-election in 1980 is a 9 universal year. One might venture to say that he was numerologically destined to the position. With all the nines surrounding his name and election, it is not difficult to surmise he has come to bring many things in our political system to a finale. If he follows the directives of his soul, he has an opportunity to plant a tremendous personal idealism and enlightened New Age realism into our political structure. If he yields to the temptations of power and pride, our country could face a period of traumatic upheaval and readjustment in our political system. The nine soul number indicates a man sensitive to the finer vibrations and aspirations of the intuitive consciousness and New Age idealism.

Whatever one's political persuasion, students of the Light can contribute immeasurably to consciousness by sending thoughts of prayer, love, and Light to President Carter, and leaders to come.

Another example, perhaps will help to clarify your understanding of the procedure.

```
M A R G A R E T      J A N E       P A U L E Y
4 1 9 7 1 9 5 2      1 1 5 5       7 1 3 3 5 7
      38 = 11          12 = 3         26 = 8
       7 = 7            6 = 6         16 = 7
      31 = 4            6 = 6         10 = 1

         10               31           1950
        (1)              (4)            (6)
```

Integrated Self = 22 = 22

Soul = 20 = 2

Personality = 11 = 11

Life Number = 11 = 11

Here is a very powerful chart of a lady who is going to influence the lives of many people. A progressed chart of her name indicates this popular network newswoman will likely make very significant changes in her career during 1980-81 and 1984-85. She could very well someday become a leading advocate for positive social change in the turbulent years of transition ahead. Using her name as an example, examine the descriptions herein to see if the material provided fits what is known of this dynamic person.

In the following pages you will find complete descriptive examples of what the numbers mean in your name.

THE PERSONALITY NUMBER

1 PERSONALITY NUMBER

Yours is the number of individuality, self-reliance, and originality. You are going to add to whatever interest with which you become involved. You are driven by strong will power, and when you have a definite goal in mind you have enormous productivity. Without such determined intent, you are less than enthusiastic and will settle for adequate accomplishment. A one is prone to self-centeredness and wants to be first in all things. You can become selfish and contrary if things do not roll your way.

You will likely have to deal with domineering elders (mother, father, or both) in childhood. Read the one life number for added insight; the experiential components of behavior are very similar to that in the personality number. In the rebellious stage, your separateness and belligerence can be very annoying. You find it difficult to accept orders from others and may choose to go against the wishes of the group, just to assert self-identity. You hide your insecurity behind brash and assertive outer expression. You love to give directions and will listen to others while seldom taking advice, smugly relying upon your own intense convictions throughout. Once you are convinced of a better way of doing something, you are ardent in praise and can quickly stir up enthusiasm in those about you. Your natural drive to the top has you seeking positions of supervision, leadership, and authority.

When confidence has been undermined in early years, the one personality lacks initiative and confidence, bemoaning lost chances because of bad luck or unjust circumstances. Ones will brag about their abilities rather than produce. A very passive orientation to life develops in the personality, and the individual no longer trusts self-initiative, preferring to let his spouse, parents, society, or government take care of his needs.

You are rather blunt, often witty, dignified, and to-the-point in communication with others. You prefer close one-to-one friendships to having many which are superficial. You are demanding, seek change from routine, and enjoy being around other go-getters. At extremes, your self-centered value system can find ways of justifying exploiting others or taking what is desired without respect for the value of self-creativity.

It is best for you to maintain a close companion or spouse who is also strong willed, supportive, and patient. Despite all the bravado about individuality, you need the security of a steady relationship to get the most out of life. When the relationship goes awry, you are prone to quick fits of temper, caustic bluntness, and isolated silence. Usually you recover quickly and bounce back to a normal self. If insecure, you become a stickler over cleanliness, regulations, and petty whims. You need affection and can give totally to your mate. You tend toward directness in romance and approach it with a straightforward intensity. There is little time for small talk and subtlety. Loyalty and attraction are key elements to a satisfactory relationship with you.

When balance is upset, you can become tyrannical, domineering, even brutal with those immediate to your life.

You are at best in professions or employment where you have freedom to be original and independent. It is difficult for you to take orders, so you could be most comfortable in your own business. Explorers, inventors, managers, designers, entertainers, small businessmen, and athletes are typical people with the one prominent in the chart.

Typically, ones are robust and healthy. This however can be jeopardized by overwork without times of rest and relaxation. You are inclined to overestimate the limits of your abundant energy. Ones are prone to headaches and arthritis. The one is an intense male energy and in a woman's chart suggests strong animus.

2 PERSONALITY NUMBER

This is the number of cooperation, diplomacy, and tact. You work very subtly and behind the scenes to accomplish desired objectives. You attain success through diplomacy, not by forcing issues coercively. You are able to adapt comfortably to varied circumstances and to people from diverse social, political, religious, and ethnic backgrounds. You are at your best being agreeable and sincere with trusted associates.

In your early childhood, you likely encountered considerable criticism and pettiness around you. (See the 2 life number experiences, for the life number and personality run very similarly to each other). This has left you unusually sensitive and your nervous system responds to tension and disagreement. There is a subconscious desire to avoid friction, which manifests in outward attempt to establish harmony wherever you are. It should be said that this is not the *only* reason for you to seek harmony; one of the strongest, however, is subconscious karmic pressure. You seek a balance against transgressions in a previous life where you lashed others with an abrasive tongue. You may wonder sometimes why you became the center of someone else's unexpected criticism.

You are naturally gregarious and prefer to be in the company of others. It hurts you deeply to be misunderstood or rejected because of disagreement. Fear of others' reaction or of what they might think is a negative attitude worth confronting and releasing. You can benefit by taking an attitude of detachment and noncritical acceptance of others' actions. As an adjunct to your persuasive manner, you accumulate and quote facts readily. At times this recitation of information cloaks the doubts about your own intellectual capacity. You can use facts accurately and profusely to enhance your bargaining position. At worst, you can manipulate data to support your opinion.

Twos often appear easy-going and indecisive compared to more aggressive types; yet underneath, is a grim determination to meet opposition convincingly.

Your exterior can be gentle and calm, but underneath the sweetness and smile is a touch of masculine strength and tenacity. When thwarted, you can become very cunning and scheming to get your way. People may have the impression that you are contrived and hypocritical. When you notice this, be wary of becoming withdrawn and secretive while slogging in a mire of self-pity.

Your charm and manner attract people who want to be of assistance. You know you will succeed because of an innate belief that good triumphs over evil. You have the ability to attract the type of people to get things done. Whereas ones are aggressive and want to rise to the top, twos are found more often in second echelon positions, finding their strength in a role supportive to leadership. This does not prevent you from being at the top; it does mean your drive will articulate itself in a less obvious manner.

In personal matters, twos tend toward an easy-going style. If pushed too far, they can become vindictive and contemptuous. An innate ability to see both sides of an issue clearly enhances qualities as negotiator and peacemaker. Twos come alive as mediators and are constantly working to establish accord between opposing elements.

Twos enjoy social activities with their necessary games and rules. You are most comfortable in marriage for you need the understanding and are uncomfortable alone. You are likely to choose a quiet, reserved, and supportive spouse who is immaculate and orderly around the home. In romance, twos are very susceptible to the details pertaining to the partner and the milieu. They enjoy the delicate touch and intrigue of tender interplay. Little things like small physical flaws in the partner's body, or a dripping faucet can break the spell of the moment, disrupting the two's pleasure. As parents, twos are patient and considerate; however, if disharmony prevails, they become critical and nagging about petty circumstances.

Twos are typically found in such careers or professions as politics, public relations, statistics, psychics, technical fields, and religions. They work best in groups. The two is a very feminine energy symbolically, and when appearing in a man's chart, suggests strong anima.

The twos' penchant for critical speech makes them prone to sore throats and tonsil and thyroid conditions. Two also relates to brain and nervous system, so people under the two influence react emotionally to strident or raucous conditions which can activate nervous disorders. At extremes, gall bladder infections and cancer may develop in the negative two vibration.

3 Personality Number

Three is the number of joy, beauty, and self-expression through words or creativity. Your natural demeanor is cheerful, entertaining, and sociable. You enjoy having friends about and are a natural host or hostess. Threes work in the realm of imagination and creativity; they will elaborate and exaggerate in conversation, preferring to overlook the drab and mundane.

The three disposition is optimistic, hopeful about the future. You can cheer up a lifeless party and dissipate gloom. But, be careful, it is easy to spread your many potential gifts thin, making you superficial and contrived.

You enjoy the good life and can naturally desire lavish surroundings. You may have gaudy tastes. When harmony prevails, your innate sense of artistry creates a tasteful environment. If you put luxury, ease, and self-indulgence ahead of productive creativity, you can become immersed in shallow, egocentric and worrisome thinking.

You are a natural with words, and can be fluid, funny, and fascinating at your best. On the other side of the coin, you are very capable of talking too much, but saying little. Words are a natural part of expressing your creative self. There are often circumstances in your childhood environment inhibiting your self-expression and natural born talents. (Read the 3 life number since oftentimes the life number and personality number are very similar).

Insecure threes are superficial and restless in their search for knowledge. They need to discipline themselves in order to locate the essence of wisdom which runs below the surface. When restless, they can get caught up in fads and crazes. Avoid these negative experiences. If unable to feel productive, threes can lose their sense of value to others. They then become detached and distant in relations, perhaps even unable to maintain warm interpersonal contact. Below the cheerful good-natured exterior, you have a dramatic feeling of self-importance. When out of proportion, you are capable of great melodramatic episodes, elaborating upon your disappointments and hurts. When properly channeled, this self-esteem can propel you to great heights of attainment and prestige.

You are a good friend, and friends are important to you. Threes are mixers and need company around them. You are trustworthy, although you may forget what you have previously stated. You are particularly comfortable with and attractive to the opposite sex. A perpetual romantic, you find yourself often entangled in adventurous affairs. Your life is full of incredible and intriguing experiences; if you teach, write, or counsel others, this provides a rich pot-pourri of anecdotes that you can draw from for examples. You are quick to pick things up, but need practicality to balance imagination. With other steadying influences in the chart (8's and/or 4's for instance), you can become quite successful in expansive imaginative business pursuits.

In romance, threes enjoy colorful surroundings and cheerful verbal interplay. They innately want to please their partner and can adjust to his/her little whims. Lighting, music, and considerate manners help set a mood which glamorizes the overall experience.

Emotional harmony is a must for any sustaining relation or marriage. You are deeply affectionate and self-sacrificing in love and marriage, but become quite stubborn if not shown appreciation. The home is quite artistically decorated, radiating warmth and making guests feel welcome. The three seeks peace and balance in the home and usually prefers a mate who is strong and responsible.

Threes are attracted to careers in areas such as the arts, media, and sales, law, education, social work, clergy, beauty, jewelry, entertainment, and travel, among many.

Three in health relates to the voice and sexual anatomy, both of which are symbolic of creative functions. When guilt and confusion about sexuality exist, threes are prone to disturbances with the creative organs. When emotions are uneven and disturbed, kidney conditions may flare up. Subconscious conflicts disturb the yin-yang (anima-animus).

4 PERSONALITY NUMBER

The four vibration is one of loyalty, dedication, dignity, honesty, and hard work. Your natural drive causes you to perform the work at hand steadily and methodically. You desire a solid foundation in your home, community, and business; hence, you gather respect in return.

Fours do not take much time for fun and pleasure and prefer to be left alone to perform the task at hand. This can become a fault because it is very easy to slip into a narrow rut, and you are probably one of the most difficult personalities to change habits. Often an early childhood environment places exaggerated emphasis upon working. (Read the four personal year for other clues to your personality). You are a bit tight with finances and personal belongings and read hardship into situations that may not justify your stringent evaluation.

The symbol of four is the square, and they can be just that. If anyone has boxed you in, it is you. If you feel harshly restricted by circumstance, you can be quite vocal. Your temper builds over a long period of time, and then — Boom! If you do not like your work, everyone around will feel it and suffer. If you do not receive compensation or praise for your labors, your self-image suffers and you can become quite jealous and envious of others who seem to get more than they deserve. Your general attitude is conservative, and this number is often intolerant, even hostile toward people who seem not willing to earn their way in life. Thrift, orderliness, and prudence are given top rating on your list of priorities. Much of your self-image is based upon your accomplishments and the achievements of your family. Property, proper social standing, and success are very much related to your personal security. It is unlikely that you would take risks which might jeopardize that security when your subconscious instincts are active.

You take pride in your work. Unfortunately, you are not above censuring another's work while ignoring the fact that yours may be no better. You are not one to waste time; often you can be found tinkering around the home, car, or where there is a need. You like routine. Imagination is not your forte. Your practicality, organizational poise, technical adroitness, and industry help you get ahead in life.

You are most comfortable when working for an industry or cause in which you can put your trust and esteem. You will gladly work at your best to help others; this can cause others to take advantage of your labor. You are steadfast, honest, and generally dependable.

It is not easy for you to mingle with others, trading small talk. Your fixed attitudes draw very opinionated definitions of right and wrong without much tolerance for people you place in the latter category. If your firm baseline is shaken, you can become scattered and defenseless. The quickest way you know how to react in that condition is defensively, argumentively, and stubbornly.

If fours are approached logically and patiently, an amiable solution can be reached — especially if it is practical. You are not one to rush into anything brashly, which will normally give you security. But many self-initiated kicks in the rear are deserved for big opportunities left untried.

It is not easy for you to spontaneously enjoy the fun in life. You have to work at it! In romance, you are ardent but control your passion. You are loyal and enjoy a constancy in companionship and technique. You are uncomfortable playing the field with the variety of games and guises required for selecting a compatible mate.

In marriage you find solace and security. A productive wife and children help to build your ego. Loyalty and sacrifice come easily if you are proud of those you protect. At times, you give no quarter and rule with a military-like discipline. A comfortable home life is a good tonic for relaxing you and giving you relief from the tension and strain of your labors.

Professions and careers harmonious to the four vibration include electricians, craftsmen, builders, chemists, scientists, farmers, naturalists, bankers, military people, accountants, office workers, and police.

Health problems associated with four include neuralgia, hardening of the arteries, tendonitis, bone disorders, backaches, and baldness (men).

5 PERSONALITY NUMBER

Five carries an atmosphere of change, restlessness, curiosity, sensuality, and freedom. You are witty, carefree, and enjoy travel and meeting new acquaintances. Fives deplore monotony and are a spring of nervous tension looking for an outlet. You enjoy crowds and events of speed, competition, and excitement.

You crave change innately; this is an excellent impetus for growth. However, you need to take time to learn and absorb from the lesson at hand. (See the five life number for added insight). Your abandon can sometimes lead to trouble and disregard for legal and moral codes. It is easy for you to run from your problems by overindulgence in sensual stimulation (drugs, alcohol, and food, or sexuality).

This points out another distinct proclivity in the five personality. When insecure, a five will repeat the same experiences over and over in an almost infantile manner, failing to learn from the experience itself. They wish life to stay as it is, and fear growing up into the next phase of learning. Fives like to roam constantly, and it is hard for them to stay attached to people or places for a long time. You see life as a gamble, and taking chances is your game. You will dabble in philosophy and religion, but usually not very deeply; you prefer to be unorthodox in your beliefs.

You are adroit with words and ideas which enables you to blend with all sorts of characters and seem like one of the crowd, almost any crowd.

Fives are fascinated by events around them and prefer to participate in jubilation rather than be left out of it. The attitude is generally progressive, independent, and willing to adapt. If anything holds you back, it's the fact that you are capable of so many diverse aptitudes that you have difficulty in concentrating on one in particular. You can become impatient and critical with slow-moving situations or delays. You'll find yourself most uneasy around the four vibration and to some extent with the seven.

Fives enjoy the company of the opposite sex and are usually surrounded by friends of both sexes. You are not one to probe very deeply below the surface and you become uneasy when someone attempts to delve into your psyche. It is not so much because they may find some deep hidden secrets, but because you often have not looked very far

yourself and do not want to be exposed for your lack of
depth. Consequently, fives are apt to use quick wit and
unusual repartee to avoid threatening issues (see the five
life number for more traits related to the five).

In romance you are flirtatious, fickle, and fun. Fives
prefer sexual variety in mates and methods. Sometimes
your curiosity leads you into the far out and possibly kinky.
It is difficult to tie you down, but you have a lot to give
while you are around.

In marriage you need a lot of latitude for your varied
interests. Fives like activity and a mate who is versatile.
Athletic and outdoor activities are important to your physical well-being and fitness. It is not easy for a five to adjust
to the demands of family and home; but, if content, you can
be an entertaining and colorful companion.

Vocations compatible with five include entertainers,
civil servants, speakers, salesmen, travel consultants, to
mention a few. If you work in an office, you will need ex-
cuses for leaving your desk to circulate with co-workers.
Tour guides, clerks, owners or workers in stores handling
many goods, athletes, and circus people are a few more
positions in which a five would find interest. A wide range
of possibilities exists for this busy number.

Health matters related to five include disabilities of the
senses (eyes, ears, skin, etc.). Nervous ailments can arise
if you remain overactive. Problems with the liver, kidney,
and intestines can arise from over-indulgence.

6 PERSONALITY NUMBER

Six is the vibration of responsibility, service, domesticity, and establishment of emotional harmony. Your
thoughts turn naturally to others and the needs of those
close to you. Wherever someone is in need, a six desires
to serve and be of assistance. A six is considerate and sympathetic. Sixes enjoy comfort, and harmonious surroundings, but do not need luxury to be content.

As a six, you are reserved but can become alternately suspicious and gullible in the company of new acquaintances. Sixes try hard to live within the conventions of society, yet will alter their patterns if it suits the immediate needs. When threatened emotionally you can become most illogical, defending your actions almost to the point of irrationality. Sixes have an excellent knack for placing themselves mentally and emotionally in another person's state of mind and emotion. Empathy, used positively, helps many associates of sixes through troubled times. On the dark side, this empathy can also be used very subtly to manipulate others by aggravating their insecurities. You are somewhat of a martyr and tend to fight lost causes with a quixotic zest.

Sixes can become overly sensitive to negative feelings around them, slipping them into moody and discouraged states. You are capable of deep affection and sacrifice, but attachment to another sometimes hides your own deep insecurity. The inner anxiety can be seen in angry outbursts of righteous indignation when the loved one does not respond with the loyalty, affection, and concern you believe to be your due.

Sixes are naturals as counselors once they have resolved their own problems or have learned to set aside their own conflicts sufficiently to empathize with the troubled friend. You find it difficult to stand idle when you see someone suffering. Be careful else those you try to help may become dependent or draining on your energy.

A feeling of duty to others seems to be an intrinsic part of your nature. If you learn to serve selflessly and without regret, you have a chance to etch the slate of Karmic record deeply.

Sixes live from the heart and feel very intently what is right or wrong. You are adamant when injustice occurs, and demand fair treatment for all of life's citizens. Some may mistake your need to serve as weakness. You take offense when not understood, and can readily dismay others at your seeming hurt and pettiness over trivial matters.

Friends are very important to you, and a refreshing evening with congenial friends can be a real lift to your spirits. You are easily influenced by the approval and praise others lavish upon you. Sixes are faithful to tradition and to those who share a similar respect. Often you think you know what is best for another's well being. When this tendency grows out of hand, you can become overbearing and a nuisance by interfering uninvited.

In romance sixes are sentimental, considerate, and protective. They are idealistic and need emotional harmony as a prelude to sexual enjoyment. When doubt enters into the relationship, they can become possessive and jealous to an irrational extent.

Sixes are well suited to domestic life. In fact, they need it to operate most securely in all avenues of self-expression. They are good providers, and their natural inclinations to please causes them to lavish luxury and goods, along with affection, upon the ones they love. Harmony in the home may come after more than one marriage (see the six life number). Once the right mate is found, however, the home can be a source of joy to all who enter.

Career and professions harmonious with six include — among others — nurses, teaching, counselors, artists and musicians, in fields of cosmetics, or apparel, doctors and food businesses.

Sixes are susceptible to stomach disorders from excessive worries and anxiety. When rejected, problems with heart and gall bladder may occur.

7 PERSONALITY NUMBER

The seven vibration is one of intellectuality, skepticism, wisdom, detachment, and aloofness. Your wisdom lies within the memory of all you have been, and you prefer to go within for solace rather than turn to others.

Your personality emits a strong sense of self-knowledge. Your temperament is judicial and stern with very strong opinions about what other people are doing. People nearby generally intuit your attitudes; words are not always necessary when a personality as strong as yours asserts itself. You have a knack of appearing unable to understand exactly what someone else is saying, which keeps them off guard and makes it difficult for them to change your mind. On the other hand, you are a deep thinker and know how to project your beliefs with force and courage. You are logical, cerebral, honest, and cannot be persuaded to deviate from your asserted position.

The certitude of your attitudes makes you reserved and aloof when dealing with emotional situations. You are less creative than many other personality types in the artistic context. Your originality is in your thinking. Sevens can get caught up in causes, or overlook practical factors if they become too intellectual. Lack of practicality can hamper your aspirations in business, leaving you unable to inspire feelings of originality or worth in the employees. When handling personal relationships you prefer to stay detached or indifferent; you often sense that you may be hurt by emotionally sticky attachment.

Your mind enjoys delving into the mysteries of life, death, the universe, and virtually any question or problem coming to your attention. Highly scientific in your approach to life, you sometimes overestimate mental knowledge and then become arrogant and snobbish. Sevens can bring tremendous wisdom to light when they are willing to blend intuitive profundity with reasoned knowledge.

Discipline and mental emphasis prevent you from enjoying superfluous or frivolous moments in life thoroughly. You dislike noisy gatherings and party atmosphere. You are dignified and poised in public, usually garnering respect for your achievements. When discussing familiar topics, you are convincing and at ease; however, in other topics, you can shoot from the hip impulsively and regret statements later.

You do not like being pressed for personal information, yet enjoy digging into someone else's intimate affairs. There are some hidden skeletons in the karmic recesses of your mind that you keep closeted in the subconscious. This makes you suspicious of other peoples' motives and at times cynical.

Sevens approach romance almost as seriously as they do the rest of their life. Intellectual rapport with their mates is an important ingredient to romance. When the cool exterior has been pierced by trust, they are loyal and capable of deep feelings. The love nature is enduring and sincere.

Mental compatibility is a sought-after quality in the seven's marriage. Seven can be difficult as a parent and spouse because of his/her tendency to withdraw into detached emotions.

Positions in which sevens function best include scientists, analysts of all kinds, *writers*, educators, and investigators. Sevens love to delve deeper into whatever they get their minds into and often come up with rich new insights.

Health conditions related to seven include glandular imbalance, pancreas and spleen problems, and in cases of severe cynicism and bitterness, cancer.

8 PERSONALITY NUMBER

Eight is the vibration of executive ability, financial success, power, and leadership. You enjoy the competitive world and are at your best when in charge of a successful venture.

This is a powerful personality and it attracts respect from both other leaders and subordinates. You are driven by a strong inner will, but have a sense of expediency which allows you to put on a tactful face at the most effective moment to get things done. You are materialistic, and vague philosophical speculation has little appeal to you. You have a knack for spontaneous enthusiasm, even to the point of passion, that you can turn on when you want to.

Eights possess a distinctly independent belief in their ability to handle any situation at home, or in business. You tend toward conservatism in thought and have some fairly strong personal opinions about those who deviate from your conceptual beliefs.

Eights derive influence from self-control, so your success runs parallel to the amount of self-discipline you maintain. When you stumble, not often, it is because you surpass the discipline and push fate too far.

Eights have an excellent insight into what motivates other people. This enables you to be an excellent manager but can also cause you to use others for personal gain (See the eight life number for more insight about eights and authority).

You have a great deal of pride and use it as a covering to hide your deeper emotions. You hesitate to demonstrate any form of tenderness for fear others will see it as weakness. This could cause a loss of prestige and of the keen competitive edge upon which you thrive. When you are callously detached from emotion, your attitude toward others can become hostile, sullen, even intimidating.

Your lack of regard can make you ruthless and can develop into seeing another person as something to be used for your gains. This comes from an internal distrust of self that can make you overly suspicious about others and impossible to deal with rationally.

The evolving eight is learning that money, just for wealth and power, comes at great expense to self. When money is sought out of greed, you will encounter totally unexpected setbacks and forces which confront your will. As a result of the turmoil, you become increasingly aware of new laws of manifestation and management. Once in the flow of your authority, you demonstrate the true mastery over self and situations. Once harmony is acquired within, your life demonstrates integrity, influence, and success.

Eights need a goal no matter what their interests are. Even in leisure hours, they are competitive. Relaxation is very important to your system and brings necessary rejuvenation.

Eights will sometimes seek romance and sexual activity to bolster a suffering self-image. This can be especially true of a man when his job or profession is not going well. An eight seeks a partner of similar ambition. Eights can become mechanical in lovemaking, are able to arise for the moment, but the spell wanes quickly, and it is back to work.

Eights seek an able partner as a spouse. They enjoy all the trappings of the good life, status symbols as indicators of success. If out of tune, eights run their home and family in tyranny.

Positions compatible to eight include stockbrokers, executives, charity organizers, engineers, athletes, management, and vocational teachers.

Health factors relative to eight include ulcers, indigestion, hardening of the arteries, and high blood pressure.

9 PERSONALITY NUMBER

Nine is the number of sacrifice, generosity, tolerance, idealism, and altruism. Nines are the dreamers and optimists who set a tone of hope and aspiration for the world.

Nines live in an inner world of ideas, ideals, and dreams. You find it hard to be practical; although you do not pursue material possessions, you seem to be provided with what you need. You are an idealist with a brooding awareness of the need in this world for broader intuitive thinking, expression of deeper feelings, and more humanistic science. You are not at home in business unless it offers an opportunity to serve a greater cause for mankind.

Your temperament is artistic, mystical, and poetic. There is a wholesome spirit of humbleness within nines because they are aware of greater cosmic forces at work in their lives and in the universe. Your mind works in generalities rather than detail. You are emotionally impressionable and generous, which lets people impose upon your time and energy to their advantage. You must learn to overcome urges to envy, spite, and revenge, by learning the law of forgiveness and release (See the nine life number for more insight).

Nines' extreme emotional sensitivity can lead to moodiness and depression. Your behavior will go from periods of elation and joy with hectic activity to listlessness and lack of initiative. When emotions become negative, you tend to take life too seriously and not let go of the source of the trouble. You turn fearful and self-conscious. Once the nines learn to let go and flow with higher consciousness, they are enlightened and inspired forebearers of the New Age.

You will have a chance to travel and experience life firsthand. Your opportunity for service is unlimited once you find the group to which you belong and the direction of your purpose. Your consciousness will have to grow with the coming tide of change on Earth. You can intuitively feel it coming like the uncertain calm before the biggest storm. If you do not fear the changes, you can awaken and prepare man for the changes through inspired art, music, writing, psychic wisdom, or leadership.

You have come through much sorrow, disappointment, personal loss, and perhaps illness. It has not been easy but as the awakening of the soul and higher guidance touches the personality, you will move from self-centered aspirations to a greater understanding of the overall cosmic purpose. As you aspire to serve that purpose and let go of attachment to the world, your role will come gradually into focus.

You enjoy friends who are far-reaching, sometimes unconventional, and idealistic. In romance, nines can fall in love passionately with an ideal, but as soon as the bubble is burst by reality, they plunge back into life; another ideal mate is on the path—be ready. You seek the sympathy and praise of your lover and can be very giving in return.

Nines have perhaps more difficulty than others in marriage, not because the cosmos has put a whammy on them, but because of their search for ideals. Too often the nine is disappointed when discovering the mate is not what was expected. You may fall short yourself from the ideal image you believe is you. Nines seek love and security, but will experience more unhappiness until they truly learn to "Let Go and Let God".

Vocations and careers harmonious to nines include inspired artists, writers, reformers, speakers, fashion, humanitarian efforts, explorers, inventors, and ministers.

Nines experience health problems through extreme emotional fluctuation which weakens the physical system, specifically, nerve and digestion disorders.

11 PERSONALITY NUMBER

The eleven personality is similar to the two personality, which should be studied in full. Some exceptions develop as the eleven potency is awakened in consciousness. Eleven intensifies the desire to serve humanity, bringing reconciliation and peace to the world. The eleven gives the drive which often leads the individual into positions of considerable influence and public prominence. When ambition and personal selfishness interfere with the altrusitic goals, the individual may suffer repudiation from the masses. Numerous famous politicians, evangelical leaders, entertainers, and scholars have had eleven prominent in their charts. Interestingly enough, as noted earlier in this chapter, President Carter has the eleven integrated self and the two personality. History will reveal which level he expressed most completely.

The eleven pursues ideas and can forget the human touch necessary to make idealism work. They can become fanatical for a cause and hurt people's feelings, trying to make the world feel better. In extreme cases, it leads to deception of the public and dishonesty.

22 PERSONALITY NUMBER

The twenty-two personality is very similar to the four, which should be read in total. Those with this number are often attracted to institutions or large movements which aim to bring mankind's greater cosmic destiny into form. In the twenty-two personality, the self can sometimes become greedy, lustful for power, or aligned with darker forces who desire control over mankind by keeping the masses divided, confused, and insecure.

At their best, twenty-twos are capable of uniting and working with people to bring the New Age into form on Earth. They may go through many menial and unimportant positions in their early years, but this can be a test that teaches them humbleness and respect for those who will do the little jobs later under the direction of the enlightened twenty-twos.

The twenty-two personality feels he has some added responsibility, and until higher awareness is opened he can wander around with a great feeling of self-importance and little to show for it.

33 PERSONALITY NUMBER

The thirty-three personality is very much like the six. (Read the six again). Thirty-threes feel the suffering of the planet's population and are attracted to institutions and organizations involved with education, health, counseling, and related fields of service. They very often are involved in research, seeking better ways to make men whole. Many thirty-threes are becoming aware of unique psychic or intuitive abilities that they are unveiling in an effort to better understand the esoteric anatomy, as well as the physical. Their contribution will shed light upon the inner gifts of spirit with traditional forms of healing and counseling.

Thirty-threes can also be found in teaching. They are, in fact, found in all arenas of life, but they contribute to a better world by working to relieve suffering in whatever they do.

THE SOUL NUMBER

One Soul Number

The number one soul works diligently, bringing the personality into accord with Divine Will. There is a strong inner drive to express yourself in original and individual ways. If your soul is restless, expect behavior and personal characteristics similar to the number one personality. You want to take charge of a situation and feel like you have a solution to every one's crisis, an attitude more admirable than practical.

The intensity of your willful drive can create the impression you are lacking emotional sentiment. This is particularly true when the personality number is seven, four, or eight. You have a strong belief in individual rights from misuse of authority.

Soul number one has an elevated feeling of self-importance; you *are* important, and — when in harmony — this gives you the confidence to perform well. If the flow through the personality is impeded, this self-identification leads to conceit and intolerance of people who are deemed inferior. You long ago chose this vibration for its thrust and initiative, necessary to accomplish innovation and renovation. You, consequently, are naturally impatient with people who are resistant to change.

This life will bring you more than an average share of willful contacts. Now is the time to accept the will in others; learn to unite the two individualities into synchronized effort. Once a wholesome understanding of your will has been attained, there is little need to compare yourself to others' standards or to compete. Rather, your higher standard provides the most accurate indicator of success.

You have come to take action. You will often walk alone among the many who live a life of reaction. How you channel and express this intensity of soul, of course, depends to a great extent upon the number of the personality. Through a seven personality, you most likely are an original thinker; through an eight personality, you might devise new business methods or ways of earning money. You possess the drive to accomplish much. It is important to work with other innovative people, despite probable conflicts of ego.

Two Soul Number

If two is your soul number, there is emphasis in consciousness upon cooperation, companionship, and the need to work with others harmoniously. The personality through which the two expresses Will yields excellent clues as to the prime area of cooperation. The primary bridges of awareness you have come to establish are those between (1) heaven and Earth, and (2) spiritual and material realms. It is particularly important for those having this soul number to find a quiet time to meditate each day. As you do this, you begin to construct the stronger bridge of cooperation between Higher Self and personality. Learn to listen to the inner voice of your higher intuition.

The two vibration is less aggressive than the one, so your gains come from negotiation rather than force. You are careful not to give away your position until the exact proper moment. Because of your capacity for discretion, others of considerable power will rely on you to handle responsibility and influence behind the scenes. Whatever your calling, you will have a chance to bring others together and help unite the world by your contributions. Sometimes your inclination for tact prevents you from speaking your true feelings. This is a patient vibration, but if you are too complacent people around you can get away with considerable mischief at your unsuspecting expense.

Those with this soul number can strengthen their natural spiritual and psychic sensitivity, already considerable, by a study of the symbolic and metaphysical sciences. Particularly, you might benefit from study of the symbolic arts such as Tarot, numerology, astrology, palmistry, Kaballah, I Ching, dreams, or related skills. Twos often develop into fine clairvoyants and psychic channels.

There is contentment with a harmonious home; while you enjoy the pleasures of money and fame, you are not overly ambitious, pursuing them just for their own sake.

You need to give less attention to *what* others are saying and doing to you and more attention to its impact on you. Uncover and release the disharmony in you that has attracted unkind criticism and hurtful remarks. Ask your higher self to help you to recognize the cause of disharmony; then work diligently to eliminate the tendencies and flaws within your being. You will think best of yourself when you see your problems from afar, and critics will soon recognize your calm as harmony.

THREE SOUL NUMBER

The three soul seeks to express joy, hope, and beauty for all. It enjoys the pleasant side of life and strives for a beautiful and colorful environment in which to express itself. Your natural touch is to creative expression; and the work, hobbies, or avocations of your life reflect the added little touch you give to each circumstance passing through your life.

Threes will benefit from an in-depth study of the yin and yang energy patterns. They have a knack for recognizing the needed touch to bring harmony and balance into a situation out of synchronization. You intuitively know how to meet someone's needs and are a natural host or hostess.

Threes are artists on canvas, with the written page, or with music. Many artists with the three soul number are entering into an inner plane awakening, producing psychic or cosmic art. This can include portraying symbols of the soul, inner body energy patterns such as the aura or chakras, or musical pieces which are in resonance with the inner consciousness.

You have come to use the word. You must work diligently to eliminate the subconscious blocks which prevent
you from using the word to its fullest glory. Let a strong
inspiration from your heart be a prelude to your speech.
Clear your mind of doubt and resistance to the guidance of
the soul. The spoken word from the heart has healing qualities which may produce unrecognized benefits to those
around you. The most important place to measure your improvement is in the home and with those closest to you.

You respond to life from the heart and can be hurt
easily; however, because you are a well of perpetual optimism, life will seldom keep you down for long. You are
entertaining and love people, pets, and children. Company
and close friends are important to your well-being.

Look to the Personality number for channels of your
creative potential. Even the act of looking within is creatively natural for you. If it is seven, your creative talent may be
more scientific; or if it is eight, for example, you may do
very original work in advertising or sales.

FOUR SOUL NUMBER

The four soul is learning to appreciate the value of a job
well done. You are known for your reliability and pride of
work. You can sacrifice much personal time and effort if
you believe in the work you are doing. Fours will work for
the benefit of others, even if it means giving up their own
aspirations.

When four is the soul number, you will increasingly feel
the need to find your inner work. You will feel something
deep within yourself compelling you to seek out the work
which you can do, with quality above anyone else's, to serve
the Plan. This inner conviction may lead to work that is not
glamorous or likely to attract much public attention, but
in the end, this soul could never be happier than performing its destined calling. No one else will be able to do this

for you nor be able to help you. Others *can* point the way and shed light upon the experiences through which you have passed. However, the inner work is an individual process. When you follow the guidance of the soul and higher self and pass the outer tests, you will come under the tutelage of inner plane teachers. The preparation includes riddance of self, ambition, pride, sloppiness, laziness, and those qualities which interfere with perfected labor.

Fours are natural administrators and obey to the letter the commands from their superiors. Be careful not to be misled. You are methodical and thorough in your labor and take pride in work well done. If anything, there is the need to incorporate a more open attitude of flexibility and of change.

You are loyal and dependable to family and loved ones. Fours make faithful companions, but can have difficulty emulating sentiment and emotions. You do not care for lying or deception in any form and are discouraged by those who fall to pretense and flattery. Fours are awkward at handling situations which involve subterfuge or deceptions.

Once you have a goal in mind, you are tenacious and persistent. Sometimes you hide your personal insecurity by pushing too hard in work. This can become an obsessive — compulsive syndrome, and your underlying insecurity should be recognized and released. As with the three, your soul purge will bring a new peacefulness.

FIVE SOUL NUMBER

"Let freedom be!" cries the heart of the five soul number. Participation in life is very central to your evolution at this time. You are here to accomplish a lot of living, but when five is your soul number, it is particularly important that each lesson of each experience be incorporated, understood, and then released for yet further growth.

Freedom is a requisite to free will. Through the opportunity of free will, we can choose to ignore, defy, or cooperate with Divine Law. The soul at this juncture is caught between the dictums of the Law of Self and the desires of the personality or lower self. This position is one of working out lower desires through the test of life. The temptations of flesh are strong; the temptations of the mind and its desires are intensified and challenge the soul. Now is the time to learn the lesson of desire and leave those desires to hear the higher self. In a way, it is time to leave the body behind.

When you understand this, you will no longer strain for mental domination over soul or seek sensual experience for personal gratification of lower self. Rather, you will learn the laws of acceptance. That is, you will learn to call up the Divine Self for proper experience, accept that opportunity, and utilize it in loving appreciation for the Creator who is the provider of all that is to be experienced. Then you will inherently desire to use these experiences for all the glory of the Creator and share experiences in a manner that assists in the awakening of others. Zeal is your forte.

The tremendous range of activities encountered by fives makes them indispensable as teachers and lecturers; they draw from personal experience to accentuate their lessons and instruction, making it come alive in a witty and anecdotal fashion. You roam the world working with all classes and races of humanity. Much of your wisdom comes not from scholarly studies, but from your personal contact with people in all walks of life. This contact keeps you flexible, progressive, restless, and anxious to participate in yet another phase of your growth.

You have a responsibility to share your growth with others. It will not be easy to take on an intense involvement with others; yet, you should learn to stay with each relationship long enough to receive and share the full lesson concomitant to the relationship. Be proud of the strength and knowledge you have to share.

SIX SOUL NUMBER

The six soul focuses life upon the home, family, and the company of close friends and loved ones. You work best when sharing the responsibility of your assignment with others. Six souls feel deeply and are concerned with those who suffer needlessly through home life or personal circumstance. You spontaneously respond to assist others upon call. Empathy marks your every relationship.

People are comfortable around you and can turn to you with confidence to discuss their conflicts and suffering. This is probably because you are a natural counselor. Many sixes are, and will be, opening their inner awareness as counselors. Sixes are often able to tap the akashic records to help in the recognition of past life trauma which still troubles the subconscious. If your awareness has not led you into the akasha, you are still most likely able to get inside another's consciousness, to help relieve discomfort.

Marriage and home are central to your unqualified harmony. You seek a perfect mate and can be disappointed when any sort of flaw shows up. Often metaphysical students seek such a union; however, it is more likely that you may have chosen a spouse who is not favorably disposed and, in fact, may be antagonistic to your pursuits of soul. But there is a purpose in this madness.

You have chosen your husband or wife for some need. If the two of you were completely compatible, it would be so easy to say "aren't we so spiritual and perfect". That could be true, but too often such couples slip into a self-righteous habit of patting each other's back—and fail to grow. On the other hand, when there is challenge on some levels, both mates grow rapidly if sincere and searching. Each assists the other, often through adversity, to better define and recognize personal needs. If you see only weakness and rebel prematurely, a beautiful chance for evolvement may be overlooked.

Your intellectual outlook is broad and flexible, but your life-style and emotional make-up are inclined toward the conservative and traditional. You want to correct all injustices around you and make up for the wrongs that have plagued mankind for eons. There is a good chance you will help many this time around.

SEVEN SOUL NUMBER

You prefer to be left alone to seek the quiet and wisdom deep within your heart and soul. Your rejuvenation comes from tranquil interludes of meditation and introspection. It is well that you take this time, as philosophers have said, to "know thyself". Within your inner self is a vast storehouse of evolutionary knowledge. You have come now to tap this memory and to bring the deepest secrets of man and cosmos to light.

The seven soul is learning to set aside the rational, concrete mind of the lower self, not totally, but long enough to hear the communication from the universal mind. The concrete mind must patiently be instructed as to its proper role of waiting to support and digest the promptings of higher mind. True meditation is simply listening quietly to the soul and higher self. The mind will assert all sorts of hindrances and tirades in attempts to prevent losing dominance it has held for ages. The reasoning mind need not be disdained, but it should become an adjunct to the soul and universal mind.

You enjoy probing the deeper realms of psychology, religion, science, philosophy, or metaphysical studies in an attempt to solve the deepest mysteries of man and universe. The seven soul often possesses a tremendous inner wisdom or gift of spirit. You will enjoy the invitation of your soul to recognize and mature this exceptional spiritual gift for the glory of God and benefit of man.

The clamor and noise of the hectic world outside are distracting and irritating to you in your quest for wisdom. A seven soul can be considered distant and unfeeling by those closest. You may have to work diligently to establish a manner of presenting your wisdom in an entertaining and humble manner. You have very strong opinions about your wisdom which can surface as arrogance. You find it uncomfortable making "small talk" for the sake of convention.

Sevens benefit from being out in nature frequently to recharge their batteries. You are slow to change your attitude and way of living. It will not be easy learning to express emotions and trusting your feelings. Subconscious emotional blocks must be overcome in order to accurately tap the intuitive mind.

EIGHT SOUL NUMBER

You are best deployed where power, money, management, or material challenges are concerned. When you learn to accept the laws of manifestation and work with them, you will attract money for very beneficial causes. If you seek money purely for selfish gain, it will likely slip through your fingers as fast as it came.

Look at your attitude toward money. Does the possession of wealth mean more to you than other values in life? Do you feel superior to those who have less? Does the material wealth affect your attitudes toward friends and acquaintances? Once an eight lets go of the need for money and accepts the universal flow, he will have as much as could possibly be needed. There should be no anxiety and no fear of loss. By learning to give and use money with love for the Divine supplier and with love toward all who share in the flow, you come into the divine law of supply!

Eights seek power. The above laws apply to your urge for control. Once you let go of the ego need to have power, the world will recognize just how powerful you truly are. Then higher direction guides you through the complexity of decisions necessary to truly become a New Age leader.

You have the stamina, poise, and confidence to achieve anything you set out to do. You are generous to those you feel have earned it, but do not give hand-outs. You dislike weakness and inefficiency. You have an opportunity to pass on your skills and thus enable someone else to develop confidence and competency in his calling. You have an excellent ability for recognizing potential in others. Life will bring a chance to determine which way you will use this gift, selfishly or genuinely to assist in the awakening of another person's potential.

There is definite potential for executive leadership in large organizations. Your calling may come in business, community, work or government. Whatever it is, you will take control and leave the situation greatly improved by your effort. You have the vision to handle the leadership required for the demands leading into the new era.

NINE SOUL NUMBER

You must learn to let go of every need, and only then will you have all you could want. You have come to serve God and man in whatever capacity the higher self directs. Learn to visualize yourself as acting as the higher self would have you act. Then as you perform the duties of life, you will soon find yourself naturally acting in accordance with inner guidance.

Nines dream of a world where there is no misunderstanding, no criticism, no ego threats, or no other causes of disharmony and of distrust. It is possible to be part of such a world, but one must let go of those human characteristics which underlie these discords. You are one who has the chance to lead the way by *living* this dream. How can you free yourself? You can do so by visualizing yourself cutting loose from the hang-ups and traps of the personality. In addition, by application of forgiveness and acceptance of grace, the process of cleansing can be accelerated to further enable you to attain detachment.

Nine in this position blesses you with a tolerant, sympathetic, and understanding viewpoint. Nines often develop into inspired artists, poets, inventors, or psychics. Once the personality no longer distorts higher consciousness, you can develop very accurate, intuitive, and prophetic abilities. Your generous and emotional nature can put you into predicaments because of an almost inviolate gullibility.

Satisfaction in personal love does not come easily because you are learning in degrees to move toward an impersonal, universal love. The suffering of personality can be made easier by knowing that your fulfillment in the end will far surpass that which any mortal condition can offer. The emotions will be unsettling as you strive for the final release of personality.

Nines dream of a utopian world. Despite the less-than-perfect current world condition, you should not give up your dreams. Your message and inspiration may well be the spark to move many others into an awakening of the new dawn.

Follow your intuition, follow your dreams, and the world will follow you.

ELEVEN SOUL NUMBER

The eleven soul and two soul numbers are quite similar, and the two soul number should be read also. Elevens with awakened souls possess the capacity to work on the inner planes and consciously bring information back for useful application. It can be very easy, however, for them to be so inwardly focused that they are impractical functioning in our everyday concrete world. Many excellent channels and psychics have eleven prominent in their charts. They may work consciously with devic beings or inner plane guides, thereby bringing knowledge or guidance.

Your idealism can become so saturated with zeal that you lose touch with the individual on your way to aid the people. Once you have a cause, you are so sure it is the best that you may not be the most tolerant of souls in your attempts to convert the world.

This is a highly kinetic energy which gives you facile intuition and inventive ability. There is a great capacity to inspire the populace, and once your feet are planted in common sense, you may find yourself in a position of prominence.

TWENTY-TWO SOUL NUMBER

Along with the qualities of the four soul number, the twenty-two soul number blends the idealism of the eleven with the formative discipline of number four. This combination makes you an inspired dreamer and builder. Twenty-twos, when illumined, read the etheric and inner plane blueprints and prepare the foundation for the golden cities of the New Age.

Once illuminated, the twenty-two taps and consciously controls inner plane forces. He recognizes other Light workers and works with them on inner and outer planes toward fulfillment of the plan on Earth. Your mental foresight and discipline allow you to be part of the forces molding mankind's evolvement.

Prior to the call of service, you will likely hold positions in many types of work. Your inner self knows you are an important soul with a masterful task, and you may wonder why the world does not recognize this. Until you have earned the right, through study and application of higher instruction, to know your true work, you tend to foster a feeling of inferiority. You then underestimate your worth and diminish your own capacities.

THIRTY-THREE SOUL NUMBER

In addition to the qualities of the six soul number, thirty-threes serve as counselors and teachers not only to individuals, but to the mass consciousness. To the awakened, this can bring access to the akasha and inner records. In preparation, you would benefit from a good solid investigation into the secret teachings and world history from the esoteric perspective. From such a study, you would assist the reawakening to memories of civilizations and Earth.

THE INTEGRATED SELF

ONE INTEGRATED SELF

You are attuned to Divine Will and flow in rhythm with both the Divine and human aspects of will. By now you have learned to work with all brothers and sisters and you no longer need to dominate. Nor are you intimidated by expressions of will in those with whom you interact.

This does not mean you will be totally at ease with everyone you meet. We must recognize that some vibrations do not touch each other in total compatibility. It only means you have a healthy respect for individuality and no longer need to be angry or judgmental about another person.

Your keen sense of originality and of innovation is an inspiration to many; your ambition is to awaken originality in all you contact. You meet greatest success at the forefront of endeavors. You will be called upon to lead, direct, and manage. Your powers of concentration and of visualization are very keen; others know this of you. You are strict about habit and behavior but are willing to change to improve yourself. Once you have set your sights, your one-pointed focus enables you to complete the job quickly and fully.

TWO INTEGRATED SELF

You are comfortable functioning between both worlds — inner and outer. The ease with which you tap the inner planes provides you with an almost uncanny foreknowledge of events affecting your life and the lives nearest you. You are able to perceive inner plane cause, producing outer plane effect.

Your role is one of mediator, bringing heavenly decrees to mankind on Earth. You also serve as peacemaker and reconciliator between factions of disagreeing humanity.

You seek personal tranquility by delicate persuasion rather than by force. There is a charm of character which causes others to be at ease in your presence.

You give tenderness and sympathy and need the same in return. Your innate intuitive insight enables you to know just what others need—a kind word, or the appropriate bouquet of flowers. You work best in association with others and benefit from growing through group consciousness.

THREE INTEGRATED SELF

You are a constant source of joy, spreading your good news through word, music, painting, or pen. Your inspiration and vivid imagination are apt tools to bring greater light into a weary world. You can put across an important moral in your teaching, using popular thought and language. You have overcome hesitation and inhibition of your creativity. This allows you to express a full range of creative interests wherever your higher guidance leads.

Your previous learning enables you to flow harmoniously to the male-female polarity. This innate attunement gives you insight which enables you to help others you perceive as being out of balance. Your artistic and creative work has the impact of stimulating the upper chakras, thus elevating the aspirations of mankind.

Your natural integrity and cheerful disposition are like a healing tonic. You are sincere and patient in friendship. As your creative fire is elevated into the higher chakras, you may experience a waning of sexual drive. Consider it a growth rather than loss; you are compensated by increased creativity above the sexual plane.

FOUR INTEGRATED SELF

You know what your inner work is and you proceed happily in the performance of your role in the Plan. Others may encourage you to take time out to have fun, but they do not realize the great enjoyment you experience doing your assigned task to the best of your ability.

Fours at this point in consciousness can tap the universal blueprint to comprehend the design for Earth. With higher inspiration, they become the builders of form on Earth, working to establish the Kingdom on Earth.

You are a natural organizer, but your systematic and methodical nature may appear too cumbersome to the more rapid vibrational numbers. Once you have set a deadline, you will work feverishly to complete your project on time. Your work is an extension of your word and trust; you take pride in what you do and it touches all of your work.

You are recognized for dependability, endurance, and your grasp and effective usage of factual data. Self-control and discipline are central to your life style, and you expect the same from others.

FIVE INTEGRATED SELF

You have finally released the shackles of life and live ebulliently in your complete state of freedom. You have learned that freedom comes from natural adherence to Divine Law. The temptation of the senses and cunning of the lower mind have been mastered; your consciousness by now has expanded the inner senses and curiosity of the intuitive mind. Through projection of inner being, you can travel and explore happenings throughout the world on many levels.

This capacity for extended sensory awareness makes you a valuable source for new ideas, rapid solutions, and alternative methods of dealing with the innumerable changes and challenges coming in the transitional years just ahead. You will have opportunities for travel, mingling with people from diverse backgrounds and viewpoints. Your ability to draw upon these human encounters for storytelling enables you to be most effective as lecturer and teacher.

You are in touch with your dharmic guidance and are free to move with each life experience with confidence and joyous anticipation of each event which takes place.

SIX INTEGRATED SELF

You have come into an understanding of the role you have chosen to serve mankind. Each day the pleasure of rendering assistance echoes through your heart in thanksgiving for this chance to serve God and man. The hours may be long and material rewards meager, but the struggle of selfless services pays rich dividends on the karmic ledger sheet.

Family, home, and close friends are paramount in your life. You live in accord with higher ideals that many find impossible to accept, let alone attempt. You seek an ideal home and spouse. When fully integrated, the six individual has learned to accept self and others; only then are the ideals truly available to you.

You are a natural counselor and guide and are sometimes referred to as a cosmic mother or cosmic father. You are generous rendering assistance and have learned to give with no expectation of anything in return. You benefit from incorporating knowledge of music, color, and vibration into your emotional counseling of others.

SEVEN INTEGRATED SELF

Your inner perception and meditative nature allow you to delve deeply into the future of man. Your far-reaching insight enables you to ponder and prepare philosophical ideas that are literally ahead of their times. You may be left very much alone in your thinking, but a few will grasp your advanced concepts. Expect to be appreciated only occasionally for ideas ahead of their time.

You prefer to keep to yourself and should make more of an effort to share your thoughts. You can be a convincing and articulate spokesman on abstract matters. You are scientific and thorough in your intellectual interests. You excel in specialty work of a scientific, abstract, or metaphysical nature.

You work quietly behind the scenes, preparing the fours and eights with the necessary foresight to get the concrete work done. You can see long range plans clearly and enable the more practical to aim toward that future.

EIGHT INTEGRATED SELF

People naturally turn to you for leadership and respect your decisions. You have learned to exercise authority according to higher guidance in conjunction with Divine Plan. Life will automatically put you into positions of authority, even command. As long as you see the One Source as your commander, your success will be unlimited.

You are a living example of how to work the laws of manifestation through proper visualization, expectation of Divine Assistance, appreciation for that received, and application for the greater good of mankind. Once in this flow, all your mystical and spiritual needs come at exactly the right moment. You are a master on all levels of expression, and you will have the chance to help many more work toward that good.

You give your skill and leadership to mankind purely for the goal of building a better world. Eights are often called into situations which have broken down and need revitalized leadership. You like nothing better than to meet such a challenge while allowing others to find faith and confidence in their potential.

NINE INTEGRATED SELF

You have come to a turning point in consciousness where you have now had an opportunity to accumulate the mastery of each vibration, allowing you to serve as a universal helper. A difficult point, this: you must learn to be in the world, but not of the world. Your intuition tunes to the utopia blueprint being prepared now in the inner planes. You will have a part in making these dreams become reality in our world.

When you have learned to let go of the need for possessions, power, wealth, and self-gratification of the lower self, the same will come to you easily and appropiately. You share your universal love and gifts generously with deserving recipients; assist others with their responsibilities; help the poor and hindered; and give encouragement to the downtrodden.

This is a highly intuitive, inspired, and artistic vibration. You are poetic and prophetic in your use of words and expressive mode. Your eye for beauty and standards of perfection give you a disposition that reaches for the stars, and there is a good chance you may become one of the first to catch one.

Eleven Integrated Self

You are driven by the notion you have a particular destiny to serve the human race. No one can dissuade you from your course once you have recognized the way. Develop caution, and discretion to keep the newly-found path. Even the most idealistic of efforts can go astray when working with the mass consciousness.

People will seek you for counsel; you can supply them with logical and common sense information blended with intuitive insight. Your impersonal perspective enables you to solve solutions without being involved in emotional entanglements. You can see the possibility of considerable improvement in the world and work tirelessly to bring about needed change.

There is strong likelihood you will reach a level of public recognition, but you are content to serve in God's role, no

matter how meager the role may appear to the world
around you.

TWENTY-TWO INTEGRATED SELF

You have probably worked in many different positions
and jobs in your lifetime, always feeling within your heart
that someday you would have a particular task to fulfill.
Now you have begun to see your role in the Plan and can
start the inner work on your evolutionary sojourn. You can
see into Earth's plan, perhaps deeper than most of humanity. With that access to inner design, you are a part of those
constructing the future institutions and organizations which
will soon again serve jointly with the hierarchy and angelic
hosts to reestablish God's Plan on Earth.

You will be joined with other Light workers at the appropriate time. By inner illumination, you will know them;
and they will know you. You are truly a master mason who
has a chance to participate in building a new world, stone
by stone, following divine order with each addition of etheric
mortar.

THIRTY-THREE INTEGRATED SELF

As you reach this level of self-growth, you will finally
be freed from restraints. Now you can serve mankind with
no limitations. It is like a fond dream coming true. You will
be part of an organization or group whose work it is to care
for and heal thousands. There will be little time for you to
think of yourself; even the inclination is gone.

You would be wise to accumulate as much knowledge as
possible about the divine origin and history of mankind
from direct experience with the akasha. This research will
be useful for your teaching and counseling. Much of your
work will be involved with the astral or emotional level of
mankind. You would benefit from a thorough knowledge of
the esoteric anatomy, particularly in relation to the feeling
nature.

THE PLANES OF EXPRESSION

Another dimension into understanding one's self is provided from an additional breakdown of the letters in your name at birth. The letters are categorized into four sections which then reveal the fundamental tendencies of your intellectual or mental character, the emotional temperament, the physical proclivities, and your intuitive or spiritual inclinations.

To determine the numerical significance for these levels, use the chart below:

PHYSICAL	D	E	M	W					4
EMOTIONAL	B	I	O	R	S	T	X	Z	8
MENTAL	A	G	H	J	L	N	P		7
INTUITIONAL	C	F	K	Q	U	V	Y		7

= 26 Letters of the alphabet

The letters from the full name at birth are placed in the appropriate level, and the total for each level computed. From this we have clues as to how one reacts and works in the four levels of consciousness. This chart is particularly helpful for vocational guidance and determining compatibilities in marriage, partnerships, or business. Using a name previously given in this book, Margaret Jane Pauley (18 letters), the example below demonstrates how to calculate planes of expression:

PHYSICAL	ME	E	E	4
EMOTIONAL	RRT			3
MENTAL	AGA	JAN	PAL	9
INTUITIONAL			UY	2

= 18 letters

In this chart, we see that she has four letters on the physical level, three letters on the emotional level, nine letters on the mental level, and two letters on the intuitional level.

As a rule of thumb, when a preponderance of letters appears on the physical plane, the individual is practical, concrete in daily matters, and concerned with material needs in the world.

Those with a high number of emotional letters are creative, artistic, and react to life on a feeling basis more so than a factual.

If heavily mental, the individual will be intellectually oriented, using his/her head for business, teaching, leadership, and related fields.

When the greatest influence is upon the intuitional plane, the consciousness is inclined to be more psychic and artistic. They live in a realm of idealism and imagination unless other factors in the chart help to ground their lofty speculations.

The reader will note that the descriptions in the following pages are broken into three descriptive *phases*. These are to be used as a guideline by which you can measure your own manifestation of attitude. When excesses are recognized you can bring about change through self-discipline or methods familiar to self. By studying the tendencies — as indicated through numerology — you can find qualities pertaining to antidotal numbers (See Chapter Three) and then apply those in your life to help establish balance, and harmony.

Following is a more detailed description of the influence of numbers through the planes of expression. These are just brief sketches, and the reader will want to add to these insights.

NUMBER ONE ON THE PLANES

PHYSICAL:

Assertive — is restless, enjoys athletics and competition, starts many projects without completing things, is overactive, dislikes delays, has headaches.

Passive—procrastinates, is careless with material goods.

Harmonious—can be a starter or leader, is original in hobbies and vocations or work, knows how to kindle interest and get others started, prefers work with variety and change.

EMOTIONAL:

Assertive—is fickle and emotionally unreliable, attempts to dominate or manipulate others' feelings, puts on a rough exterior, is restless.

Passive—is afraid to engage in emotional relationships, demands attention without giving in return, has difficulty trusting feelings.

Harmonious—enjoys meeting new acquaintances, is enthusiastic, does not care for subterfuge, is optimistic.

MENTAL:

Assertive—needs to win arguments and debates for ego's sake, forces own thoughts upon others, is stubborn.

Passive—is unsure of where he/she stands, makes decisions after it is too late, is easily talked out of personal beliefs.

Harmonious—is an original thinker, likes to solve new problems, is a quick thinker, follows own beliefs and opinions.

INTUITIVE:

Intuition hits like a lightning stroke; with 4, 7, or 8 on the mental plane, is likely to follow logic rather than trust intuition; original ideas need to be developed into reality. May inspire new directions.

NUMBER TWO ON THE PLANES

PHYSICAL:

Assertive—can get too involved with minor details of dress, work, et cetera; chooses personal items to please or impress others; enjoys sports of strategy rather than power.

Passive—lacks courage to take self-initiative, wants every detail in order before making a move, holds onto worn-out or useless items for sentimental reasons.

Harmonious—works well with others to get job done, able to see the needs of others clearly, enjoys dealing with factual information to make point, enjoys dancing and artistic hobbies.

EMOTIONAL:

Assertive—is hurt readily by criticism; speaks impulsively; is critical of others when everything does not go just so; is overly self-conscious.

Passive—has negative moods, worries excessively, withholds complaints, relies heavily on another's support, uses acerbic speech.

Harmonious—has good "feel" in evaluating people and making decisions; gives encouragement to others; is naturally at ease with various types of people; is calm, patient, and poised.

MENTAL:

Assertive—becomes encumbered with too much detail, manipulates statistics to support own opinion, is unyielding and has fixed attitude, can pursue needless incidentals to extreme, distorts logic, is rhetorical.

Passive—is unwilling to consider varying viewpoints, is intolerant, unable to communicate personal ideas, needs others' support when stating a position.

Harmonious—sees both sides to a position fairly, has good judgment when reviewing facts, plus accurate gut feeling, is a storehouse of knowledge and meaningful trivia, is logical and factual, is firm but fair with decisions.

INTUITIVE:

Needs to trust intuition and gut level feelings, is psychic, has unusual ideas and visions, is sensitive to inner moods of the mass consciousness. Intuition may help solve personal conflicts and yield a clue to enhance cooperation with those close to you.

NUMBER THREE ON THE PLANES

PHYSICAL:

Assertive—scatters talents in too many directions, is neither systematic nor disciplined, is oversexed, cannot make imaginative ideas work practically, has gaudy taste in dress and decorum.

Passive—squanders potential talents and creative abilities, is asexual, may have problems with creative organs, has difficulty putting feelings into form.

Harmonious—has lovely voice, is artistic and has creative ability, dislikes restrictions, likes beautiful attire and home, enjoys nature and natural products, travels.

EMOTIONAL:

Assertive: over-reacts to someone else's criticism of his/her work or ability, is impulsive, is superficial, emotions overcome reason under pressure, has variable emotions.

Passive—feelings are hidden under fears of criticism, has repressed emotions, is unable to plan ahead, is listless, is vain about personal dress and belongings, is oversensitive to criticism whether real or imagined.

Harmonious—is expressive, is a good friend, is pleasant, spreads joy, is adventurous in personal affairs, works for appreciation and needs recognition, is intuitive.

MENTAL:

Assertive—ideas and thinking may be too imaginative for practical value, unable to convince masses of personal view, colors facts with personal feelings and opinions, has controversial ideas.

Passive—is unimaginative and dull; thinks things out, but acts on impulse; exaggerates ideas and facts to compensate for feared inferiority; is confused by emotional issues.

Harmonious—creative and imaginative in thinking, much feelings go into decisions, is not too serious, takes life as it comes, is colorful and lighthearted when discussing philosophical ideas and concepts.

INTUITIVE:

Is artistic in comprehension of intuitive and psychic impulses, is inspired in art or speech, must overcome sexual guilt to best receive impulses. May open up clues to outlet for talent.

NUMBER FOUR ON THE PLANES

PHYSICAL:

Assertive—overworks self, is harsh as a boss or supervisor, overestimates skills to compensate for poor self-image, takes work seriously, can pay too much attention to procedures without getting the work done.

Passive—is stubborn about alternative work procedures, is lazy, feels his/her work is below one's dignity, is uncoordinated, must work hard to discipline body.

Harmonious—is dependable, is loyal employee, executes others' directions well, is capable, is economical, dislikes waste, does job well.

EMOTIONAL:

Assertive—possessive with personal relations and personal belongings, is domineering, controls emotions, resents regulations and authority, has conflicts with aggressive people.

Passive—temper builds slowly and explodes when pushed too far, dislikes restriction, uncomfortable unless in control of emotional relationships, forgets to consider others.

Harmonious—is loyal, is patient, overcomes others' negativity, has difficulty enjoying spontaneity of feelings, is generous, is warm-hearted with family.

MENTAL:

Assertive—studies long and hard so he/she will not be shown up, pride of thought, has to be shown to believe, dislikes speculation.

Passive—has fixed, opinionated ideas and prejudices, refuses to change mind even when facts prove wrong, hesitation and over-caution causes him/her to miss opportunities, is envious of those who are successful.

Harmonious—is thorough and exacting, is analytical, has managerial ability, is technological, can carry a project through from idea to finished product.

INTUITIVE:

Is uncomfortable with mystical and intuitive experiences, does not follow through on inspiration unless practical, prefers conventional religion and studies, has inventive ability. May shed some light upon new career or work opportunity.

NUMBER FIVE ON THE PLANES

PHYSICAL:

Assertive—is on the move often; cannot stick to a job or to personal responsibility; seeks escape in sex, alcohol, drugs, or gambling; suffers from nerves; takes chances.

Passive—fears change, does not like to perform in front of many people, is always tired, has difficulty making new friends, has sexual problems.

Harmonious—has good dexterity and physical prowess, enjoys travel and people, has sales ability, benefits from working with many people, is adaptable to changes in circumstances, is a good speaker.

EMOTIONAL:

Assertive—dislikes getting too close emotionally, has many types of adventures, can misrepresent feelings, is overly frank and brusque, seeks risks for kicks, has disregard for others.

Passive—has difficulty letting go of outworn relations, uses others and then leaves, can be cruel and cold, unable to enjoy and benefit from life experiences, has unpredictable outbursts.

Harmonious—can be comfortable with different people and make them feel the same; is able to adjust to different temperaments; likes to probe and analyze others' feelings; is impatient; has variable moods, but not deep or for long.

MENTAL:

Assertive—cannot stand monotony, is deceptive, uses intellect to prey on less fortunate, likes to study bizarre and unusual subjects, changes opinions frequently.

Passive—has sluggish mind, prefers pat answers and social norms to independent thought, needs to learn mental discipline, is repetitive.

Harmonious—is flexible, curious, and witty; mercurial thinker; needs to get out of set routines; investigates many subjects, but none very deeply; is quick to catch on to things.

INTUITIVE:

Is naturally attuned to Divine Law; must listen to dharmic guidance; doubts intuition, but uses it at times unknowingly; picks up on many interesting incidents. Can shed insight into the true motives of new acquaintances and friends.

Number Six on the Planes

PHYSICAL:

Assertive—gets into others' ways, worries more about something than actually getting it done; is exacting; has poor taste in clothing and home decor.

Passive—is upset with less than perfection in self and others, takes short cuts, over-evaluates own importance to boost ego, is usually somewhat frail physically, must work diligently to build body strength.

Harmonious—often displays artistic touch, chooses career of service or assistance to others, is willing to handle responsibility, enjoys pets and plants, works for human welfare and justice.

EMOTIONAL:

Assertive—is too concerned about little setbacks in own and others' lives, remembers embarrassing experiences longer than necessary, feelings are hurt easily, is irritable and cranky.

Passive—worries about potential pitfalls and misfortunes, can be a hypochondriac, gets touchy about certain personal issues.

Harmonious—knows how to work effectively with other peoples' problems and worries, brings harmony into home and working environment, can keep another's trust, has high integrity, is calm.

MENTAL:

Assertive—is sensitive to criticism about ideas, carries many imagined and unnecessary burdens, lets world conditions and suffering upset his/her mind, meddles in others' business.

Passive—has callous disregard for another's situation, is self-centered in thinking, is unable to solve problems effectively, is lethargic.

Harmonious—handles responsibility with efficient and confident ease, is a problem solver in personal or business matters.

INTUITIVE:

In inclined to conventional, personal religious experiences and faith; must learn to live and express own ideals rather than living by someone else's standards; may have breakthroughs in understanding how to serve mankind. May show the best way to serve.

NUMBER SEVEN ON THE PLANES

PHYSICAL:

Assertive—is timid, prefers to be reclusive, analyzes all events rather than accepting and enjoying them, prefers individual activities to team sports, is rigid, does not accept things at face value.

Passive—does not prepare endeavors thoroughly; takes too much time to make decisions; can become aloof, rude, and critical.

Harmonious—is analytical and thorough in work conducted, is scientific in nature, is reserved, is usually conservative, does not enjoy crowds or noise.

EMOTIONAL:

Assertive—is reserved and aloof, has difficulty establishing new friendships, stays in the background on social occasions, is disgruntled.

Passive—has difficulty making conversation with new acquaintances, is very secretive about personal feelings and experiences, over analyzes feelings, represses emotions.

Harmonious—has deep and long-lasting feelings although not easily expressed, is loyal, uses discretion and caution, struggles to make thinking and feelings compatible.

MENTAL:

Assertive—analytical mind is so intense, everything goes through the mental microscope leaving very little spontaneous enjoyment of life; isolates himself/herself and is reclusive, over-asserts personal opinions.

Passive—weighs everything analytically and then acts on impulse, holds resentment too long when intellectually humiliated or embarrassed.

Harmonious—is an excellent technician, scientist, or analytical advisor in many fields; likes to examine and investigate ideas and situations with scientific precision and thoroughness; can communicate ideas well when discussing a familiar topic; enjoys quiet and peace.

INTUITIVE:

Can tap deep cosmic mysteries of the universe and man, are natural occultists and metaphysicians, can become a crusader of some inspired revelation, is inventive, is artistic. May lead one to inspirational literature or ideas.

NUMBER EIGHT ON THE PLANES

PHYSICAL:

Assertive—has to dominate any situation, uses money for selfish and greedy ends, can be dishonest, is competitive in sports and hobbies, wants recognition even if unearned.

Passive—has no desire or ability to make money, has fear of taking leadership and responsibility, does not like to depend on others.

Harmonious—has natural ability to determine potential in others, has executive ability, knows how to make and use money productively, is often successful as leader in large corporation or government, can achieve considerable recognition.

EMOTIONAL:

Assertive—wants to dominate all relationships, has unpredictable outbursts, is stubborn, does not admit errors, is satirical and caustic.

Passive—worries about possible losses and misfortunes, self-conscious around those deemed superior, needs to appear invulnerable, wants symbols of success for ego gratification.

Harmonious—has deep and loyal feelings, takes charge in a crisis, enjoys being needed, works hard for family.

MENTAL:

Assertive—does not like to lose an argument or debate, wants to dominate others' thinking, is belligerent, is powerful leader, is frank and outspoken.

Passive—gets right to the brink of success and makes mental errors; gets things organized, but does not carry through; has overgrown pride seeking recognition; is disloyal when not given recognition.

Harmonious—is a good organizer and leader, has sharp business and commercial acumen, works hard to improve skills and profits, is excellent financial or business counselor, works hard for success.

INTUITIVE:

Enjoys leadership roles in church, lodge, and/or metaphysical organizations; applies intuition directly to leading and business; at best, highly inspired leaders for the New Age. Can aid one in decisions or organization or leadership.

NUMBER NINE ON THE PLANES

PHYSICAL:

Assertive—pursues less aggressive careers, is artist and/or poet, is colorful in style of dress, enjoys radical and unconventional friends, gets interested in work because of ideal, is impractical.

Passive—can grasp broad ideals, but needs direction when dealing with details, has difficulty reconciling ideals to reality of the world condition, has fluctuations in emotions which hinder attainment.

Harmonious—is artistic and colorful in conducting work, likes to work for an ideal objective, is generous, is tolerant.

EMOTIONAL:

Assertive—emotions fluctuate from feeling good to feeling depressed with little apparent reason, dreams and worries keep consciousness unsettled, feelings are hurt easily, is overdramatic.

Passive—becomes discouraged without approval and support, seeks others' attention, has difficulty relating personal feelings, emotions confuse reason, is withdrawn.

Harmonious—is inspired, is highly intuitive, has fluctuating moods, is colorful and poetic, is idealistic in love, is tolerant, is compassionate, seeks to assist mankind.

MENTAL:

Assertive—extreme idealism can prevent finding realistic solutions, needs to plant feet on firm soil, is gullible, plans far ahead, is selfless in giving of ideas and assistance.

Passive—mind tends to wander which makes it difficult to keep in touch with the work being done, worries because cannot change the world situation, is unconventional in thinking and habits.

Harmonious—is original and inspired thinker, is visionary, can see future plans clearly and inspire others to make them become a reality, likes broad plans and ideals rather than details.

INTUITIVE:

Is highly inspired, can tap inner planes and symbolism thereof, needs to discipline consciousness to be effective channel, awareness can help awaken mankind. May bring entirely new visions for serving and uplifting human needs.

ZERO ON THE PLANES

When no letters appear on one or more planes (rarely more than one), this does not mean you are without body, feelings, mind or intuition. It more often indicates the individual will have to consciously work to harmonize attributes on the particular level where an absence of letters occurs. The individual subconsciously is blocking the attention needed for the level and must purposely determine a method for dealing effectively with that level.

PHYSICAL: wants to dream and speculate; avoids hard work, getting hands in soil, and physical discipline; tires and bores readily.

EMOTIONAL: has difficulty communicating feelings, as well as accepting one's own emotional nature; is lacking in patience, sympathy, and tolerance.

MENTAL: cannot reason confidently; distrusts pure, unfeeling logic and cold facts, lacks curiosity and inquisitiveness about life.

INTUITIVE: distrusts intuition and vague abstract impressions, is self-centered in own belief structure, would benefit from meditation and consciousness expansion techniques.

MORE THAN NINE NUMBERS

In some instances, such as with very long names or when there are two middle names, more than nine letters can occur on a plane of expression. This cannot be ignored. The double digit is reduced to its single digit value for interpretation. However, the concentration of energy on the particular plane will show a likely achievement in life of extraordinary proportion. For an example, on the physical plane, it may indicate a great leader; on the emotional, a teacher-healer or counselor; on the mental, some area of genius; and on the intuitional, an inspired teacher or inventor.

WORKING WITH FOREIGN NAMES

Upon occasion, the student of numerology may be requested to construct a chart for someone born in another country where the name was in the native language. This can create some perplexities for the aspiring numerologist, considering texts written in our country deal with only the English alphabet.

To construct a natal chart in the native language, simply set up the chart according to the Pythagorean system of numbering from one to nine. The first letter will be given a value of one, the next two, and so on, through the foreign alphabet in the manner presented with the alphabet earlier in Chapter Five.

When working with most alphabets the above method should work out adequately to allow the adaptation of the Pythagorean method for interpretation of the chart using the descriptive paragraphs in this book or any other one chosen for study.

Working with certain languages may remain a bit mystifying because of unique dialectics or phonetical structures inherent in the native tongue. In most instances there should be a little difficulty when following the instructions given.

Meanwhile, a useful chart can be obtained by taking the Anglicized name and working the numbers of the outer you, inner you, and accomplished you as presented in Chapter Ten.

VI

DEALING WITH KARMA

The doctrine of karma is quite complex and would take considerable space to discuss completely. I intend this chapter to specifically outline some principal themes to clarify karma, particularly as it relates to numerological interpretation.

Karma is very intimately interwoven with the doctrine of reincarnation. The soul seeks to evolve by absorbing experience from this plane. In successive cycles, the soul incarnates into a personality structure, learns about life, adds to its wisdom, and finally withdraws for introspection upon the inner planes. The personality (physical, emotional, and mental bodies) provides vehicles through which the soul interacts with the lower planes. This cycle repeats itself until the soul finally reaches a point of mastery over the lower vehicles. At that point it no longer incarnates into the physical realm, but is expressed through the higher octave invisible bodies.

Through the personality, the soul accumulates and eventually masters the various challenges, experiences, and lessons of life. One symbolical method of describing these life lessons is through numerology. This is not to say that there are nine simple lessons to learn. The interaction between the numbers creates shades and subtle mixtures of life experiences; however, for purposes of clarity and definition we concentrate on the primary phases of growth through study of the nine basic numbers.

One fundamental law of karma is force which impels consciousness (be it in a one-celled microbe, animal, man, or angel) to progress toward the next phase of cosmic, universal, planetary, social, human, animal, or biological growth. In humanity, this law expresses itself through human will. It is the will factor which urges and compels expansion and unfoldment through life's experiences.

A second fundamental law of karma is that of cause and effect. "As you sow, so also shall you reap," is a pertinent allusion to this law. In the process of learning, we often overdo or avoid the lesson at hand. This creates imbalance and perpetuates karma. Finally, through study, higher guidance, and attunement to the soul, we reach a point of balance wherein the lesson is mastered; and there is balance and harmony. Once this dharmic balance is reached, the lesson is completed, and one is free to move on to new experiences. There eventually comes a time when the soul has accumulated and balanced out all of the Earth plane lessons. Then the soul is free from the wheel of karma and enters a new cycle of experience in a higher realm or level of consciousness.

Almost every number in the chart has karmic implication in a sense. Each number shows potential skills and deficiencies. If that lesson were not important to our growth, we would have chosen otherwise. The very fact we are embodied at this time indicates that we are still working out imbalance (karma).

Strangely, the primary determinants of karma in numerology are revealed by the numbers *missing* in the name at birth. This defines where specific imbalance exists. The absence of a number reveals an area of life which will require extra attention to balance the lesson indicated. It is sometimes believed that a person with no numbers missing has no karma. Such thinking is incorrect. Later in this chapter, a special description and explanation will discuss such a condition in the chart.

Each number missing represents a karmic lesson not learned. This lifetime is your opportunity to correct the situation or balance the condition. The absence of a number or numbers merely indicates that in previous life or lives you have gone to excess or failed to master the lesson at issue. You know that this book frequently touches the theme of balance, and its lack in both directions. Now it applies to our experiential progress. As previously stated, every number in the chart has a karmic implication. The missing numbers help define which karmic lessons are in need of the most attention in this life cycle.

The interpretations for missing numbers will help you understand how these missing numbers reveal very important insights into the nature of your character and behavior. Each karmic lesson will be described separately.

The use of assertive and passive descriptions in this chapter dealing with karma are designed to help the reader recognize more accurately the lessons that have been out of balance and now need harmonizing. The passive description *suggests* the *meaning* of the lesson was likely avoided in previous existence or existences. The assertive paragraph suggests the lesson of the number was overdone. By reading the two, your own inner guidance should help you recognize which is applicable.

An entirely new approach to delineating the karmic impact is also detailed following individual descriptions of the karmic lessons. This is the karmic accumulation number. The number of karmic accumulation is determined by adding all the missing numbers into one total (do not reduce the number to a single digit unless the total is over twenty-two). For example, if the numbers eight, four, and three, were missing from the name at birth, the karmic accumulation number would be fifteen $(8 + 4 + 3 = 15)$.

The karmic accumulation number gives perspective on individual overall reaction to the weight of the necessary lessons. It should be emphasized that the dynamics of karmic numbers are mostly expressed through our lives subconsciously. Only a few are obviously conscious traits.

The karmic accumulation hints at a lot of tendencies expressed through previous personalities. Some of these may still remain in the subconscious and reveal themselves through the current personality. By recognizing these traits consciously, one can transmute the negative and integrate the positive traits into the present life expression for richer unfoldment and living. If this is not accomplished, then one can become bogged down by weight of the past and never really accomplish desired intentions of this life cycle.

Remember that these traits and karmic tendencies manifest through the personality and will reveal themselves with differing hues and nuances, depending upon the personality number. They will become particularly pronounced when assessing stress patterns or during the personal year or month that corresponds to the karmic number that is missing. I hope the descriptions in this chapter will be of particular value, helping you to understand and more harmoniously cope with the conditions individually chosen in this lifetime.

It is recognized the descriptions of this chapter are potentially upsetting and possibly depressing. We need to be reminded that karma is self imposed illusion. Illusion is the prelude to enlightenment! The first law of karma brings us to a discomforting awareness, and the soul finally breaks through with truth. Use your imbalance as a springboard to growth, now.

The descriptions for the karmic lessons are not intended to be an indictment, and not every statement in each description need apply. Perhaps just one minor aspect needs harmonization. Discretion is needed when using these to evaluate another person's chart and life. When studying them for your own personal edification, read the descriptions and watch the reactions in your own emotions or intellect. If you are honest with yourself, those which apply will cause a reaction. If you want to ignore or deny certain ones, those may very well be especially applicable to your life. The crux of your self-examination lies in finding an honestly objective stance from which to see your emotional/intellectual/reaction.

KARMIC LESSONS

Number One Karmic Lesson

Assertive—There has been a tendency in past lives to dominate or control the will of another person or many people. Too much individuality has been a problem in the past, indicating a lack of concern for others. You have had difficulty trusting others and difficulty working cooperatively to finish the job.

Passive—There has been inability to trust your self-confidence. You have relied upon others to make decisions and have not been willing to face decisions or take hold of opportunities that presented themselves. You have been jealous of others who were decisive and successful. There has been an attitude of over-conservatism and fear of taking a chance.

Current Opportunity For Harmony—Life will bring strong willed people into your experience with whom you will have to struggle to find your own self-confidence and beliefs. You will be given many tests to strengthen your own individuality; and, if you benefit from this, you will find yourself becoming increasingly more respectful toward the will and individuality of others. This is the first step toward cooperation of wills.

Number Two Karmic Lesson

Assertive—A past life pattern of criticism, caustic tongue, and impatience is the indication with this lesson. You have lacked ability to work harmoniously with others and have been divisive and isolated in your attitude. Too much attention to detail and lack of patience are also suggested.

Passive—There has been a tendency in your past to avoid details and become slack in attitude. There was carelessness to settle matters like appointments, and a decided lack of concern for others. You lost your own self-identity through attempts to please others, thereby losing awareness of your opinions and beliefs.

Current Opportunity For Harmony—Life will bring to you people who are highly critical and petty. You will be the brunt of seemingly unjust gossip and rumors. Negativity will follow you at home and at work; give more attention to detail and small personal considerations. It will be hard learning to watch your tongue, thus overcoming negativity, criticism, and judgment toward others.

NUMBER THREE KARMIC LESSON

Assertive—A past-life tendency toward superficiality, wasted talent, and carelessness. You sold out your creativity for fame, fortune, or to live the good life. It is likely you have used the creative energy for gratification and indulgence. You were prone to exaggeration, jealousy, and criticism of people's talents.

Passive—This past life pattern shows unwillingness to develop or express creative abilities. There was a tendency to spread talent too thinly. You have had difficulty communicating in your feelings or thoughts to others. You possessed minimal faith in your own potential and developed a low opinion of yourself.

Current Opportunity For Harmony—Life will bring challenges to your self-expression and to your creative skills. You will be forced into situations requiring you to overcome encumbrances to your self-expression. There may be a lisp, or speech impediment, or poor posture resulting from bending under others' opinions. It will be difficult to get into the theater, orchestra, or new station or career of your choice. This time you must learn to appreciate your artistry and *work* for its fullest expression.

NUMBER FOUR KARMIC LESSON

Assertive—You have worked very hard in the past; this narrowed your vision and perspective. You became very fixed, opinionated, dogmatic, and unwilling to try new ideas or ways of doing things. Your convictions prevented you from understanding others, causing you to be stern and overbearing with those with whom you worked. Yours was a stubborn and unyielding disposition.

Passive—There has been a decided distaste for hard work and methodical labor. You preferred ease and comfort without earning your share. This indicates laziness and a searching for the easy way out. You suffer personal hangups about the responsibility for your worth.

Current Opportunity For Harmony—Success and accomplishment will not come easily, and you will have to work hard to earn your rewards. Whatever the endeavor you will likely experience several types of work before settling down into one which feels right. Any attempts at shortcuts will end in disappointment or, worse, outright failure. You must build success block by block on a solid foundation.

NUMBER FIVE KARMIC LESSON

Assertive—This is a past life pattern of irresponsible and carefree living. There was a kind of cavalier "love 'em and leave 'em" attitude. You had difficulty establishing responsibility in personal relations. Inability to stay in one place or at one job is indicated. There is a strong likelihood of sexual indulgence and promiscuity. It is also likely that there has been abuse of the senses and emotions through excessive gambling, drinking, or use of drugs. A disregard for the law is also suggested.

Passive—A past life fear of new experience, change, and progress is related to this lesson. You were uncomfortable dealing with human interaction; you possessed little understanding or tolerance for others. Fear of sex or rejection of sexuality has created confusion toward that particular outlet. Disappointments or setbacks may have driven you to sensual self-indulgence.

Current Opportunity For Harmony—Life will bring constant change. For instance, people with very different backgrounds and philosophies from your own will appear in your path. You will mix and mingle with diverse personalities and attract extremely wide-ranging experiences and situations, creating confusion and doubt. Once you learn to accept people for what they are, you will be able to seek and define your own comfortable standard of conduct based upon inner law, not social norm. You must persevere in situations long enough to absorb their lessons. Know, also, when to let go. There is a need to work out sexual guilts.

NUMBER SIX KARMIC LESSON

Assertive—You have been quite a difficult person with whom to live and share responsibilities. There has been a tendency to make everyone's business your own. You have meddled with others' lives and manipulated emotions for your own personal security. Your disposition has been cranky, cantankerous, and contentious as a spouse and parent. You have not learned the importance of sharing trust and building relationships on mutual responsibility.

Passive—A past life pattern of refusing to face responsibility to self, home, family, and others, is indicated. You were careless and non-supportive to loved ones. You resented having to provide for them rather than pursuing a career or opportunity of your own. You may have done many things, but seldom carried through to finish your obligation. You have given attention to the care and nurturing of those for whom you were responsible. Emotional instability and misunderstanding are indicated.

Current Opportunity For Harmony—Life has likely put you into a family where there is dissension and friction between your parents. The possibility of more than one marriage in your life is high if you are unable to learn the lesson now. Your emotions will be tested and strained until you are willing to face and forgive the subconscious blocks deep inside. Family, friends, and neighbors will constantly demand your time and energy, or your counseling ability. Marriage and home will bring many unexpected burdens and adjustments. You will experience considerable tribulation in adjustment to spouse and home. Learn to cooperate and share the responsibilities of life; things will fall into place.

NUMBER SEVEN KARMIC LESSON

Assertive—There has been too much past life emphasis upon intellectual effort and academic knowledge. You became specialized in certain areas of study, and—as a scholar—enjoyed the awe and prestige associated with it. As a result, you became narrow, opinionated, and severely sarcastic toward opponents or people you deemed to be below your intelligence. You subsequently lost touch with the human equation and day-to-day understanding. There was a preference for living behind high-toned theory, but with little of the layman's common sense. You have cut off feelings with excessive reasoning and become skeptical and cynical of mundane human events.

Passive—There has been a past life pattern of shallow thinking and superficial living. An unwillingness to take things seriously or to investigate life deeply has left a need for deeper searching. You have resisted disciplining the mind to be thorough and scientific in your reasoning. Another possibility is of past disillusionment in a former religious incarnation, perhaps as a nun, monk, or ascetic. Lack of deeper wisdom has perhaps led to superstition and a belief in false doctrines.

Current Opportunity For Harmony—Life will bring you circumstances requiring you to overcome these doubts and superstitions by building a solid faith, based upon intellectual knowledge and spiritual wisdom. You must work to integrate reason with intuition. Seek the deeper teachings of spirituality, science, metaphysics, psychology, and the cosmos. Along the way many adversities may befall you, forcing you to examine Truth more completely. True faith will be yours once you begin to acquire a fundamental grasp of esoteric wisdom teachings. Meditation, introspection, and self-explorative tools, which open the inner doors, will benefit your search for the answer to cosmic riddles.

NUMBER EIGHT KARMIC LESSON

Assertive—This suggests a former misapplication of power and wealth. You have dominated and manipulated others through force or intimidation. Wealth may have been squandered or employed for domination of others. This is a strong indicator of overbearing pride and personal ambition. Your way has been the only way; you sternly forbade deviation. There has been overemphasis upon your personal influence in leadership and social circles. Former greed is also a possibility with this indicator.

Passive—There has been a past life tendency to disregard material aspiration. You have not been willing to use your abilities, leading others and assisting society. A decided distaste for money and lack of courage to take financial risks is suggested. Ineptitude and inefficiency in commercial enterprise is another possibility. You have not wanted to take responsibility for anyone else but yourself. Thus, you've missed opportunities for promotion or advancement. There has been difficulty breaking free from an authoritarian parent or some deeply inbred doctrine that has dominated your consciousness.

Current Opportunity For Harmony—Life will put you into situations which constantly test your authority. You will work under intolerable authority and see misuse of power and ineptitude at every turn. You must learn to take responsibility for your own financial and business affairs. You may very well earn a great deal of money and suddenly lose it. The absence will cause great pain. In the same light, if you strain for money, it will remain elusive. However, if you value it properly and use it wisely, you could easily become financially successful. There is an obvious need to balance between leadership and bossiness. As your leadership abilities mature, you will find many people willing to respond.

NUMBER NINE KARMIC LESSON

Assertive—You have been an impractical idealist and dreamer, roaming in your personal misty world, never being able to produce a tangible contribution. Eccentricity has predominated over good taste; generosity has usually bordered on squandering. Artistic potential was dissipated by nervous tension and lack of direction. You have been overly-sentimental and romantic in personal relationships, which allowed you to be used by others. You thought you were loved for your golden heart and turned to depression and disillusionment when your pockets were fleeced.

Passive—This indicates difficulty handling personal emotions and relating emotionally with others. Your' selfless, impersonal routine smugly disguised an inability to sustain any personal commitment or to share in affection and love. You have meant well, but left little to those whose lives you touched while in that consciousness. You have been less than sympathetic toward the suffering of others, overly concerned with your own suffering and loss. You have been unwilling to face and deal with the harshness and cynicism of life.

Current Opportunity For Harmony—Life will bring you one series after another of emotionally traumatic situations which put the personality under stress until it finally reaches out to the soul for relief and instruction. Marital, job, and health setbacks will cause grief, opening the heart center, and bringing you the chance to understand and sympathize with the suffering others go through in life. You will benefit from working with groups or organizations which foster new avenues of research, metaphysical, or educational instruction. This is a difficult turning point for letting go of the personality so that it may more fully blend with the expression of the soul.

ZERO KARMIC LESSON

Does the fact that no numbers are missing from the name indicate there is no karma? Don't count on it! (No pun intended). We are all here to work for a share of balance. Generally, such a condition in the chart represents a turning point in consciousness where the individual has come to a relatively harmonious point in his growth. He or she has an opportunity to choose from within just how to proceed, having no specific push from the pressure of missing karmic numbers. If this freedom of choice is not handled well, the person may create greater imbalance, returning next time to deal anew with missing numbers.

On the other hand, he may move further from imbalance, becoming able to leave the wheel of karma and proceed along the evolutionary spiral. When such a condition is approaching, the absence of missing numbers simply is an indicator that each lesson needs to be learned and then understood in relation to others. When such an understanding is consciously sought, the sincere seeker enters into the subtle and more esoteric study of numbers. More will be said about how the absence of missing numbers influences our consciousness at the end of the following discussions about karmic accumulation.

PUTTING KARMA INTO PERSPECTIVE

A warning: Sometimes students just starting to learn about reincarnation and karma will read evaluations like these describing karmic patterns. They become overly wrought with anxiety and discomfort because they interpret this to mean they are guilty of doing everything described in the karmic descriptions. Or perhaps they will mistakenly believe that is all the karma there is for them to deal with in this lifetime.

There have been authors of numerology books who have stated that we live nine lives and learn one lesson each time. Nothing much from available authoritative sources supports this opinion.

From my study of the works of the great akashic readers, such as Edgar Cayce and more recent channels, a definite trend emerges, suggesting that we live many *more* times. The author is currently a personal and professional friend of numerous channels who are, to the best of my judgment, tapping the akasha with success and a high rate of accuracy. From what has been gathered from their collective opinions, it appears that the number of lives *has no* exact limitations. Although there may be many exceptions, the average for most mortals seems to range from 150 to 250 lives. Therefore, we may just be working on a recent imbalance or one that has been embedded in the subconscious for many, many lifetimes and is just now coming into resolve.

This information is rendered to assist your understanding, not to upset it. If you are troubled by something said, seek your own inner guidance for clarification. It is probable some aspect may have been overlooked herein and your own intuitive insight can add other valuable perspectives.

KARMIC ACCUMULATION NUMBERS*

ONE KARMIC ACCUMULATION

You are intent upon doing things your way. This can make you aggressive, at times almost militant. Your keen independence and self-reliance make it difficult for you to accept advice and you are prone to disagree with superiors. Normally enthusiastic and impulsive, your inspiration

*See page 139, paragraph 3.

is of short duration. When things do not work out immediately, you become discouraged and allow negativity and
procrastination to undermine your efforts. Part of the reason for your short concentration span is that you have been
too reliant upon others or allowed them to dominate. Now
you will struggle in the sustained effort necessary to accomplish your goals. Until you overcome these tendencies,
you will find yourself lacking in ability to concentrate and
think logically.

You are naturally popular and will be placed in a position of notoriety—where you will exercise authority and
leadership over a number of people. This could even lead
you into a position of considerable prominence and an opportunity to make a lasting contribution to society. It is not
easy for you to sit still because of your abundant energy.
Once you have learned to direct this nervous dynamism
constructively, there will be little to stop you from attaining success and recognition.

You can succeed in commercial enterprises if you use
your originality, ingenuity, and resourcefulness. However,
you can also turn right around and become rash and impulsive, causing you to lose a profitable transaction or to
offend someone who could be of help. Your dislike for supervision makes you seek self-employment. Business breakthroughs will come *after* many setbacks and at considerable
expense to your vitality.

In friendship your individuality cannot be concealed.
You do your own thing, and those who have similar interests stay around to enjoy your fellowship. If they have differing interests, you shrug it off and move on to new
acquaintances. Once you do establish a bond, trust is vital;
and your word is valued and respected. You appreciate the
chance to meet new people and can be socially dynamic
and entertaining. You have strong convictions on right and
wrong, and cannot easily be dissuaded.

In love and romance, you can be fickle. Are you constantly seeking a new mate? Once you think you have the

right partner, you want to dominate the relationship. Thus, you'll probably be best off selecting a mate who is willing to go along with things, not over-assertive. Your emotions can get away from you in love affairs, and you rush head-long into them with little thought to possible consequences. You can be intense and passionate, but lose interest quickly.

In marriage, you will work hard to make the partnership satisfying. Peace and harmony will not come easily, however; and you most likely will end up with an equally strong-willed spouse who is a constant challenge and protagonist. You are demanding and strict as a parent, but want to see your children have the best possible opportunities in life.

Two Karmic Accumulation

You are doggedly determined to resolve life conflict and find peace and harmony. You seek to give and receive kindness and consideration, and you are willing to assist another unselfishly. At your best, you are discreet and tactful in speech. You handle situations with diplomatic aplomb. Because of your sensitivity, you respond readily to kindness and consideration from others. On the other hand, your need to help sets you up for being used by those relying upon your aid, rather than performing their own tasks. When injured, you turn your attention to your employment and immerse yourself in work as a substitute for emotional conflict.

With this combination, consciousness can be split; and you may at times have trouble knowing which way to turn. Your outer personality is agreeable and willing to give and take; however, your attitudes run deep. So it takes an act of parliament to change your mind. A strain of seriousness runs through your sense of humor, often overwhelming it. You are conscious of human weakness and frailty and exhibit great sympathy. You will take the opposite side of an argument, just to keep conversation lively.

Where business is concerned, you are not one to make bold and pioneering decisions, preferring to evaluate and take a more conservative path. You are not overly ambitious for material gain; although, you do have a kind of material luck that keeps you going. If you are weighted down with responsibility and decisions, you will juggle for time and seek opinions, thus missing the boat. You prefer working with labor and personnel problems more than with the commercial aspect. Memory of dominance by others and heavy responsibilities early in your life triggers a subconscious rebellion toward heavy pressure. This makes it difficult for you to make up your own mind.

You retain friendships by playing a follower rather than a leader. Your willingness to lend an ear causes friends to seek you out to discuss personal problems. There is a decided dislike of dissension, so you will go out of the way to avoid antagonizing someone. You solve conflicts that arise by diplomacy rather than by force.

In romance and love, you are loyal. Mating games are not sport to you! You are conservative toward love affairs, even prudish. It is easier to stick with a relationship that's going fairly well than to break up and risk hurt and rejection trying to establish a new union. You seek a strong and dependable spouse you can turn to for strength and security. You work best with a more aggressive mate who takes charge of domestic decisions. Your approach is persuasive, yet tactful, thus maintaining peace through reasonable debate. You enjoy children, but will have many quarrels and disagreements with them when they try your patience.

THREE KARMIC ACCUMULATION

Deep in your heart you want to create and bring beauty and joy into the world. Your early years will involve frustration, repression and/or inhibition of talents you want so much to share. You have a high degree of personal magnetism that attracts artists, freethinkers, malcontents, and generally creative types of people. Your moods swing quickly but seldom go up or down to extreme, and the fluctuations do not last very long. This lack of emotional control can be crucial, preventing you from sustaining a creative drive long enough to gain success and recognition. You have an extraordinary imagination and know how to dramatize events with flair; capitalize upon this by entering the field of writing which catches the public attention.

You would do well in creative or artistic enterprises, but you are not cut out for the purely commercial and technological end of business. Most likely, there will be many different positions until you settle into one of suitability. Your personal affairs and moods keep your mind drifting away from the routine of your job. When this happens, you appear distant and detached from coworkers and your supervisor is inclined to reprimand you because you are not paying attention to your responsibilities.

You are fond of company and socializing, and friendships are very central to your life. Because you are swayed and influenced so much by their opinions, you will find that destiny brings many opportunities through your acquaintances. You are flattered by and responsive to friendly overtures and respond warmly with a refined affection to those who awaken it within your heart. However, when out of harmony, you can become careless and unconventional regarding your affections and personal love. There is a strong attraction for sensuality, but when boredom sets in, you may experience rapid change in lovers with much hurt and disappointment. You are unable to give completely; you then are surprised when your lovers terminate affection. You can be secretive and flirtatious and at the same time desire a loyal and loving mate of your dreams. Once hurt, you can pass through a phase of total disinterest in sexual needs, preferring to express your drive in hobbies or work.

You would be most comfortable with a patient comprehending mate who is willing to boost a dubious self-image.

You are prone to feel everyone recognizes your flaws while overlooking the many commendable strengths and talents you possess. A happy marriage will be long in coming, but once found gives you the chance to be a colorful and inspirational spouse and parent.

FOUR KARMIC ACCUMULATION

You are a fixed, determined, and hard-working individual. Life allows you very little time to enjoy the luxuries of fun and amusement. Without some restraints, you can become a "workaholic", which could be detrimental to health. Your childhood was likely burdened with some form of heavy work which caused you resentment. You have respect for authority and would like to be considered one yourself. You deal with emotions similar to how you deal with life. When challenged, you may react with stubbornness, anger, and seething resentment. You like to be one of the crowd and are very much aware of people's motives. When you experience or witness injustice, you can become moody and develop a deep simmering dislike, even hatred. Because you think you have everything working so well, you do not handle opposition well. You can become outraged and indignant because you do not feel that anyone has the right to change the precision machine you operate.

Although you are inclined to be somewhat obstinate, you are fundamentally practical, organized, and particularly good at maintaining the daily routine of business or office. The subconscious tendency is to become restless and try changing the routine to suit yourself; however, you have learned to discipline yourself and work for the good of the organization. Because of your loyalty to the organization, you may be called upon for a supervisory role which you can handle well. Your preference is to be left in a job where you know the routine and do not have to deal with greater responsibilities and personal problems of the employees. A tendency for moderation and conservatism runs deep in your consciousness, and you may almost reach the top of your work, although you lack the intense self-sustained drive necessary to reach the top of the competitive totem pole.

In love, romance, and marriage, you are loyal and intense. You are faithful to your partner, as a rule. When your work is not going well, and your mate is not supportive or encouraging, you are vulnerable to the charms of another admirer, willing to build your pride and sense of worth. Once attached, you are a potent and conscientious partner. You take pride in home, family, and possessions, and work hard to be a good provider.

FIVE KARMIC ACCUMULATION

You are extremely active and independent in mind and body. You do not like to stick with anything very long and jump quickly. So you are often involved in two or more things at once. You will probably make many trips and meet with many strange experiences before your life is complete. In fact, you often go out of your way to seek thrills and sometimes dangerous stunts. There is a need to use discretion where stimulants are concerned (smoking, drugs, alcohol) because your body could suffer considerably, and the likelihood of being heavily involved in overindulgence is extremely high. You are caught in excruciating dilemmas between desire and a fear of sexual and sensual habits. This uncertainty will attract numerous opportunities for you to learn to control and master these fears and cravings. You act on impulse at the moment and react childishly to any kind of restrait upon your free flowing nature in action or thinking. You may react with a temper which is of short duration and is gone as quickly as it appears.

Your career and business endeavors are likely to be multiple and varied because of your restless nature and lack of regard for monotonous routine. Sales and positions with variety and action are your forte. Your curiosity and inventive potential could produce a new product, perhaps, or method of merchandising. You prefer not to work hard for a living and would like to make easy money.

This indicates an individual who will be popular and lively in society. You are not prone to develop many deep friendships, preferring to stay on the move in order to meet someone new. Personal magnetism works favorably in your friendships, but your emotions can create sorrow.

In love and romance, you have a kind of carefree spirit others find appealing. You are a natural at flirtation and prefer not to be tied down. You live each moment fully with a devil-may-care attitude about tomorrow. You enjoy the sport and intrigue of new love affairs. Unfortunately, you confuse sexual and emotional needs. You are aware of your sexual charm and do not hesitate to use it. Your emotional variability can reveal a hardness which can create unpleasant surprises for your lovers. You are not likely to enjoy the restraint of marriage. Even though you envision yourself as a model of loyalty and devotion, at the same time you may very well be flirting at the office or next door. You prefer a mate who gives you a great deal of room and freedom, but most likely will choose one who prefers a homebody and attentive spouse.

SIX KARMIC ACCUMULATION

You are concerned with ways to make life easier for the human race. This concern can put you into a position where you can be used; you are apt to deceive yourself into thinking you have done so much, especially if the combination of missing numbers is 2 and 4. However, overall, you are effective in roles of service and support. At times, the altruism of your motive is dubious, and you overplay the role of helpmate, trying hard to express your concern, particularly if 1 and 5 are the missing numbers. Your charitability and concern often cause you to overlook the needs of those closest to you, or even your own misfortunes, because of your absorption with other people's needs.

This generosity in your blood excludes highly competitive business and commercial enterprises as a livelihood to render hard-nosed, impersonal business decisions. There may also be little aggressiveness toward acquisition of power or wealth. If involved in business, you are able to accomplish transactions without stepping on toes or hurting feelings. This enables you to make close friends among associates.

Friendships are compulsory to your well-being, and you are blessed with a few very endearing friends for most of your life. You adopt many of your opinions from those close to you, feel their joys and misfortunes. It is true you have been imposed upon too often, but this should not leave you distrustful toward everyone. At times, you have been known to push another's good will a little bit too far yourself.

Tenderness and concerned understanding permeate your attitude toward love and romance. You prefer one emotionally rewarding relationship rather than passing affairs. This emotional need can be your source of aggravation when your partner falls short of the same sincerity.

You long for a happy marriage and will work hard to make a go of it. There is a strong attachment to the home and, even though you may travel, you look forward to returning to domestic surroundings. You work well with a spouse who is willing to take charge of domestic decisions, and you probably have opinions on home management yourself. Loyalty is uppermost, and you are loyal to the union even after your mate has lost interest. You would rather stay in a poor marriage than go through the legal/emotional hassle of getting out of it. There may be anxiety and difficulty with children and subconscious blocks preventing a complete bond of trust. Part of your discomfort may stem from your childhood with emotional confusion arising from detached or unsympathetic treatment from one or both parents.

Seven Karmic Accumulation

There is a deep philosophical and secretive aura surrounding you which piques the curiosity and interest of
people you meet. You pursue new studies with intensity
and leave very few stones unturned in your search for the
essence of a matter. You are quite set in your judgments
and opinions, so anyone wishing to change your mind had
better beware. Your wry wit and pointed sarcasm are
appreciated by some, feared by others. Your outer appearance of intellectual prowess hides a turbulent emotional
sea, whose tides you fear may be so extreme you keep them
behind a mental dam. The seven karmic number is a very
intuitive indicator and, in your periods of introspection, you
will learn to trust the message from within. Your analytical
mind explores every angle of behavior and prepares a
logical course for each event. However, when emotions
become involved, all of your logical preparation falls apart,
and you act impishly on impulse.

Your business drive is fettered by a fundamentally religious and philosophical nature. It is difficult for you to
worship Mammon, and the value system of economics is
alien to your inner being. If you do enter business, your
analytical ability and suspicious nature allow you to make
cautious, if not dramatic, decisions which may get you close
to the top of the ladder because of consistency. You would
enjoy any kind of investigative research, or analytical employment.

This is not the most compatible indicator for friendships.
People find you somewhat haughty and intellectually aloof,
which makes it difficult to be close to your feelings. Once
a friendship is established, you are intensely loyal, and
many turn to you for insight from your reserve of wisdom
and mundane comprehension. You are threatened by the
fact others may learn about your emotional insecurity;
therefore, you put up a mental defense. Once they have

accepted you, you allow deep feelings of loyalty and concern to be expressed. So the benefit is ultimately both yours and theirs.

In love and romance you need a mate you can intellectually respect. Mental rapport is important to inspiring excitement in the rest of your system. You are possessive and fervent once attached.

It might be best to choose a lighthearted mate to offset your seriousness, but if your spouse does not reach certain intellectual standards, you can become disinterested. You may, in fact have more of an intellectual companionship than a strong emotional and physical relationship. You enjoy the debate of minds and thrive on the verbal entanglements. This combination may leave you a little uncomfortable with children, their noises, and problems, especially with the numbers 2 and 5 missing.

EIGHT KARMIC ACCUMULATION

You are constantly seeking ways to bolster your ego and success image. An aspect of pride makes you believe you deserve to be in a position of authority: however, at the same time, you are unwilling to put forth the effort making you worthy of the rank. At negative extremes, you can become ruthless to the point of inflicting pain upon others. You put on an air of bravado and confidence that masks a very deep-rooted fear: you may not in fact be able to handle the situation. There is an enormous drive for success, and most likely you will end up with a significant position and sizeable earnings — unless greed enters your heart. You become uneasy and dissatisfied readily with the way things are progressing and then doubt the ability or motives of those with whom you are associated. This indicator suggests one constantly on the move, teaching business, charitable, or civic affairs. The early years of your life presented numerous adversities and impediments, forming a subconscious attitude of defiant belief that you can meet any challenge.

Most of the previous statements apply to your business as well as general life attitudes. You have difficulty with bosses and managers and need much leeway to make decisions. You will not be in the lower echelon for long, no matter what kind of organization you have chosen. You have a knack for contributing ideas for better technical production, more effective utilization of personnel, and you exercise sound judgment in the expenditure and investment of money. Unfortunately, your personal financial decisions may not be as fruitful.

You play a convincing charade about friendships, acting as if you can take 'em or leave 'em, especially with 3 and 5 missing. Underneath this act, you want to be liked by all, and secretly you need acceptance from others to have peace of mind. Because of your need to have supportive friendships, you develop loyalty and will offer helpful advice about any impersonal topics. When friends get too close to your emotional framework, you become uneasy and temperamental. A strong competitive drive makes it difficult to accept friends and social acquaintances for what they are instead of for what they have.

Oddly enough, this businesslike attitude also permeates your romantic life. Your detached emotional nature generates a sort of indifferent attitude. You would do best with a strong-willed mate who is ambitious but able to give *you* constant boosting. If your goals are too similar, competition rather than compatibility will no doubt prevail. When support is not given or the marriage falters, you easily justify outside love affairs or indulgent habits.

NINE KARMIC ACCUMULATION

This is a most challenging indicator because you must learn to recognize and let go of restraining insecurities, possessive attitudes, and relationships which are no longer moving in a direction compatible with your evolution. There is a deep yearning for emotional contentment, especially with 6 and 3 missing. However, emotional fears are lodged deep within the subconscious, and it will take some traumatic encounters with life circumstances to bring them to surface awareness. You seek a comfortable home and stable marriage (especially 6 and 3); and yet, something inside does not let you become personally attached to either of these. You are besieged by feelings of loneliness and isolation, even when among others, especially with 7 and 2 missing. Your idealism does not always have the impact you would like upon the mass consciousness.

This is not the most aggressive indicator for business. You prefer to let others handle the responsibility and leadership while you provide the inspiration and support. You would be good in motivation and public relations or personnel work, rather than on the competitive battlefield. No matter what your business may be, the work you enjoy most will have to do with some aspect of religion, consciousness development, advanced science, metaphysics, social reform, or related fields.

You are capable of establishing friendships with people of totally paradoxical interests. You hope to maintain closer relationships with all your friends, but life brings you new friends rapidly, and even they will move on to new things. You are apt to be emotionally affected by negativity from other people. In fact, your generosity and desire to help often attracts people who trample over your feelings, treating you with indifference or even maliciousness (especially with 1 and 8 missing). You are almost always in disagreement with people who live by conventional social norms, so you spend much time speculating about more modern, or even futuristic forms of government and society. Universal causes and thinking are important to you. You will fit well into an impersonal role, working to bring about global expansion in human consciousness.

You are highly idealistic and sentimental about romance. You will probably experience occasional spiritually platonic love affairs. You work best with a mate who is tolerant of your unconventional ideas and shares a general concern for the world and humanity. You seek an ideal union and impose almost impossible expectations upon your loved one. This is not a favorable influence for marriage; perhaps you will experience more than one before finding the right mate.

TEN KARMIC ACCUMULATION

You almost inevitably succeed, but that doesn't prevent a horrible fear of disaster every time a new project looms near. Indication of significant failure in a previous lifetime makes you hesitate to initiate new endeavors or unwilling to sustain the confidence and effort needed for success. The author recently worked with one chart with 4, 7, 8, and 9 all missing; this adds up to 28; 2 + 8 equaling 10. The description for this combination could hardly seem more appropriate.

You have great ideas and initial enthusiasm; however, subconscious fears can prevent you from completing a lot of your schemes. There is a curious fluctuation in your temperament from excessive confidence to overwhelming insecurity about your abilities. In one instance you are inspired about great projects to help mankind, and in the next you become completely self-centered. You can become easily convinced that certain of your opinions just happen to be exactly correct which then makes it difficult for you to alter a course of action, be it for better or worse. You will encounter intense resistance when attempting to push your opinions forcibly upon those around you (especially when 2-8 are missing).

Your cycles in business will also fluctuate from near success to the brink of failure until you learn to resolve the underlying fear of failure. Your enormous talents can go to waste because you lack the confidence to develop them thoroughly. You are best working cooperatively with others and are often indecisive and discouraged. Once you have been told how to do a job, you are capable of much achievement if left alone to work independently. Even though you desire a role of leadership, it does not come easily. You are excellent in work which inspires others. However, once things are underway you prefer to move on to new territory.

You need many supportive friends around you and attract individuals who also have considerable unexpressed abilities. Your choice of friends is very important because some could easily prey upon your weakness and self doubt. You would benefit from being around people who use metaphysical, self-help, and growth techniques with maturity and wisdom.

Your behavior in love and romance is changeable and insecure. You seek a partner who recognizes your needs and gives you the confidence to push a little harder. You may seek love affairs to bolster a sagging self-image. You work best in marriage with a mate who is flexible and supportive. You are not particularly domestic and prefer not to be tied down to all the demands of family life. You have an abundant vitality and recover easily from illness. (See also one karmic accumulation number).

Eleven Karmic Accumulation

This indicator suggests one who is highly idealistic and intuitive. You possess a comprehensive awareness of the needs in society and therefore work to cultivate a favorable public image. Your destiny will probably at one time put you before many people. There is a natural inclination toward religion, occult, or metaphysical studies; will you follow it? The suggestion is that in an earlier lifetime you may have misused psychic or intuitive abilities; if 3 and 8 are missing, for political expediency or manipulation of others; if 2 and 9 are missing, because of misplaced idealism; if 4 and 7 are missing, you may have let intellect dominant intuitive development; with 5 and 6 missing, you may have

unwittingly misled others because of your own opinions and
hang-ups. You enjoy inspirational and advanced thinking
but, at the same time, cling to old and tried ways. Once
you have taken a stand on an issue, you will go to unpre-
cedented sacrifice to defend it. Once you have established
the law, you expect everyone to fall in line and abide by it.
This is a failure to see that they may not share either your
opinions or zeal.

Business success and attainment can come to you if you
use patience and tact rather than force. Generally this combination is not conducive to business pursuits. You are better advised to seek a career in religion, social reform,
education, government, or consciousness instruction. Your
heightened powers encourage leadership. There is a natural
inclination toward awakened, modern thinking and far-
sighted ideas; but you can doggedly persist in defending
some cherished personal belief. It is not easy for you to
admit mistakes. Just do it, and be free to move on in truth
and confidence.

When this indicator appears, the individual will attract
friends from diverse and seemingly incongruous backgrounds. Your intensity and magnetism will draw or repel
new associates with equal strength. You innately want to
reveal the glory of higher wisdom and universal truths, but
you must guard carefully against twisting and coloring
truth to support your personal rendition. You may unwittingly attract eccentric personalities and consciousness
leaders of dubious motive which could be sources of considerable trouble. Unchecked, the vibrations of this combination can breed excessive eccentricity and unstable proclivities.

A similar idealism influences your attitudes in love,
romance, and marriage. You expect your level of awareness
to be returned immediately. You seek an ideal union and
see yourself as nearly perfect. In fact, you can become quite
an undesirable partner because of moodiness, lack of patience, emotional volatility, and the constant push to have

your mate live by your standards. You are constantly dreaming about the perfect soul mate. (See also the Two Karmic Accumulation).

Twelve Karmic Accumulation

Life will bring you numerous occasions where you will be required to make a sacrifice. These occasions may be consciously recognized and dealt with accordingly, or they can be a subconscious pattern evolving. The latter might not be as easily understood because of its deeper content. You live in a kind of constant anticipation that the things near to you may be gone tomorrow. This constant emotional anguish creates suffering, real or imagined; and the discontent leads you to sources of self-discovery or emotional outlets. You possess a natural flair for drama and are like an actor or actress on the stage bemoaning your torments, especially with 3 or 9 missing.

You may have to take care of an invalid relative, go into military service, or take over for a coworker right at a moment in life when you most desire free time to further a personal ambition. Who knows why you are constantly being called upon to take care of someone else's needs?

Just remember: as you sow, so also will you reap. Your natural, creative, and artistic inclinations may at some time be utilized as a means of conveying what you have learned to others. You could very well end up writing or lecturing about the lessons you have learned from your struggle with life.

In business and employment, you are placed in positions where you do a great deal of extra work, often behind the scenes, while someone else gets the applause and promotion. You have difficulty staying in one career because of your restless and creative nature. Success and professional recognition will most likely come later in life and after considerable struggle and sacrifice.

You seek friendships and enjoy social events and being popular. You tend to dramatize your experiences and respond impulsively to excitement of the moment. Friends enjoy your spontaneity and flexibility. Your desire to please places you in positions where you are unable to say no. Then you readily discover you have become somewhat of a sacrificial martyr, spending much time taking care of their lives.

Working out the knots in love, marriage, and romance will be constantly trying. Your lovers, spouse, and children will require an inordinate amount of attention. You sometimes wonder if you will ever get away from the demands of kids, activities, illnesses, wife's club activities, husband's job demands, and in-laws' interference. You can easily feel discouraged and unappreciated, with good reason.

THIRTEEN KARMIC ACCUMULATION

Probably no other combination directs as much attention to the work ethic as this vibration. During other lifetimes you have not worked to your best ability, or you may have worked just for your own selfish ends, especially with 5 and 8 missing. This indicator suggests a time to consider others and to enter work with others in mind.

You must learn to complete the work you have come to do. You have the capability, but often give up or avoid the responsibility of the job at hand. This is an indicator of learning to enjoy work for the sake of work, and nurturing healthy respect for discipline and accomplishment. Your role may not seem of significance to society, but you are now learning to serve as one becoming attuned to the Divine Plan for Earth. There is a tendency to hold yourself back. It is as if you possess a lack of ambition and kind of humility that prevents you from attaining the limelight. It is not that you lack capability or opportunity, but just that you seek to do your job well and may lack glamour or imagination in the process.

In commercial and business endeavors, you may find it emotionally hard just working to make a living. You may face several setbacks, even failure, before finding the meaning of work and a truly meaningful job. You push yourself harder and longer than coworkers. When serving in a supervisory position, you expect the same from your subordinates.

There is likely to be much sadness and unexpected disappointment through friendships. The pattern of most friendships that develop will be intense and loyal; however, they will be of relatively short duration. They do not end with animosity or hard feelings, but destiny simply spins a different web of fate. You leave saddened, pondering the circumstances which separated your mutuality. You are considered stubborn; oftentimes misunderstandings occur because of your set code of conduct. Despite a fixed attitude, friends can count upon you and respect you for solidity.

The romantic and marital details of your life bring periodic cycles of frustration. You are loyal and ardent in love, but may experience an unfortunate love affair while seeking attention after reversals in your career. You suffer a great deal through your love life because of an innate discipline of emotions, preventing you from giving and accepting love fully. There may be weird estrangements from spouse or family, resulting from incompatibility even though there is still love.

Fourteen Karmic Accumulation

This combination brings a major turning point in consciousness. It is one of regeneration and growth through much tribulation and rearrangement of character. You have resisted learning from past life experiences and have a difficult time growing out of the illusion and enticement of the senses. You are ambitious but are clever about the political approach you use to gain prominence. Your subconscious karmic pattern is to seek freedom, intrigue, and personal kicks. Your present desire is to fit into social conventions and expectations. This leaves you with a very formal, but outgoing, manner which constantly has to monitor the surging quest for freedom and indulgence.

You must learn to accept past mistakes and move on to new experiences. No amount of mental or emotional reexamination can alter the past; however, you need to review it long enough to discover and eliminate the underlying cause for self-inflicted errors. You seem constantly to fluctuate between desire for complete freedom and the need for security. This constant strain can disrupt your health if you are not careful. You are curious about life and hate to miss any experience.

The possibility of success in career and business is quite high. You would do best to work with people because of your extensive interests and adaptability. You are ambitious; however there is a likelihood that you will change goals, just before you reach success. If things get out of hand, your aspirations may cause you to become involved in underhanded or dubious circumstances. This combination indicates the probability that you may earn a great deal of money. It could just as easily be lost, unless you purposely concentrate on financial planning.

Your exuberance and vitality make you a popular and sought-after friend and social acquaintance. You do not like to be tied down and move confidently among people from diverse backgrounds and social standing. Your peppy style brings cheer to others. On the other hand, you can be inconsiderate and hurt others, unknowingly perhaps, by your actions and impulsive statements. You are not so much malicious, it's just that you're insensitive to undercurrents and must guard your tongue to prevent tactless and revealing slips of speech.

You constantly search for the essence of love. This keeps you flitting from one romance to another, seeking that nebulous happiness. You can confuse sex and love and

get yourself into ambiguous situations regarding your affections, loving more than one person at a time — one near,
and one alluringly distant. You disdain the thought of public attention being given to your personal love affairs. Happiness in love and marriage will be elusive, so you do well
playing the field. Keep it that way until you are certain a
partner is totally right for you. Only time is a proof.

Fifteen Karmic Accumulation

An aura of ignominious humility looms around you and
you work to appease a subconscious guilt associated with
past life mistakes. An unfettered ego and insolent treatment of those disagreeing with your ambitions are to blame.
Your public manner suggests consideration and sympathy,
and you work hard to truly cultivate these qualities. Your
emotions are greatly unsettled, and you become overly
upset and embarrassed about the most inconsequential incidents. You will encounter people with powerful egos on
many occasions; from these experiences you will learn
much about people's problems and needs for identity.

You are, of course, in most cases witnessing the type of
attitude you have held in a previous life or lives and will
acquire first-hand insight as to the negative impact it can
have upon others, especially with 2, 5, and 8 missing. When
you let pride or ambition get out of hand, something or
someone will come along to put you right back in your place
in a hurry. This can include being fired from a job or perhaps coming down with an illness. Then you will have time
to reflect and recognize unbecoming ego needs within your
character.

You work hard to establish stability, consideration for
others, and a down-to-earth attitude about life and people.
You dislike the disruptive nature of disagreements and
work quickly, but patiently, to dissolve hostility. There is a
need to help others, and you have a meddlesome practice

of trying too hard to help others. Stay out of the way unless asked to help.

Your preference in business or career is not in the more
competitive sectors. You are best working with people in
a manner that enables them to accommodate life more
easily. You work long hours with unexcelled diligence and
are willing to take on responsibilities, which may not be
yours, with patience, diplomacy, and desire to serve. Again,
beware of overdoing it.

You enjoy making new friends and are often called upon
to counsel and to cheer others. Your considerate attitude
and desire to get things together in your life are appealing factors. Sometimes you become blind to the way others
manipulate your trusting nature. You are learning to be a
good friend. But to be a good friend you should not *have*
to try so hard.

In love, romance, and marriage, you seek a happy and
harmonious relationship, but you are likely to attract a jealous, possessive, and domineering mate. You are strongly
attracted to your mate and the thought of domestic harmony.

Many obstacles may delay your harmonious relationship:
parental disapproval, insufficient funds, or interference
from a job. There could be more than one marriage. You
must learn not to nurture grudges, but seek to overcome
strain of disagreements.

SIXTEEN KARMIC ACCUMULATION

You are constantly looking over your shoulder, expecting a catastrophe or unexpected disruption in your marriage, work, or personal life. There is a need to build a
stronger faith through deeper investigation of universal
laws. You think often about emotional matters, but are
prone to hasty and erratic decisions where emotions are
concerned. A predominantly intellectual attitude motivates
your impulsiveness more than does physical restlessness.

You will learn to deal with your emotions after unexpected and sudden mishaps in life.

You enjoy intellectual debates and derive great satisfaction from coming up with some point or fact in an unexpected thrust. You benefit from learning to concentrate your interests on one thing at a time. You can make impulsive decisions which even surprise yourself; and, once made, you may stick by them even though you suspect the results will be disastrous. You will very likely encounter complications in obtaining a higher education. At some point in life you will experience disappointment because you have not completed the proper degrees or scored well on some standardized test. Even though you may not have obtained a complete formal education, you must trust the wisdom within yourself.

You are conscientious and hard working in business and career. You desire recognition more than money; yet, you possess a reluctance toward aggressiveness and have some timidity in accepting your worth. You can, therefore, fail to reach full job potential. The fear can stem from a past life pattern of overdoing your role and falling into disgrace of some kind. Once overcome, you may very well attract public recognition and success deservedly.

An intellectual detachment characterizes your friendships. You enjoy people around you who are also deep thinkers and/or constantly searching for further understanding of their psychological and spiritual nature. You enjoy close friends, but would rather be alone than with a noisy group. You aren't much of a conversationalist because your mind is made up on most matters. You are generally a considerate friend, often witty, sometimes sharp tongued, usually stimulating.

In love and romance, you first seek an intellectual rapport; on other levels, you can be somewhat impersonal. Your constant search for the perfect combination may lead to a variety of love affairs before settling down. You are idealistic about love and explore different ideas about sex and love relationships; this can complicate the personal experience with your mate. Your desires for a perfect union put unrealistic demands upon your spouse which can hardly be fulfilled. Once you have overcome the emotional complications and learn to unite head with heart, there is a chance for harmony and security in love.

SEVENTEEN KARMIC ACCUMULATION

It may take you some time in life to replace an innate sense of pessimism and despair with an awakened sense of optimism and faith in your future and the world condition. You have the drive and energy upon which to build your confidence and inner strength. If your plans and actions are not built upon an honest and legitimate foundation, you could tumble from a position of great authority. This is a plateau of learning where power should be used constructively.

There will be disagreement with people in positions of authority who misuse their power or who fear to alter the prescribed ways to progress. Interestingly enough, you are subject to the same resistance within. You do not like to be told what to do by another and will have difficulty working comfortably as a subordinate. Your ambition is powerful and you will persist with hard work (sometimes beyond endurance of the physical body) to achieve your goals. Part of your drive for attainment is compensation for subconscious fear of losing your identity (by getting lost in the crowd, by becoming another automaton in our technological society, or by failing to leave your mark in the world).

Your career and commercial talents are marked. You have a capable mentality and good sense of organization. You have the foresight to visualize a project and then anticipate the needs and outcome of the directive you have set in motion. You are persistent and can be tactful enough to obtain the cooperation necessary to complete the requirements of the job. Be careful that impulsiveness and pettiness of ego do not interfere with your work.

This is a curious combination for friendship. You want friends, but you want them on your terms. You alternate between a come-on and a put-off. Your blend of outward optimism and latent pessimism affects the way you deal with friends. You like friends, but do not go after them. Rather, they seem to find you. You work hard to make things work and just as quickly become indifferent, expecting things to fall apart. In one instance, you may demand too much, then turn around and avoid any feedback, making friends feel unneeded. Those who persevere find you a loyal friend and enjoy your buoyant, boisterous, and practical side.

Your lively nature is unsettled and fickle, and you seek love affairs as an outlet when the breaks do not go your way and you are down on life. You could very well marry for social or political reasons rather than follow your heart, creating a cold or unfulfilling union. You are likely to marry more than once or engage in an attachment to someone below your social or intellectual level. When the finer emotions rule, and you find a strong independent mate, you are a loyal and dynamic partner.

Eighteen Karmic Accumulation

A strain pervades your character in distinguishing between practical idealism and naive gullibility and deception. You see life through beautiful rose colored glasses, which cause you to overlook gross flaws in self and others. An innate generosity can put you into a position where you give too much of self, not always to your best advantage. Watch out that this generosity does not become obsessive, causing you to blame yourself for everything that goes wrong. The suggestion is that you have deceived others in a past life pattern and now must conquer deception and deceit in self and by others. This will be difficult because you easily become confused when strong empathetic emotions are aroused. Turmoil within keeps the body tense and emotions on a raw edge. You will benefit from a system of multiple consciousness discipline applied every day. Your intellect is expansive and very logical; however, at times you show complete disregard for convention, becoming argumentative and negatively eccentric.

As you may suspect by now, this is something less than a stellar indicator for business. You handle routine and technical work, but emotional inadequacies and insecurities may prevent your intellectual concepts from clearly teaching the heart of those you wish to enlighten. You would derive a much broader satisfaction providing humanitarianism, creativity, and assistance for those in need. You may possibly one day work with an organization which is involved in psychic, occult, or metaphysical teaching and investigation. It may take some time to start this association because you can be afraid to join a meaningful organization for fear of some unknown hindrance to your growth. This makes you feel guilty for failing to learn a subject that can be helpful in preparing you to do beneficial work. Be rid of the guilt and get on with it!

Your attitude toward friendship is precariously balanced between an ambivalent need for friends and outward reserve. You often associate with eccentric and individualistic friends, and often fail to recognize glaring flaws. You can appear very distant; this does not make it easy to become your friend. Your feelings run deep, but you are afraid to let them show. Excessive control over your feelings causes misunderstandings.

Your romantic needs and sensual desires are all related to your sexual enjoyment. Your ability to respond sexually is linked blatantly to emotions which have both positive and negative influence. You depend a great deal on others for contentment and may suffer when they fail to live up to your trust and expectations. There is a likelihood of considerable melodrama and hidden intrigue in your love life. Marriage relations will have hidden circumstances that need to be resolved for mutual harmony. Desired harmony will not come easily; there is a strong likelihood of more than one marriage.

Nineteen Karmic Accumulation

This indicator suggests the misapplication of will in a previous life pattern. The will was directed in a forceful and domineering manner to control others. Consequently, when this number occurs you can expect to meet many willful people in home and work who constantly challenge, doubt, or defy you. One or both parents will be domineering or authoritative to an almost unbearable degree. Your behavior can fluctuate from acquiescence to brash aggressiveness. Life should teach you to respect individual will and to work cooperatively with the will in others. You are driven by a desire for complete freedom on the one hand and security through another person on the next. You sometimes feel you know it all and become very impatient with dull or unexciting beliefs of others. When you turn to others for advice, things usually do not work out. Little by little, you have learned to make up your own mind and follow your own decisions.

You will have the opportunity to overcome selfish concerns and underlying eccentricity through a refinement of emotions and a more magnanimous attitude toward mankind. When it appears, grab it and hang on.

Your capable and forceful nature is quite suited to the demands of business and a challenging career. You will be best in work with diversity and much activity. You are more likely to be an employer than an employee. You have developed a genuine concern for those working for or with you and will work to advance them once you have overcome ego threats in self. You *can* climb to the highest peaks but may collapse to the depths when ambition or pride thwart your personality. You will constantly run up against conservative business supervisors or associates who are stuck on the treadmill of tradition without your imagination.

The hasty vibration of this number makes you one who changes friends often and moves on before establishing much depth. There is little art or style of accommodating new acquaintances and your cautiousness makes it hard for others to move toward you. You easily use friends to further your own goals. You get along best with those who make the least demands upon you as a friend.

Your love life may be just as changeable as other friendships. You are direct in relationships, not prone to much preparation for lovemaking. You can give of yourself in the mood of the moment, but lack patience to maintain long-term relationships. Learn that it is more difficult to give love than to receive it. As a marriage partner, you can be difficult to understand because of rapid change in moods, ideas, and beliefs. You may one day become excited about something and forget about it the next. You will likely attract a strong-willed and contradictory mate.

TWENTY KARMIC ACCUMULATION

You are at a point of developing a greater social awareness and consciousness. Sensitivity within self needs to become directed to the awareness of needs in society or community. The suggestion is that you have experienced public embarrassment in a previous life because of personal mistakes or overdone ambition which created injustice for others, especially with 3, 8 and 9 missing. Another karmic pattern suggested here is that of a person who held a position of prominence and used it to attack and chastise opponents. Somewhere back there you misused authority. With this indicator there are subconscious proclivities to lose consideration and patience toward others. You must guard a careless tongue and root out your judgmental criticism of differing life styles and beliefs. Your personal and moral convictions are well defined, but you sometimes twist your opinions to justify questionable actions. The hypersensitiveness and nervousness of your temperament can be unhealthy if care is not exercised.

The business nature with this indicator is not as aggressive as it is persuasive. Your actions are political rather than directly forceful. This indicator suggests a likelihood of serving a public role sometime in one's career. The ministry, government, large corporate operation, or philanthropic or social reform are most appropriate careers. You work at being humble and can be self-effacing. You are cautious and discreet with an almost morbid fear of being caught off guard by the public. Loosen up, this is a tension you don't need.

The manner of expression with friends is warm, direct, and can become demanding when ego gets in the way. You enjoy hobnobbing with a variety of personages with a fondness toward people in general. Beware of becoming so involved with yourself in conversation that others are merely a source of feedback to your personal opinions. You can be stimulating and witty in relaxed moments, but when you *try* to come off as clever and witty, the results may appear contrived.

You are less aggressive and more romantic in matters of love than many. You prefer an established emotional background as part of the prelude to interplay. You enjoy the romantic, elegant, and sentimental trappings of love. In fact, these are essential in stimulating continued interest in your partner. You seek refinement in your mate, and social standing can be a factor in your choice of spouse. You are repulsed by crude or routine attitudes toward the relationship. At best, you are a concerned, sympathetic, and tender lover and partner.

Twenty-one Karmic Accumulation

Despite the many tribulations that befall you, there is a recurring awareness within that you are approaching the end of long study in the classroom of life. There is at the same time an urgency to complete tasks and some indifference about where to go. This is a number of synthesis in body, mind, and soul. You are approaching a turning point in evolution but have some major hurdles to overcome. Life will call upon you to share and describe your wisdom, but it will not be easy to convey the ideas or words you want so deeply to share. Your ability to evaluate life from so many levels and perspectives causes you to change your mind often about the same subject.

A kind of vague guilt complex haunts your life. Do you have a feeling that you should be accomplishing more inner growth and development? At the same time, life will put demands upon you that seemingly make it impossible to pursue those goals. You often overlook the fact that the most important growth comes in the situation at hand when you learn to apply esoteric law to apparently mundane tribulations. You are extremely impressionable about your environment, and you are psychic and mystical in your attitude toward life.

Business interests will be varied, and you are likely to make many changes in your career direction. You tend to prefer work of a humanitarian nature. You will likely encounter hidden resistance and secret antagonists in the pursuit of career goals and ambitions. You are at best working in areas that deal with ideas rather than physical effort.

Friendship brings mixed experiences. You enjoy the merriment and good times of friendship because of your gregarious nature. On the other hand, friendship will likely bring many behind-the-scenes upsets. It is not easy for you to establish really deep friendships. (You hold back part of yourself while professing to pour out your heart). You struggle to balance your extroverted needs with the worries, disagreements, and emotional upsets that are attracted to you. You enjoy people from the arts, communications, writing fields, theatre, and educational professions in particular.

In love and romance, your moods fluctuate considerably. Emotional equanimity is important to romantic interests. Without it, your sexual and emotional cycles alternate between intense activity and disinterest. Your prefer a mate whose refinement of feelings enables the tender and delicate facets of love to emerge. In truth, your inner being craves the spiritual union of the male and female aspects of your being into the full realization and marriage of cosmic consciousness.

Twenty-Two Karmic Accumulation

You are entering a cycle of self-mastery and expansion of soul. When this number results from the total missing lessons in the name, it is time to get your life in shape. Be careful not to fall into a pattern of growth slippage. When this number is the total for the soul life number, and personality in particular, the indication is that you have a very important role of mastery (through application of higher law) in this lifetime. In earlier years you were troubled because your work did not seem to be of a magnitude worthy of your self-opinion. A kind of overinflated outer confidence hides a subconscious feeling of inferiority. Once the soul consciousness is more fully awakened, you will begin to more fully understand your inner work and dissolve this covert insecurity.

You possess a natural ability to meet obstacles head on, and deal with problems before they grow to insurmountable proportion. Your fixed determination to achieve a goal makes you alternately open and accessible, then rigid and unbending in your reaction to opposition.

The aspect is high for career. Your persistence and tenacity make you a valuable asset to the organization. You are flexible enough to recognize new procedures or products that improve business. Your integrity and balanced sense of individuality, perseverance, and organizational skills enable you to be effective in virtually any commercial endeavor. You will be most satisfied once you are performing the inner work that the soul has come to fulfill. Expect difficulty in learning the spiritual laws of prosperity and use of money.

Your interaction with friends is rather clouded while subconscious motives mix with your conscious desires to create somewhat ambivalent associations. Although you enjoy and desire friends, ofttimes the obligation to them prevents you from accomplishing what seem to be more important interests. Your greatest happiness comes once you have begun to attain soul awareness. Can your friends share this aspiration of spiritual expansion and growth? You are highly judgmental; once this is controlled and directed in a tactful and considerate manner, you can effectively show them deep insights about themselves.

Your attitude in love and romance might be called "enlightened detachment". Your spiritual drive causes you to be less romantic, rather distant in the day-to-day expression of affection. You seek a mate who balances with you on the emotional, mental, and soul level. However, your tendency to impose certain spiritual expectations upon the loved one may inhibit your partner from progressing into his/her own desired pattern. At your best, you are a patient soul capable of giving deep love to your mate.

THIRTY-THREE KARMIC ACCUMULATION

You are very sensitive emotionally to injustice and suffering you see in the world. It is like a burden around your neck, and you want to solve every problem and help every person. This is sometimes your biggest problem; because of this intensity you overdo. In some ways this blocks your effectiveness. Can you recall a specific instance of this situation? You may waste time and effort persuading people they need your help. Let the natural healing capacity be summoned spontaneously.

Your subconscious feelings of guilt and emotional turmoil surface to occupy a tremendous amount of your conscious time. It will take equal time, and turmoil, to bring these hang-ups to harmony.

These conflicts have a similar distressing impact upon your business attitudes, friendships, and family life. You are a very emotional being with highly fluctuating moods. This makes you difficult to be with; one cannot be sure when your ups and downs will occur. Once your life becomes centered, you will be effective in work with organizations of healing and service.

ZERO KARMIC ACCUMULATION

What does it mean when no numbers are missing in the name at birth? Is there no karma at all? These questions arise often; my insights are based upon personal experience. And, yes, karma exists!

None of us would likely have chosen to incarnate presently if there was not some karmic imbalance in our evolution. As a general rule, a name with no missing numbers suggests a dharmic lifetime rather than one which is heavily karmic.

What is a dharmic lifetime? This means roughly that rather than having to spend so much time straightening out past imbalance, the individual will be able to concentrate more upon the furtherance of evolution and soul growth by opening new avenues of unfoldment and work; so zero is a karmic plus for the thinking person.

This is a plateau period of one's evolution; you have to consciously make a choice as to how you wish to progress in consciousness. This is not as easy as it appears, because there is little push from within, and fewer specific needs to fulfill. You do not have the missing numbers to provide a focus or impetus for specific action. Unknowingly, one can begin to drift and lose control of destiny. If no effect is directed purposefully to your growth, then in subsequent lifetimes new missing numbers could occur and your wheel of karma would spin along through new cycles. With this combination, the individual has the chance to decide and accomplish what he/she feels from the soul to be most significant for unfoldment action. Use it fruitfully.

As we approach this New Age when many of the Earth's humanity will be completing the need to incarnate, this indicator in the chart may have particular significance. When no numbers are missing, and all other patterns are balanced, there is a suggestion that if this life is handled well, it may be the last incarnation. This is a condition that depends on your handling of life, and is not fully dependent upon the implications of the chart. Just because a number or numbers are missing does not eliminate the possibility of completing the karmic wheel in this lifetime. It only leans more heavily in the zero aspect.

My experience is that in order to most effectively expand soul growth when this condition exists in the chart, the individual should learn to handle, master, and balance out the qualities of each number. It will require, first, mastering the numbers separately and then understanding the relationship of each number to the others. Of course, this means the numerical qualities must be learned and applied in life with other people and situations. Just learning the qualities from reading books and studying in the classroom is not enough.

With the above concept in mind, one way to evaluate the karmic accumulation is to add all of the numbers together. By doing this, we derive the following total: $1 + 2 + 3 + 4 + 5 + 6 + 7 + 8 + 9 = 45$, or 9. The remainder of this section applies to the chart with no missing numbers.

This is a life pattern where personality shortcomings must truly be brought into conscious focus and harmonized. You have a tremendous depth of awareness and take life events with a purposeful responsibility. A distinct sort of detachment and impersonal feeling pervades your attitude toward life; it is literally as if you have been through it all before and have begun to tire of earthly routine. It is difficult for you to sustain a prolonged interest or enthusiasm for mundane activities because the soul cries out to be free of this dimension, to move along in its destiny. All of a sudden, the sobering thought may overwhelm you—what a task it is to finish up the demands of this earthly plane.

You can be suspicious, critical, and moody. These qualities must now be transmitted into ones of optimism, hope, and a trusting faith in higher guidance. Your logical procedure is to generalize by bringing the overview of wholeness down to each small part. When an adversary starts to pick at the details of your structure, you become uneasy and at times defenseless. Because of your expansive outlook and understanding of so many viewpoints toward life, it is easy for you to switch views or to succumb to another's viewpoint for the sake of harmony even though you still disagree. Let this ambiguity work *for* you.

Motivation is an ingredient that often haunts you for there seem to be so many things you could do; yet, it is hard to decide. Be careful that your desire for release from this plane does not lead you into escapist behavior.

If you have not discovered your heart's desire, the deeper teachings of metaphysical and related studies will be of great guidance and comfort. Learn to give thanks for all that comes to you and visualize the perfection in yourself, others, and each situation that arises in your life. You are closer than ever to the possibility of attaining that perfect goal.

OFTEN OVERLOOKED DETERMINANTS OF KARMA

Missing numbers in the name at birth provide insight into the karmic lessons that need to be given particular attention in this life experience. It has also proven useful in my work to determine the missing numbers in the personality which, of course, are ascertained by working with just the consonants. Especially in charts where no numbers are missing, this evaluation can provide another clue to the dynamics of individuality and behavior pattern. The missing numbers are added together, and then the proper karmic accumulation number (using the consonants) should be studied. The reader needs to understand that this evaluation should not be given quite the same status or significance as the karmic accumulation number for the full name.

It is, however, a valid tool to gain added insight into the nature of the person whose chart you are interpreting, be it your own or that of another's.

Another way that a secondary karmic accumulation number can be determined is by adding the three numbers of the soul, personality, and life numbers together (first using master numbers if any—then by reducing master numbers to single digits). For example, from the name James Earl Carter Junior, the sum of personality (2), plus the number of the soul (9), plus the number of the life (9) equals $2 + 9 + 9 = 20$, which is not reduced.

Truthfully, the use of this total is as much a dharmic indicator as karmic. That is, the number demonstrates a path toward balance, as well as suggesting where imbalance has previously occurred. For that reason, the reader must use these numbers discreetly when delineating a chart. They should not be employed as an indictment regarding past behavior but, more importantly, as a guideline to right action (dharmic) during this life sojourn.

Keeping in mind the statements of the previous paragraph, the subtotal of the personality, soul, integrated self, and life number can also be taken separately for evaluation of secondary karmic accumulation numbers. For example: using Carter's chart, the subtotals are for personality, 20; soul, 27, which is reduced to 9; integrated self, 56, which reduces to 11; and life number, 18. *Remember* that the overall weight or *significance* of these numbers *is not equal* to the total of missing numbers *or* total of the life, soul, and personality numbers added together. They do apply, however.

The reader may become confused comparing all of these numbers, each of which suggests different attitudes in the life style. Remember that the karmic lessons indicate the nature of imbalance that is being worked upon in this lifetime. On the other hand, the karmic accumulation number is written in an attempt to capture some of the behavior patterns that the individual may express, taking into consideration the different lessons.

When using the total of personality, soul, and life number added together, the karmic influence is implicit rather than the more obvious influence of the total from the missing numbers in the name. This sum tacitly suggests previous imbalance, as well as the dharmic pattern for current establishment of right action. The behavior patterns briefly described for the karmic accumulation numbers do have influence upon the personality and affect the soul growth throughout life.

When evaluating the subtotal of the soul number, personality number, and life number individually, know that the influence will be more cyclical than definitive of the whole life experience. Use the karmic accumulation number purely for interpretation. The behavior will become more evident during personal years, triune cycle, or pinnacles where the numbers coincide. Also, contact with individuals having like numbers in their chart will trigger the qualities suggested in your karmic accumulation number.

VII

RECOGNIZING THE STRESS NUMBERS

In this chapter, we examine a new system of numerological evaluation. The stress number serves to accentuate differences between two numbers. It helps to define the tension between the vibrational qualities of the numbers being compared. Stress numbers are like points of tension or opposition which need to be overcome before the two numbers of comparison can best function harmoniously.

The difference between two numbers also yields insight to the compatible facets of each number; how they can be harmoniously directed by purposeful recognition and cooperative application. In this chapter I choose to concentrate upon the subconscious and stress factors of numerical differences rather than the potential compatible element which also must be given attention. I feel that the reader should be able to reach self-understanding of the compatible potential more easily than delving into the rather disconcerting elements of the unconscious framework.

The stress numbers have been divided into two groupings: the intrapersonal stress numbers and the interpersonal. The intrapersonal number is calculated by subtracting the smaller of two primary numbers from the larger of the two. In this instance, primary number refers to the personality, soul, integrated self, or life number. When calculating, all the numbers should be reduced to a single digit. First, compute the difference between the personality (P) and soul (S); then between the personality and integrated self (IS); then between the soul and integrated self. From this set of calculations, you will have three stress numbers (unless two of the primaries are the same). Finally, compute the difference between the life number (LN) and personality number; then life number and soul; and then life number and integrated self. You will then have a second set of calculations composed of three additional stress numbers, giving a total of six stress numbers.

Let us say your IS = 8, S = 5, P = 3, and LN = 6. The stress numbers would be computed as follows:

Difference between S and P or 5 - 3 = 2 Stress Number
Difference between IS and P or 8 - 3 = 5 Stress Number
Difference between IS and S or 8 - 5 = 3 Stress Number

Difference between LN and P or 6 - 3 = 3 Stress Number
Difference between LN and S or 6 - 5 = 1 Stress Number
Difference between IS and LN or 8 - 6 = 2 Stress Number

You will note, the combinations which provide the stress numbers are also purposely written out. Now refer to these numbers by combinations using the intrapersonal description on the following pages. The combinations are arranged in numerical order purely for purposes of systematic arrangements.

Interpersonal stress numbers are computed by subtracting the difference between the primary numbers in each chart. That is, when comparing charts, the major stress number is the difference between the two personality numbers for the integrated self and the two life numbers. An example is given below:

Chart A	*Chart B*	*Stress Number*
P = 4	P = 2	4 - 2 = 2
S = 7	S = 1	7 - 1 = 6
IS = 11 or 2	IS = 3	3 - 2 = 1

A further use for stress numbers when assessing compatibilities between charts is to compute the difference between the numbers on the planes of expression: Physical,

Emotional, Mental, and Intuition. If a further comparison is desired, you can subtract the difference between the personality number of one chart and the life or soul number in another. You may also devise effective ways of your own for using these stress combinations.

The intrapersonal stress numbers provide a method of examining potential cross currents within the individual's psychological make-up. Stress numbers help to pinpoint likely subconscious tensions between the needs and actions of the personality, soul, and higher self. By consciously recognizing these stress areas the combination can be then transmuted into a cooperative dynamic flow between the three fold structure of consciousness, personality, soul, and higher self.

The interpersonal stress numbers are indicative of the differences between the two charts that should be understood for reaching greater compatibility and cooperative blending of the two vibrational qualities of the involved primary numbers. They point out where resistance will occur between two people, but they also reveal the easiest avenue for working harmoniously.

As I mentioned earlier, the descriptive paragraphs emphasize the subconscious and karmic traits. You will think of wholly new ways to apply the stress numbers because this new area of interpretation will require much further investigation and application. My desire is to get subconscious conflicts recognized and resolved for more effective living. Therefore, the emphasis from now on is upon the negative side of the stress numbers.

The interpersonal stress numbers are particularly useful in understanding marriage, parent-child, employee-employer, or other relationships. Used wisely, it provides insight to overcome the difference. Use the number of difference to build a more complete union.

The question may have arisen in your mind about the meaning of two numbers in the chart being the same, i.e. a two soul number and a two personality number. Or two people's charts, each having the same life number which provides no stress number. We have already discussed many times how each number has an assertive, passive, and a harmonious quality. When two exact numbers are compared, the possibility of stress arises from the increased likelihood of going to the extremes. When two people have the same numbers, it is similar to people having the same sun signs or similar aspects in the astrology chart. They may fail to see the imbalance in their mutual life and commit excesses or omissions blindly together. Another possibility is that when one fails to recognize a negative in himself, it is so easy to overemphasize and pick on that idiosyncrasy in the spouse or partner. On the other hand, the ideal situation would be that when one partner moves too far out of balance in one direction, the other partner may be going the opposite way, and this cycle could work to teach both the lesson of harmony and mutual growth.

The following pages describe all possible combinations of numerical differences. With experience you will probably want to develop your own interpretations. These are given to be of assistance; like all written descriptions they are by no means final or all-inclusive. These descriptions (particularly the intrapersonal) may not seem to fit at all. These are subconscious negative patterns; and after age 29 and the Saturn return, the negative qualities should begin to become recognized and eliminated, in which case the positive element of the difference becomes more pronounced in behavior.

When you read the descriptions pertaining to the interpersonal stress numbers, it may appear that in certain instances, the role described will seem more applicable to the other individual involved. Just remember, we choose the opposite sometimes to learn balance, so roles can often seem reversed. That could indicate where balance is necessary.

The descriptions for the interpersonal stress numbers are admittedly quite general. They are intended as guidelines to help you establish your own concepts. The dynamics of the stress between a 5-9 soul combination would differ from a 5-9 personality combination or 5-9 life number comparison. The reader should use his intuitive understanding of these different levels of interpretation when evaluating the stress numbers.

INTRAPERSONAL STRESS NUMBERS

COMBINATIONS WITH NUMBER ONE

1-2—Stress Number (1). There is conflict between assertiveness of will and fear of social criticism. You are struggling within yourself to find your own self-convictions. In competition or under stress, you are argumentative and critical. A karmic pattern of working out a tendency toward gossip or scandalous accusations may return, directed *toward you* in this life. You want to dominate relationships; and you find conflict with an intensely self-willed spouse, relatives, or friends. You will find it difficult to establish direction and conviction particularly in your early thirties. It is likely you were raised in a dogmatic and critical, religious, or socially active family that left you caught between strong personal ambitions and indoctrinated conscience.

1-3—Stress Number (2). There is conflict between self-will and creative urges. This combination makes it difficult to express inner feelings articulately because of conflicting undercurrents. Conflict is likely with the father or dominant female. You are unable to convey or express artistic or creative insights. Because you are lacking in conviction, you will say what seems momentarily appropriate. This demonstrates a superficial friendliness. You need to work toward less critical speech and lower resentment of talent in others. When others direct malicious gossip and harsh criticism toward you and your endeavors, you are hurt very deeply. If you nurture resentment, you can delay your own advancement.

1-4—Stress Number (3). The tension here arises between indulgent self-desires and karmic obligation to accomplish the work at hand. You resent any interference with selfish ambitions. You will have difficulty finding creative avenues to resolve obligations. It is necessary for you to develop patience and more understanding of the feminine energy. You have a false sense of self-worth and desire positions of prominence without going through hard work to earn deserved recognition. You are misdirected and extravagant toward practical endeavors. You are selfish about your own needs. There is a haughty attitude and a desire for display. You are prone to an uncertainty in disposition, are slow to make decisions, and quite stubborn once they are made (for better or worse!).

1-5—Stress Number (4). There is tension of will and of freedom. You are unable to consistently face life responsibly. Work to discipline instinctive impulses toward carefree and selfish living. Frustration is compensated for by overworking oneself on insignificant projects. You seem to provoke quarrels at home and with others close to you. It is difficult to admit being wrong, and there is a karmic carryover here of self-opinion and lack of tolerance. You are prone to criticize most people who are doing the very things that you get away with. You rebel against rules and regulations imposed upon you by society. There is fluctuation here between pride and self-dignity and between courage and timidity. Thus, you find yourself wavering between silence or speaking out emphatically where you recognize injustice and wrong action. This is not an emotional combination. When you let your emotions out, they are violent and explosive. You are at your best once you have found a wholesome and heartfelt direction toward your predominant life goal.

1-6—Stress Number (5). There is strain between will and emotional needs. You must learn to find proper expression of freedom. In the past, you tended to avoid responsibility. Life will not allow you to pursue a free choice until you learn to recognize responsibility and fulfill obligations which arise. There is likelihood of separation or conflict between your parents when you were very young. Jealousy and possessiveness may have contributed to that divisiveness. You attract a spouse who is alternately overbearing and the next moment indifferent. There is a fear of change, but life will put you into a position that demands rearrangement of your attitude. You prefer a spouse who reflects your own opinions.

1-7—Stress Number (6). Emotions are caught between the impulses of will and a fixed tendency of the mind. The individual is emotionally contradictory and retreats from emotional discomfort into a self-justified intellectual excuse. This stress pattern is deeply touched by the suffering of the world and, at extremes, becomes unstable because of keen sensitivity to astral turbulence in the environment. There is a likelihood of detached parents, particularly the mother. Did she put her needs ahead of yours noticeably often? The conflict between these two emotionally restrictive numbers suggests difficulty in dealing with others in work or in exchange of opinions and ideas that contradict your biases.

1-8—Stress Number (7). There are tremendous power needs here with an almost unbearable sense of pride and desire for attainment. You need to learn wisdom as an antidote for selfishness. There is an irrational impulsiveness, a seething venom within which attracts hostility from contradictory people. It is likely that two strong-willed intellectual parents had difficulty expressing emotions. There is an almost ruthless need for power and control. Karmic tendency is toward misuse of power and will in past lives. With this stress pattern, one is completely out of harmony with the feminine energy and prone to vastly overcompensate with powerful male ego. You can be completely inconsiderate of others when on the way to the top. Proper use of intellect to investigate deep causes of inferiority is one means of dissipating tension.

1-9—Stress Number (8). There is a pull between extreme opposite polarities. Self-will is pitted against altruistic needs to serve the mass consciousness. You seek attention to build ego. There is a likelihood of dissension with authority. You are cynical toward successful leaders and covet influence. You use self-deception and unscrupulous means of tricking the public. You take advantage of others' dreams and idealism to attain your own ends. You are indifferent to the plight of the poor and helpless. Until a proper perspective is placed upon wealth, you will likely experience financial reversals. You can offset the negative here by altruistic application of your individuality to help others. But it will take rigorous effort.

Combinations With Number Two

2-3—Stress Number (1). With this stress pattern, you tend to be torn between self-criticism and creative potential. There is a fear your ideas will not be accepted by the public. You need to strengthen your self-confidence and will. You likely express a fake sense of pride to mask the self-doubt indicated. You are plagued with sensitivity, apprehension, and worry over minute details and inconsequential trivia. You lack the male drive to initiate positive action. Do you receive much criticism from coworkers? You must use your own strength of will to discern what is significant to your life; then go after it, regardless of outside criticism.

2-4—Stress Number (2). You have conflict between your work and the expectation of others. You must learn to see both sides of issues clearly and objectively. Develop your intuition to solve indecision. It is easy for you to give excessive attention to material goods and achievement. Your tendency is to let details bog you down, preventing completion of your work. It is very easy for you to hide your lack of confidence behind self-created details and petty regulation. You will adhere to the letter of the rules rather than use them constructively for achievement. You confuse goals, and values plague your desire for accomplishment.

2-5—Stress Number (3). Tension between impulsiveness and social restraint is found in this stress pattern. You need to express yourself in a cheerful, positive manner. This suggests a past life pattern of sexual indulgence and misspent creative talents. You are overly sensitive to public criticism: Why can't people keep to their own affairs? It is difficult for you to recognize how critical you are of others who are trying to express their own creative talents. You are likely to overindulge at the table when under pressure. This combination indicates conflict between conscience and impulse regarding sexual needs. You are highly condemning toward others' transgressions; deep down you are envious because you would like to be in the same position. You must seek harmony toward the proper expression of your own creativity and sexuality.

2-6—*Stress Number (4)*. There are crosscurrents of emotionalism. You are torn between what others demand and what feels proper to your own being. It is likely you were caught between a solicitous parent you did not respect and an emotionally inhibited parent whose love you wanted very deeply. You will have to work at establishing emotional equilibrium, which will not come easily. You can deceive yourself easily where emotions are concerned and can be hurt deeply when you discover a loved one is manipulating your emotions for selfish needs. You should best avoid psychic or occult studies until getting a grip on your own emotions. You have likely toyed with others' emotions in earlier lives and must learn to be forthright and honest in relations, rather than trying to please or manipulate.

2-7—*Stress Number (5)*. A seething desire for self-gratification is caught between intellectual and social censors. Your mind and emotions tell you that it is no longer necessary to crave that which you know is not best, and yet you are tormented by sensual and sexual fantasies. In earlier lives, you may have attempted to ignore or prevent sensual and carnal desires for religious or social reasons. However unfortunate, damning a desire does not terminate it. Now a war rages between temptations of the flesh and the religious and intellectual upbringing which teaches purity and lust-free loving. In a man's chart, there is intellectual disrespect for women, but a latent physical desire for them. In a woman's chart, there is dissatisfaction when sensual desire cannot be controlled. You must work out sexual conflicts by learning to identify within yourself what is proper action for your own lifestream.

2-8—Stress Number (6). Emotional tension arises from conflict between personal desire for recognition and public acceptance. There is a karmic suggestion of past misuse of wealth and power. Criticism by coworkers and associates brings disappointment from those you most want to please. Promotions and increased earnings will not come easily, and you are likely envious, even jealous, of people who seem to get ahead with little effort. You are not easy to get along with if things are going against you; you may take out this aggravation on loved ones closest to you. You can become sullen and morose for long periods of time. Your masculinity suffers when you cannot produce up to expectations in career and profession. You must learn to let go of the need to *prove* how important you are to others. Let them find you in proof of your actions.

2-9—Stress Number (7). There is mental confusion between your public image and your idealized concept of yourself. You have a rigidly defensive belief system in what you are doing. Once underway, it is hard to persuade you to alter course. You may err in isolating yourself from what outsiders are thinking. There is a fixed determination to follow your intellectual decisions which can create emotional upheavals with employees and coworkers. If the emotions were not confused, it would be easier for you to trust the more refined feelings of the heart and soul: your intuition. Until the higher intuitive mind is developed, this combination leaves you torn asunder by emotional demands and intellectual rigidity.

COMBINATIONS WITH NUMBER THREE

3-4—Stress Number (1). There is conflict between creative talents and work environment. You may have shown

talent as a child that was stifled by parents or circumstance. You need to assert self-will to fulfill creative proclivities and would be best in crafts or an artistic career.
A past-life neglect of talent is suggested when this combination occurs. Rather than assert yourself to make something of your creative skills, you are inclined to pursue
pleasure and material security. Conflict with male energy
prevents the development of courage to face the adversities of your endeavors. You are likely to develop phobias
about losing your personal possessions and money. Be careful to avoid grudges. You have a quick temper and can be
resentful about destiny passing you by. This dominating
laziness makes you vulnerable to the unscrupulous.

3-5—Stress Number (2). There is desire for unconventional indulgences and a fear of family and social opinion.
At extremes, there are licentious and exotic cravings for
stimulation. You easily confuse sex and love and become
involved in depleting relationships. Your physical eye dominates the inner eye when choosing a mate; passion may
rule over discretion. You may be mistreated by casual partners. You can be impetuous and caustic when threatened.
You are intense, angry, and volatile inside. There is a likelihood of difficulties in marriage. You tend to attract anti-
establishment and unconventional friends. This can be excellent combination working skillfully in communications.
When transmuted, there is a strong indication of success in
art, writing, communications, or sales.

3-6—Stress Number (3). Responsibilities and emotional
crises keep your life upset. Marriage and partnerships can
be a genuine hassle and frustration. It is likely that emotional conflicts in your parents' marriage had an impact
upon your early childhood. You are alternately indifferent
or overly-involved in others' emotional problems. You would
be best to get your own ship in port before attempting to
steer others. It is difficult to deal cooperatively with your
partner or spouse when the relationship becomes too emotionally entangled, particularly where possessiveness and
jealousy enter. You can turn within and ignore others when

under pressure, preferring sulking to dialogue. Do you find it easier to build your security around a stable person near to you than to find it in yourself? You must uncover and release emotional conflicts from early childhood.

3-7—Stress Number (4). You want to create and express profound ideas for the world, but opportunity for working out your dreams comes belatedly or after much struggle. When mind and heart blend, this is an excellent combination for literature and writing, but the mind needs steadying or one is fickle and unstable. This stress pattern suggests one of your parents was intellectually biased and one emotionally dependent. You benefit from marriage and working with others, but prefer your own ingenuity. You feel you are worth more in your work than your job usually indicates. When intellectually threatened, you become autocratic and respond with an acerbic tongue. Love and desire for material acquisition can intefere with natural creative ability. Indecision can plague you when head and heart are at odds.

3-8—Stress Number (5). This is a struggle for freedom between creative potential and the strident authority restrictions imposed by self or others. You have a militant attitude toward restrictions and rules. You are prone to brusque and impulsive reaction. Although you enjoy telling others what to do, you are resentful of advice from others. You tend to blurt out accusations or contrary statements; then you suffer in regret. Sexual desires are strong and can put you in compromising situations. Is sex a barometer of your success? Money slips through your fingers when your self-image suffers in an attempt to buy esteem. You are not much of a respecter of conventions, and this disregard tends to be repulsive to those of finer taste and sensitivity. A healthy attitude toward constructive creativity can help greatly to make this a powerful combination for successful growth.

3-9—Stress Number (6). With this stress pattern, there is emotional suffering through marriage, romance, and affections. Expect considerable difficulty in your emotional relationships. In marriage, you will constantly resent the burden and responsibility of seemingly unjustified demands. This can lead to love affairs, in search of the ideal mate. But this unrealistic search will haunt you until you realize you are incapable of being ideal to someone else and release your hang-ups. The suggestion here is that you have had difficulty giving constant love in past life patterns and must strive to earn love now by giving it ceaselessly. Be careful, however, not to become a false martyr. There is a tendency to be careless with little things like payments, appointments, and birthday-anniversaries.

COMBINATIONS WITH NUMBER FOUR

4-5—Stress Number (1). In this stress pattern, there is a very difficult tension between desire for play and the need to work. You must seek constructive direction for will through adversity. This is not the best combination for business; you alternate between miserly restriction and impractical spending. You want to be recognized for great work and may take short cuts or exaggerate credentials to get that recognition. You must work diligently to recognize the source of your insecurity. It is likely that there was a conflict with the father in your early years. In your efforts to advance, you are prone to attract dishonest or misleading characters who have quick and appealing solutions. Many reversals will force you to examine your motives and seek your true place in the scheme of things.

4-6—Stress Number (2). There is emotional tension from work and home. You find yourself repeatedly beset by your spouse, boss, and your own self-criticism. You attract a possessive and envious spouse and friends. You tend to acquire trite symbols to build your self-image, such as trophies, awards, and conversational items of little use. You have the power to organize and supervise if self-doubts are overcome. You are afraid of losing your money or possessions and the security you derive from things around you. You put one face forward in public, but you are considerably more stubborn and intolerant in private. You are

prone to harbor grudges and easily criticize others. Then
you turn right around and express amazement that people
are so critical of you and your work.

4-7—Stress Number (3). You have difficulty learning to
properly express feelings because of a strong intellectuality
and a tough exterior veneer. There is a subconscious conflict from prenatal or early tension with the father or a
strongly masculine mother. A cynical and judgmental attitude and an emotionally manipulative personality are two
qualities in your nature you may want to overcome. Tender
feelings are blocked up, and you become secretive so you
aren't threatened. Have you tremendous pride of intellect,
even an arrogance about pet opinions and beliefs? When
your fundamental belief system is challenged, you will overwhelm rather than discuss the subject with your adversary.
You are clever at using someone's emotional insecurity to
accomplish your own needs. You will become more satisfied
within as your emotional nature is refined.

4-8—Stress Number (4). Frustration in employment and
with authority figures is characteristic of this stress pattern. There is a strong suggestion of previous misuse of
money and power. You may have been born into wealth in
a past life and you did not need to put forth much effort
to gain prominence and status. Things are different this
time around. There will be considerable resistance to your
endeavors for success, and money will come only through
hard work and effort. You expect to be treated like a king
and act like a tyrant. You have a false ego and desire to be
in an elevated status without doing the work. You will exercise poor judgment under stress and are likely to color
truth just enough to support preconceived opinions. There
is benefit from deep and sincere evaluation of your goals
and ambitions. Honesty and hard work can bring much suc-
ces and monetary security.

4-9—Stress Number (5). The combination of stress here
is between monotonous work, bohemian desires, and highly
idealized aspirations. Your excuse for transgression of
regulations is that you are "just ahead of the times". The

love nature experiences confusion with this combination. You are likely to crave your lover's body, but may end up enjoying a lovely and stimulating conversation. A strong platonic inclination is suggested, but does not rule out the physical side of love. There is an awareness of mission or duty to be served. When destiny thwarts this mission, you blame everyone around you and are unable to recognize that the culprit is yourself. When under pressure, you can be cold, revengeful, dogmatic, and spiteful.

COMBINATIONS WITH NUMBER FIVE

5-6—Stress Number (1). An intense pull between freedom, responsibility, and will exists. You can be very fretful about taking a step in any direction for fear of a mistake or failure. You strive for independence outwardly, but subconsciously you will choose a mate or position that gives security. One streak in you can be callous, cruel, and indifferent . . . you may have had careless disregard for life and property in a previous life. This is a difficult combination for giving love. Sexual passion and physical indulgence sometimes surface as a sign of emotional deprivation. Misuse of will in an earlier life has caused you to choose this combination in order to learn the importance of facing personal acts. The suggestion is that you did not receive much ego support for your own individuality as a child. You must learn determination and perseverance if you want to succeed.

5-7—Stress Number (2). You must learn to discern between sensationalism, intellect, and social or self-criticism. There is much confusion here in pleasing parents, self, spouse, and social and public opinion. You will work very hard at performing as expected in life, but may have difficulty finding your own convictions and role. Much energy is spent trying to check strong subconscious desires toward behavior patterns beyond common sense and rational thinking. Your excellent cerebral capacity becomes irrational when confronted with the strong impulsive urges of the five. This combination causes one under pressure to lash out verbally about neighbors' faults. Let this be a clue that it is time to face up to your own. As you work out inner conflicts, you will have a chance to serve as a peacemaker and mediator.

5-8—Stress Number (3). The primary struggle here is to use creativity properly for constructive purposes. You fluctuate between superficiality and the demands of your profession. The suggestion is that in a past life, or lives, you squandered creative talent for sensuality and superficial living. You probably find it difficult finding the motivation and direction you want out of life. Oddly, you may attempt to force situations that create discord for your ambitions rather than the attainment you are seeking. This stress pattern produces a restrained emotional make-up. The feeling is often that of being unable to enjoy the spoils of social status and good living. You need to look deeper within to attune to higher creative laws of the universe.

5-9—Stress Number (4). A tension develops here between idealism, excessive habits, and desire to seriously discipline your life. You are capable of creating a very convincing image of your idealized self. The only person who does not see through it is . . . you! Many traits and habits keep you short of your aspirations, and you will have to work hard all your life to reach most of them. Do not be discouraged; it will help to develop some common sense idealism. You rotate from overindulgence to remorse for excesses, then to an idealized state that discounts the flaws erroneously. Guilt associated subconciously with past life abuses makes you a target for chastisement and almost masochistic punishment. You have difficulty taking advantage of opportunities when they come your way. There is hesitation and uncertainty about what principles you stand for because your value structure has a rocky foundation. You benefit from studying deeply spiritual, philosophical, religious, or metaphysical systems to build an inner foundation.

Combinations With Number Six

6-7—Stress Number (1). In this stress pattern, there is a classic struggle between head (intellect) and heart (conflicting emotions). The need is to find your own will through conflict. An individual with this combination must learn to control emotions and not be controlled by overreaction and moodiness. The disruption of emotions by subconscious turmoil has the effect of distorting reasoning. You tend to rationalize to justify your insecurity rather than applying reason to recognize its origins. Your friends and mates are most often also emotionally inhibited and intellectually unsure. Have you often become intimidated easily? Not knowing exactly how you stand on the issue under debate causes indecision. Because you then feel humiliated, the next time it occurs you become belligerent and unyielding on some petty point. Until you establish a solid sense of will and confidence, your consciousness will be split between the forces of mind and emotion.

6-8—Stress Number (2). Sensitivity of emotions and a drive for power engulf you in everyone's wrath. A past life pattern of selfishness and arrogance—with caustic tongue for opposition—is suggested by this combination. Even now, you can be very self-centered and trite. There is disdain for the world around you, and you create circumstances that justify your attitude toward yourself. You show very little ability to express genuine affection. Your manner and rude tactics disappoint and injure those desiring your friendship and love. In return, others disappoint you; and so the wheel turns. Your pride and ego will be severely tested until you are willing to release your blocks and turn outward to assist the world in its attempt to shed all needless suffering.

6-9—Stress Number (3). This is another emotional conglomerate of discord with a crosscurrent of emotions running in three directions at once. You will only attain inner serenity after surrendering the little self to the directives

of the intuitive guidance from the soul. You very likely
have been a martyr in a previous life and felt others turn
against you. This has left you very caustic and reserved in
your expression of inner feelings. It is hard for you to give
of the heart completely; you fear admirers will reject the
affection. This fear works subconsciously to attract a demanding and unresponsive lover who brings that which you
feared most into your house. Your whole attitude can sink
into pessimism and sorrow. Delays and frustrations seem to
plague you at each turn. Face this combination and work
your way through this labyrinth of emotional dilemmas,
and you will be very effective at assisting other souls out of
their doldrums.

COMBINATIONS WITH NUMBER SEVEN

7-8—Stress Number (1). This highly mental combination
has difficulty finding satisfactory direction of self-will. Mental quandary and gloominess follow you; a hollow feeling
toward the values of the world pervades your life. An intellectual isolation from others leaves you somewhat cynical
toward trust and friendship. There is suggestion of an attitude of intellectual oppressiveness over others in an early
life. It put you in a vacuum this time to learn the imbalance
of willful mentality without compassion and sympathy for
others. This gives a strong sense of accomplishment and
possibility for responsible leadership. You have a good
mind, but show difficulty in expressing your ideas clearly.
You tend to resist new ideas and projects; but once started,
you can organize and complete capably.

7-9—Stress Number (2). Feelings are torn between
mind, idealism, and the demands of society. This pattern
indicates that you found yourself under much pressure
when young to live by some vague ideal your parents had
decided was their dream. The only thing is you just happened to come for another purpose. You have excellent

intellectual capacity with an added ability of intuitive and inventive potential. Your nervous sensitivity and lack of emotional refinement create difficulty working with others despite your originality and ability. You can be harshly critical of yourself and others because you are intensely aware of the misspent energy in your life and of those around you. You can create antagonism in people who could be helpful by letting your sarcasm go too far. By learning acceptance of others and overcoming your inner arrogance, you can be innovative and attain considerable success.

Combinations With Number Eight

8-9—Stress Number (1). Past misuse of will puts you in a position of choosing between selfish aspiration for power and an opportunity of selfless service for mankind. There is much self-control and desire to lead and influence people. It is very easy for you to arrange other peoples' lives and tell what is best for them. You did it in other lives, and maybe you will let go this time and do a better job with your own life. You could well be a great savior to mankind or a megalomaniac dictator. Use your originality and determination to build a better you. The world will automatically benefit from your contribution. You have a reserved and gruff exterior and excellent mind. Beneath this is a stubborn determination which helps you overcome obstacles and attain your goal. Just be careful not to trample others on your way.

INTERPERSONAL STRESS NUMBERS

Combinations With Number One

1-2—Stress Number (1). The stress here is of willfullness. The one wants independence and is careless about the two's cautions or criticisms. The two needs to respect the individuality of the one and overcome a nitpicking attitude. The two needs the one for security; the one dislikes the dependence. The one enjoys the way the two takes care of little matters, but the two dislikes the one's lack of appreciation. Because of the one's attitude, the two learns to be more independent, and the one learns to be more cooperative. Until then, the arguments and petty bickering will prevail. When they work together, the two gives support to the initiative of the one, and both set up a dynamic duo of cooperative wills.

1-3—Stress Numbers (2). Sarcasm and bickering are likely going to occur until harmony is established. The one sees the three as emotionally weak and superficial. The three sees the one as arrogant and unfeeling. The one is critical of little things the three does, and the three retaliates by criticizing the one and undermining his initiative. Threes like to socialize and go out; ones may prefer an occasional visit with good friends. Threes worry often and inhibit the one from making changes. The ones criticize the three for being unable to give up sentimental attachments and move on in experience. At worst, this breeds an environment of criticism, indecision, and disagreement over trivial issues. When in harmony, each provides valuable clues for the other in establishing more ability to see issues clearly and become more cooperative in his daily relationships with others.

1-4—Stress Number (3). This is likely to create considerable stress upon emotions and the ability to communicate feelings and personal concepts. The four is serious, structured, and unyielding; while the one seeks freedom from structure. The one dislikes the four's restrictions, and the four becomes upset with the one's careless disregard for convention. Strong emotion will flare up and explode as temper. The one is likely to subconsciously undermine the four's confidence toward work, while the four withholds cooperation with one's new interests. Sexuality might be used as a tool for manipulation; for instance, hang-ups could develop in sexual expression when these two are out of harmony. Each partner involved will struggle to express words and feelings in an articulate and comfortable manner. When in harmony, there is potential for innovative and creative work together. One or both parties involved most likely had a domineering parent or parents who worked hard and probably gave the child needed warmth and emotional support.

1-5—*Stress Number (4).* With this combination, both parties will have to work hard at finding mutual balance between impulsiveness and desire for total freedom. This is an on-and-off type of relationship where things go well at one moment then become totally uncooperative the next. If both share interests, the flexibility could be helpful. A strong sexual drive directed mutually toward a constructive goal could produce tremendous accomplishment. The one expects the five to take care of his needs, while the five becomes irritated by the one's constant opinions about his new interests. The five wants to be left to free action, but becomes upset with the one's indifference. One or both parties likely had parents who left them pretty much alone to decide their own life means and course; neither likes to be tied down to job and responsibility.

1-6—*Stress Number (5).* A struggle for freedom is the primary stress in this combination. The six clings to the one for security within self. The one dislikes being tied down to responsibility, but he needs the six to learn more concern for others. The one resents being tied down, while the six becomes upset with the one's lack of interest in domestic issues. The one dislikes the six's worrying. Conversely, the six cannot understand why the one is so sure things are going to work out all right. Each is learning the true law of freedom, but it will come at considerable cost. The one's need to learn freedom truly results when responsibility has been met . . . six finds freedom only after letting go of others to trust his self-confidence. One or both of these parties lived with a parent who on some levels rebelled against home, family, or social restrictions.

1-7—Stress Number (6). Considerable tension hinders the building of mutual trust and responsibility with this combination. The analytical seven cannot deal with the impulsiveness of the one; while the one becomes impatient with the indecision of the seven. There will be very noticeable differences in the philosophy and life attitudes, which can become pronounced when child-raising is an issue. The seven has all sorts of theories about life, but can be emotionally out of touch with the needs of the one. The one also has trouble handling emotional responsibilities and can become impatient and inconsiderate. There will be much shifting in blame when the relationship goes awry. Domestic and emotional harmony will be a struggle. Either one or both of the parties involved likely comes from a home where a divorce occurred or the parents perpetuated a conflicting relationship.

1-8—Stress Numbers (7). In this combination, the eights want authority and try to dominate. The one prefers individuality and wants no one telling him what to do. The eight needs the one to recognize the authority in everyone. The one needs the eight to learn to balance will and power. There will likely be a constant intellectual struggle, each trying to outscore the other in arguments, each using quotes and facts to support his position. If the seven energy is used wisely, it will force both to look more deeply into life studies to find mutual respect through development of deeper insight of mind and soul. One or both parties involved most likely had a detached and cerebral parent or parents who had difficulty expressing emotions.

1-9—Stress Number (8). This is a tough combination because one is selfish and nine selflessness. The difference here creates a struggle for authority. The nine expects the one to live up to the nine's ideals, and the one wants to be free. There is a constant pull between idealism and realism.

The one may attempt to dominate the nine, forcing the nine to look deeper into the principles of practical idealism. The nine needs to learn acceptance of the individuality and the one more selfless concern for others. There will be subtle little (sometimes big and not so subtle) power games played by each in an attempt to prove his own position. This can create completely different attitudes toward money and finance, creating dissension. One or both likely experienced parents who were constantly struggling for power in the home and over each other's life.

COMBINATIONS WITH NUMBER TWO

2-3—Stress Number (1). Another conflict of wills, but this time the competitive nature is not as obvious as when a number one occurs also as part of the combination. The communication interaction will be erratic, contrary, and confused. There is constant misunderstanding, and lack of clarity in communication will plague the desire to get along. The two looks at topics from more than one angle and believes the three is superficial and shallow. The three knows from the heart, so becomes irritated by the vacillation and indecisiveness of the two. There can be a problem with this combination determining who will take the initiative and leadership. Either of these parties, or both, probably came from a highly emotional environment. This could be a very creative and articulate combination when the two numbers work together.

2-4—Stress Number (2). This is a very likely combination for petty bickering. The two is seldom content with the way the four does his work. The four works very hard to please society and spouse, but is likely to be unhappy pleasing self. The four wants to set the rules, and the two upsets the four by dreaming up so many alternatives. At crux, the two is very hard to please and constantly measures success by the standards of others rather than by inner awareness. The four dislikes the two's constant fluctuation in taste and values. The two does not like the four's lack of imagination and serious attitude; the four cannot understand the two's flighty moods and whims. The combination working harmoniously balances the four's steadiness with the two's ability for cooperation and assistance.

2-5—Stress Number (3). A superficial level of communication is suggested by this stress combination. The two dislikes the five's impulsiveness and lack of regard for convention. A five becomes irritated by the two's social conventions, suspecting shallow thinking. The two shudders at the five's generalizing and carelessness; while the five is uncomfortable with the two's unreasonable attention to detail and protocol. The five seeks change and activity, and the two is slower to make friends and try new outlets. The various activities of the two and five make it difficult to establish a deep understanding and communication. They can be mutually extravagant; do you get behind in payments? The two is likely to become possessive and jealous of the meandering nature of the five. The five becomes aggravated by the two's insecurities and distrust. Both parties must establish an open and honest dialogue and exchange affection to overcome shallowness and petty pretense.

2-6—Stress Number (4). This combination easily gets into a rut of stubborn resistance instead of accommodating mutual needs. The two can wallow in self-pity making the six feel guilty, thus becoming overly indulgent to the two's whims. The six then becomes a martyr, believing you must suffer torment and pain. The two dislikes divorce; because of conventionality he will bear the aggravation in silence. Both parties in this combination are prone to nag the partner about his work and profession: the two likes more status, and the six prefers greater security through increased earnings. Both must let go of emotional and social hang-ups and work to establish mutual stability. An excellent opportunity might come from working together in a group or organization (charitable or professional) which works to assist others.

2-7—Stress Numbers (5). There is a struggle for freedom from intellectual pride and socially ingrained consciousness. The seven is infuriated by the two's constant nitpicking at his opinions and intellectual pride. The two dislikes the seven's aloofness, but can learn from the depth and wisdom of the seven. The seven wants nothing to do with the two's sentiment and emotionalism, while failing to recognize that is exactly what he is seeking to develop. Neither likes being pinned to the other, yet each clings tenaciously. Each overplays and overdramatizes his condition. Each is plagued by a vague restlessness and search for something or someone different. With this combination, both are learning to let the other be free; with freedom each can grow closer to the other because of a greater range of experience shared.

2-8—Stress Number (6). Holding this relationship together will require much attention. Competition develops between outside pressures and interests versus the attempt to hold onto a caring relationship. The eight is absorbed in career and job demands, leaving the two to feel neglected. At the same time, the two wants the social trappings that indicate success. The two seeks outlets in various causes and pretends not to appreciate the achievement of the eight. The eight often overlooks the home and family on the way to bigger things in career, while the two learns about money and commercial responsibility. This often necessitates overcoming fearful emotional insecurities. The two works subconsciously to undermine authoritarianism with subtle sparring and devious little tactics to show disregard. Both parties will have to avoid negligence toward partnership and strive to maintain their union.

2-9—Stress Number (7). With this combination, the parties involved will strive to find more significance in life. This will involve a difficult search for truth and self-understanding. Both parties in this combination are prone to the impracticality of idealism. The nine resents the two putting the blame on him, while the two cannot understand the nine's blind faith and flighty reality. Both can exhibit wide mood fluctuations and need to develop intellectual detachment as a balance to broadly fluctuating emotions. Each party can be impractical and at times irrational, blaming the other for setbacks and circumstances. For example, the nine is worried about world problems and possible war in the Mideast; meanwhile, the two worries about the leak in the bathroom faucet. Both parties need to dig deeper into spiritual or philosophical wisdoms to adequately understand their mental and divine wisdom within.

COMBINATIONS WITH NUMBER THREE

3-4—Stress Number (1). A distinctly different lifestyle and attitude challenge the will aspect in both parties of this combination. The three misconstrues the four's seriousness, and the four is irritated by the whimsical three. The three may depend upon the four for support, but the four takes work so seriously that he fails to give emotional strength. The four needs to learn to loosen up and enjoy life more spontaneously, but cannot grasp the spontaneity and illogical whims of the three. A significant difference in goals is likely. The four seeks a boost to will, but the three has so many distractions that it is difficult to sustain support. The three seeks strength of will, but the four's discipline and serious outlook are difficult to accept. Both parties must be willing to recognize the fundamental individuality and will in the other. Together, this combination blends spontaneity with discipline.

3-5—Stress Number (2). This combination breeds mutual superficiality and disregard for regulations. The fun-loving qualities in each chart create a surface level relationship with little cooperation or mutual purpose. The three is intolerant of the five's excesses, but displays its own extravagance other ways. The five is self-indulgent and tasteless, which rasps against the artistic and refined qualities of the three. Daily bickering and constant hassle over small issues become routine until regeneration occurs. Five can learn from the refinement of three; and three can learn spontaneity from five. This combination can create a mutual lack of interest in social dicta, leaving both parties out of touch with current customs. Both must rise above the pain criticism causes to unite the potentially dynamic combination of creativity and originality latent here.

3-6—Stress Number (3). This is another emotionally difficult combination that can become entangled in inhibited feelings and restricted communication. The six demands attention and dislikes the three's varied interests and time-consuming outlets. The three has trouble handling the six's domestic needs and dictates of personal attention. The three means well, but he manages to say just the thing to trigger the six's sullen and morose withdrawal. The six means well, but dampens the three's enthusiasm by playing upon the theme. The mood cycles run almost in counter rhythm, making it difficult to get together even when both desperately desire understanding. At worst, poor communication exists and very likely separation and divorce occurs. This combination must learn to articulate feelings clearly and carefully understand the deeper need of the partner.

3-7—Stress Number (4). A difficult combination for working to merge mind and emotions. Expect constant struggle against divergent philosophies and attitudes toward life. The seven does not understand the optimism and sense of knowing experienced by the three. The seven's cynicism and doubt alienate the finer sensitivity of the emotional three. Both hold stubbornly to old ways and outwardly reject the other's viewpoint. The three prefers more attentiveness; the seven prefers to be alone to pursue self-interests. The three can benefit from learning to think deeply and analytically like the seven, while the seven can learn to accept feelings and inner impressions. Neither will easily accept opportunity to balance these two dichotomous approaches. It is probable that one has come from a warm home environment and the other from an intellectually detached parental influence.

3-8—Stress Number (5). An intense struggle for freedom is suggested with this combination. The eight constantly dominates the situation, causing the three to hold in emotional resentment. The three follows intuition and comes up with insights which undermine the authoritative attitude of the eight, upsetting the eight's ego. The eight cannot learn to let the three free to follow the job of heart. The three has difficulty letting the eight be free to pursue his ambitions for success and attainment. The three becomes possessive and jealous, while the eight tries to fulfill the three's emotional needs by providing material tokens of security. The three helps the eight to appreciate the joys of the humane side of life; the eight helps the three to be more practical and ambitious toward life realities.

3-9—Stress Number (6). This emotionally fluctuating combination must seek a realistic attitude toward responsibility. The three relies upon the nine's idealism and faith, while the nine expects the three to take care of business. The three's worry tendency upsets the natural idealism and optimism of the nine; the nine's detachment creates an emotional frustration for the three. The three's varied interests and diversions antagonize the nine—who would like more personal attention. On the other hand, the nine can get caught up in ideals and causes, becoming quite indifferent to the personal needs of the three. Both parties must strive for mature solutions in areas of responsibility and support. Each tends to place often totally unrealistic demands upon the other for security and domestic tranquility.

COMBINATIONS WITH NUMBER FOUR

4-5—Stress Number (1). Four and five are like polar opposites, so this combination will undergo considerable strain in accepting the individuality and will of each one involved.

The five can abuse the privilege of freedom and individuality and resents the possessive and plodding four. The four clings stubbornly to habit and custom and becomes annoyed with the five's total disregard for rules and accepted norms of behavior. Their struggle will likely persist: expansive tendencies of five against the restrictive nature of the four. The four works so hard to make things comfortable and cozy, but the five is seldom home to appreciate the work. The five has no tolerance for the confinement imposed by the four. There will be many arguments that flair up intensely and are over quickly. The five can learn patience and discipline from the four, and the four can learn to be more independent and spontaneous from the five.

4-6—*Stress Number (2).* The old nemesis of nagging and criticism can plague this combination until an attitude of cooperation is established. The six nags the four about working so hard and neglecting the six in doing so. The four then becomes busy with other projects to get away from the six's complaining. The four expects the six to take care of responsibilities and family needs, resenting the six's interference. The four will harass the six about minute procedures or daily routines. The six fights back by criticizing the four about work and personal habits. The four does not understand why the six fails to appreciate how hard the four has worked to provide security; the six responds by resenting that the four has been spending so much time at the job and cannot express emotional support openly. The four can learn to feel from the six ; and the six can learn to discipline emotion from the four.

4-7—*Stress Number (3).* We see a dead heat when the fixed four meets with the opinionated seven. The four hides emotions, and the seven secludes feelings behind a strong intellectual facade. Both have trouble with feelings, and this creates a climate of stifled feelings which inhibits communication and flow of expression. Stubbornness will characterize the texture of this relationship. The seven chastises and belittles the four's lack of intellectual depth, while the four dislikes the pompous insinuations of the seven. The climate of communication is strained, and the disagreement is laced with pent-up emotions and unexpressed feelings which color and intensify the tension. Each has attracted the other to learn the importance of recognizing personal feelings and clearly expressing self.

4-8—Stress Number (4). Disagreements of methodology, habit, and financial attitudes are suggested by this combination. The four works hard and diligently for gains and resents the eight's flippant attitude toward money and success. The four likes to hold onto every penny; however, the eight wants the good things in life. Both are inordinately stubborn at their worst. The eight can prosper from learning discipline from the foiur; the four needs to learn to be more innovative about work from the eight. Controlled emotions in both parties make it difficult for them to recognize the partner's needs. One, or both, likely came from a home where a parent or the parents spent long hours pursuing work which left the child emotionally starved. When united in a project, these could be an unbeatable team.

4-9—Stress Number (5). With this combination there is a struggle of identity and individual purpose. This partnership fluctuates between the nine's idealism and the four's practicality. The four's rigidity irritates the nine's desire to live in dream worlds of the netherlands; on the other hand, the nine's lack of common sense develop within this prone four. Sexual guilt could very well develop within this relationship because of the blend between the conventional nature of four and possible unconventionality of the nine. The nine learns true freedom comes only from discipline; an excellent example being the four. The four needs to break from the rigid and preestablished attitudes to soar to the greater heights like the nine. Each will attempt to flee from the lessons they can gain from this combination. Yet, as with any pair, there is a tremendous opportunity for broadening of learning and growth.

Combinations With Number Five

5-6—*Stress Number (1)*. This is yet another of the dynamic combinations. The channeling of will and expression of individualism are two of the significant lessons indicated. The five craves freedom and resents the six's constant need for emotional support and domestic cooperation. The six's serious attitudes are unsettled by the five's casual behavior. The five feels inhibition of will, and the six feels that the five neglects consideration for his identity and needs. Five can learn that freedom comes from fulfilling obligations, and the six can learn to let go of overattachment to security and to family support. One or both likely came from a home where the parents were constantly at odds about philosophy and each other's expected roles.

5-7—*Stress Number (2)*. Verbal sparring and disagreement over small issues can plague this relationship. The seven sits among intellectual clouds and pontificates about the five's superficial life style. The five's zest and exuberance are diminished by the seven's lack of participation in experiential life processes. A nagging and constantly petty interplay can develop between the high and the flighty. The seven can learn to disengage pompous intellectuality and enjoy life as the five does. The five can learn to see things with more depth and insight, as demonstrated by the analytical seven. One or both partners likely came from a home where intellectual detachment by one or both of the parents contributed to emotional discomfort.

5-8—*Stress Number (3)*. Detachment and trivial behavior toward the feeling nature can become a stumbling block with this combination. The eight's formality toward emotions is not stimulating to the curious and expansive five. The eight finds the five's enthusiasm and unpredictable temperament too threatening, causing even more inhibition and controlled behavior. The eight inhibits the five's self-expression, but can teach the five to become more articulate and definitive. The eight learns to loosen up more and becomes more expressive, rather than tight and restrained. There is a strong likelihood one or both partners came from a family where prestige and attainment may have been put ahead of personal warmth. When in harmony, this is an excellent combination for successful communication.

5-9—Stress Number (4). Both partners may have had a hard time keeping their efforts grounded and functional. The nine drifts into dreams of nether worlds, and the five takes this world very superficially. Because neither is apt to take the lead in bringing organization to the relationship, they could drift together through life aimlessly. As situations crumble, both will have to learn discipline and the need to work conscientiously together to build a foundation for any mutual success. Both, however, dislike the four vibration, so a struggle will exist establishing practical realism. The scattered five will have to work at understanding the sensitivity of the nine. The idealism of the nine is confounded by the blatant indulgence and worldly ways of the five. An artistic and creative temperament pervades the actions of this combination.

COMBINATIONS WITH NUMBER SIX

6-7—Stress Number (1). Herein is the combination for building an identity from the struggle between mind and emotion. The seven's intellectual detachment forces the six to look back within self in order to resolve inner emotional insecurities. The six's constant referral to feelings perplexes the seven, and the resulting heart activity undermines the best efforts of the seven. The six's will is strengthened by self-survival, and the seven learns to be more emotionally compassionate toward the will in others from being around the six. A fundamental difference between the approach to life will bring these two into heated debate and constant sparring. The seven works from logic; the six from feeling and intuition. Both will benefit from learning to appreciate the other. One or both of the parties probably came from a home environment with a similar emotional-intellectual split between parents.

6-8—Stress Number (2). This combination breeds bickering unless each works to complement and understand the other. The six enjoys the material comforts of home, but dislikes the inability of the eight to express warmth and emotional tenderness. The eight puts time and energy into work and attainment, thereby resenting that the six does not appreciate the effort to provide security. The six worries about money and family, putting pressure upon the eight's earning capacity. The eight's drive for money and success offends the six's sensitive feelings. Arguments may ensue regarding what is the most socially acceptable etiquette and procedure. The brusque manner of the eight is annoying to the six; therefore, the eight becomes intolerant of the consistent and whining six. Through cooperation and sharing, the two can balance this conflict between the drive for success and tender consideration for others.

6-9—Stress Number (3). This is perhaps one of the more difficult combinations for establishing communication and harmonious flow of emotions. Both parties seek emotional support from the other and are often unprepared to give in order to receive. Unrealistic goals and demands lead to bonds and proposed pacts which often prove to be pure fabrication. The six has no capacity to understand the nine's impersonal idealism, and the nine feels the six holds consciousness back by trying to tie down the nine to mundane trivia. Both parties suffer from a feeling of inadequacy, trying to alleviate each other's wildly fluctuating moods. Each tends to discuss frustration lightly with the other, and both will benefit from learning to articulate feelings more specifically. This is a potentially creative and highly artistic combination.

COMBINATIONS WITH NUMBER SEVEN

7-8—Stress Number (1). Intellectual authority and personal pride are factors which bring the conflict of will to a sharp focus. The seven will use facts and figures to support a position of attack and parry. The eight intensely dislikes to be put down and thrusts at emotional doubts and weaknesses to maintain leverage. Each can be very stubborn and unyielding, and the lack of emotional balance in this combination makes for a subtle power play. The seven will try to reason with the eight; the eight uses past experience as a basis for making decisions. This combination naturally breeds a competitive rather than a cooperative climate. A good combination of reason and power can emerge when the two are united comfortably.

7-9—Stress Number (2). This combination of mental realism and emotional idealism creates a climate of mixed philosophy and confused goals. The seven chides the philosophical and intellectual weakness of the nine and cannot understand the vague mystical leanings that motivate the nine. The nine detests the constant intellectual doubting of the seven and yearns for someone to share his deep-seated idealism. The quarrelsome atmosphere strains emotional harmony, an atmosphere of nagging and petty criticism. The seven could learn much from the emotional and idealistic nine, and the nine can become more organized and articulate about ideas by being around the seven. Either or both of the parties likely came from a home where parents were at odds between heart and head.

COMBINATIONS WITH NUMBER EIGHT

8-9—Stress Number (1). The difference in direction of the wills with this combination arises from the eight's desire to accumulate the goods of this world and the nine's deep-seated need to let go. The eight interprets the nine's philosophy as undermining and unrealistic. The nine becomes bored with the eight's constant materialistic appraisal of life values. The eight needs ego support of the will to accomplish. The nine could care less about some of the eight's ambitions. The nine seeks an ideal mate and finds the eight lacking in areas of emotional sensitivity and humanitarian idealism. This is a very opportunistic combination for growth when recognizing the metaphysical potential of the two numbers together.

VIII

SYMBOLOGY OF THE LETTERS

At the heart of numerological interpretation are the letters in the name. In the first portion of the book, the numerical equivalents were given for each letter. In this chapter, attention will be directed to the specific symbolical meaning of each letter and its meaning for the natal and progressed chart.

To construct foundation for the symbolical meaning, let's review basic symbols presented in the second chapter: The full circle represents the superconscious of inclusive embracing awareness. The half circle represents the subconscious or soul. Straight lines represent the consciousness; the vertical is usually male and horizontal is female. When angled lines occur in a letter, they represent progress and an exchange of awareness. They may be assertive or responsive, depending upon origin and direction of flows.

As a further aid to delineation of the letters, think of a letter as operating on three levels. The top represents the spiritual aspect, the middle the mental-emotional, and the bottom is symbolic of the physical plane where spirit is planted on earth. Using the letter A as an example:

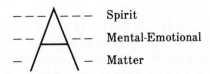

Following are individual interpretations for the twenty-six letters of our alphabet.

A (1)—The A symbolically originates on a higher plane, and its thrust is down and outward to the planes below. The horizontal bar represents an intuitive link on the mental level which forms a balanced triangle and then plunges to earth with direct force. When A appears in your name, there is an indication of independence, aspiration and ambition. The direct impact from the A creates rapid thinking and inspired ideas. You are original in action and more often start new projects than finish them. The value one of A makes your actions direct and to the point once your mind is clear. You possess a strong sense of self-reliance and independence and do not like to have others impose or interfere. Yours is a carefree and courageous attitude. You can be blunt to a fault and need to weigh ideas carefully before presenting them. However, you enjoy debates and friendly intellectual sparring with friends and coworkers. When inharmonious, the person can become self-centered, opinionated, and fiercely independent. Many A's in the name stimulate impulsive actions, adventurous longings, and a need to work at completing projects in motion. When A is the first letter in the name, it emphasizes assertiveness, leadership qualities, and willfulness. At the end of the name, the tendency is to initiate good ideas or projects too late.

PROGRESSED CHART—new undertakings, change in job or residence, breakthroughs in consciousness, new friends or opportunities, promotion, can indicate setbacks or reversals when negative, spiritual illumination.

B (2)—The B draws spiritual and physical awareness into the emotional-mental level for its evaluation. This enclosed pattern reveals shyness and introspective withdrawal. People close to you often overlook your sensitivity to criticism and antagonism. You go to great lengths to avoid a tendency toward judgmental attitudes. You are inclined to be critical and finely discriminating in your mental outlook, and you see it as a flaw. You enjoy positions that allow you to negotiate and bring people with conflicts into a position of harmony and deeper understanding. You work best with others, despite your inclination to withdraw. Learning the axioms of cooperation will prove valuable to your future. There is an inclination to carry projects to the tiniest detail; sometimes this angers more impulsive types. Your negative tendencies are self-criticism, indecision, and overzealous opinions of what is right or wrong. When many B's appear in the name, the above negative tendencies may be pronounced. As the first letter in a name, the B stimulates emotions, and brings success through constructive cooperation with others. As the last letter, the tendency is to criticize self for recognizing proper behavior only after the mistake is made. Remember that looking back is only valuable as a guide for future behavior.

PROGRESSED CHART—nervous strain, need to rest, seek harmony with others, listen to intuition, improvement in career or work, time to cooperate, do not force issues, make improvements in home, seek cause to emotional disharmony.

C (3)—Symbolically the C starts to form the circle, but it leaves an opening to communicate that which has been accumulated from eons of time and experience. A natural sense of joy and freedom flows from the possession of the C. You have noticeable originality in thought and speech and should strive to cultivate these creative abilities. You are a natural, gregarious host and enjoy the company of artistic friends. You often see only the good in things, yet are sensitive and susceptible to disillusionment or injured feelings. You benefit from partnerships, and your outward personality attracts creative coworkers. When in disharmony, you may suffer from throat afflictions and tend to scatter your creative abilities too thin. Many C's in the name suggest a special destiny; you will reach goals and lessons after much resistance, through sheer perseverance. When C is the first letter, it accentuates the voice and likelihood of exposure to the public. When it is the last letter, creative inspiration comes late and often from another source rather than from one's own fund of originality.

PROGRESSED CHART—brings new adventure and friends, inspired creative thinking, a time to enjoy life, heightens intuition and psychic experiences, study ways to improve self, new business endeavors, brings marital differences to surface, follow own guidance.

D (4)—This letter is enclosed, so consciousness is centered and directed. The soul awareness flows along all levels and brings the four quality to mundane fruition. Those of you with D in the name will work hard to overcome setbacks and mundane obstacles. With self-discipline and frugal habits, you will be able to acquire the security and personal comforts you desire. Once given a task, you work diligently—until it is completed exactly as ordered. You easily become set in your ways, critical, and temperamental. Your fixed attitudes in love and home can be difficult for loved ones to reconcile. Control a simmering temper. A practical businesslike manner underlies your actions. Many D's in the name emphasize that determined, narrow, and tenacious attitude. There can be a tendency to overestimate your capacity to provide for others. Be careful not to promise more than you can produce. When D is the first letter in the name, you take your work seriously, but will move to greener pastures if everything looks favorable. When D is the last letter, you may seek new opportunities after the best situation has passed.

PROGRESSED CHART—stresses health, be careful with nutrition and diet, business trips, strained love relations, activity with residence or property, time to ferret out locked-up emotions, pay attention to organization, a time to build a solid foundation in home, career, love, or personal consciousness.

E (5)—The E expresses on all levels; it will have you reaching for experience in all sectors of life. Those possessing the E are curious adventurers who seek experience for its own sake. The E in your name encourages experience and confrontation with active life events. You may hesitate often, but in the end, you learn much from the new people and events the E attracts. This stimulates mental activity and self-expression. You exude much energy in daily living. You may find yourself being very fidgety, intellectually curious, and with a knack for altering situations to suit yourself. You have a keen perception of events . . . but may lack a depth and concentration of thought. Oftentimes a casual interest in religion, philosophy, and the occult. You are adaptable, restless, and always on the go, especially when there are several E's. E as a first letter suggests an active mind, much attention to communications and dealing with the public, and decided ability to use words well for the ministry, sales, entertainment, or whatever your calling. When E is the last letter of the name you often reach conclusions too late or are unable to solve intricate parts of a life puzzle.

PROGRESSED CHART—accelerated activities, possible change in residence or job, many short travels, active love life, chaotic happenings with unexpected twists, fluctuations in job and business, awakened interest in religion, philosophy, and occultism, new (and sometimes eccentric) acquaintances, new job direction, desire for freedom, tension in home.

F (6)—The thrust of the F is outward on the spiritual and mental-emotional level. The consciousness is directed to spiritual and mental levels to best deal with responsibilities in life. You will attract many opportunities to protect and take care of others; although you withdraw into emotional and mental realms when upset. And you are ill at ease amid discord and tension. Your firm sense of right and wrong leaves you quite upset at injustice around you. Because of your sensitive receptive personality, you respond readily to consideration and affection. You suffer from the weight of your own burdens, at the same time taking upon yourself the problems of others close to you.

You will face many sacrifices in life. Many F's suggest a sort of higher protection, despite the numerous setbacks and responsibilities that befall you. When F is the first letter, a somewhat subdued and withdrawn behavior is suggested. You will be faced with many added responsibilities and can mature from facing them fully. When it falls as the last letter, it is difficult for you to get started; you put off even the necessary until later.

PROGRESSED CHART—adds to home and personal responsibilites, need to make emotional adjustments, learn to accept duties with willing attitude and complete them efficiently, learn to release stress, spiritual peace from fulfilling personal burdens, seek quiet of mind, community service, accentuates discord or harmony in the home, be careful of martyr complex.

G (7)—The G is almost a circle, but turns in on the mental—emotional level to dwell upon the accumulated wisdom within. Your thrust in consciousness is toward deep thought, philosophical speculation, and analysis of life issues. Your aloof and detached attitude can cause misunderstanding in people close to you. You are somewhat self-contained, perhaps not readily responding to warmth or attention. Your reserved, somewhat self-deprecating, and anxious nature can cause you to wear yourself out through negative thinking. With more than one G, you possess keen analytical ability with pronounced insight into the subtle motives behind people's outer actions. When G is the first letter, it indicates a strong desire to delve into the mysteries of life. You will work hard, but are acutely aware of your value and balk at selling yourself short. With G at the end of a name, you can become bogged down by the weight of all the accumulated knowledge and concerns you carry.

PROGRESSED CHART—examine possibilities for financial gain, guard health, scrutinize possible changes thoroughly, can bring advancement, emotional impulsiveness, search for deeper happiness, can bring expansion in business or work, overcome inward brooding and direct abilities outward.

H (8)—The H possesses two parallel vertical lines. The horizontal line represents a building block on each plane. When this letter appears, there is opportunity to climb the heights of consciousness. Remember that climbing brings the danger of falling. You have an innate executive capacity and seek out the struggle for accomplishment and success. You enjoy people, possess a refined intellectual outlook, are active, and put your point over convincingly. You are impressed by pioneering people of outstanding personality, and you attempt to emulate productive qualities you see in them. You are uncomfortable when conditions become disturbing to the point that you lose confidence and feel out of control. When H is the first letter, it enhances leadership and an ability to attract success. When it is the last letter, there is a tendency to demonstrate your best abilities and talents too late. Many H's can suggest an overbearing and self-centered arrogance.

PROGRESSED CHART—seek opportunity for promotion and advancement, use creative ideas for gains and success, selfish and greedy goals can undermine enlightened judgment, time to discipline and understand feelings and personal needs, a good time to find and establish self-identity, seek love and attention, work out internal conflicts and misunderstandings with others.

I (9)—The letter I symbolizes a straight line verticle thrust between two planes of consciousness. It is direct, intense, and dynamic. Because it is the last single digit letter, it brings one cycle to a close, resolving individuality and building toward universality. This leaves its beholder sensitive and fluctuating in temperament. You are often susceptible to hurt feelings because of your tendency toward idealism. When out of balance, you can suffer deeply through sacrifice and disappointment in personal relationships. Let your innate humanitarism and impersonal inner guidance become the focal point in your inspired musical, literary, or creative endeavors. The nine lets go and accumulates cosmic rewards. When I is the first letter in the name, it enhances quickness of thought, psychic sensitivity, and awareness of mass consciousness. As the last letter, it can bring misunderstandings, hurt feelings, and poorly defined relationships. The intensity and directness of the I can bring emotional fluctuations in the form of mood swings, depression, and discouragement.

PROGRESSED CHART—volatile emotional moods need to be controlled and constructively directed. Increased intuition and psychic inspiration are present. You must strive to understand others' needs. Nervous strain and health problems can arise; if one is not careful, worry and nervousness increase. A time for self-investigation and cleansing; abrupt and unexpected changes in job, family, and relationships.

J (10 or 1)—J is the only letter that looks back with its cup (u) holding onto the wisdom the soul has accumulated, using that as a foundation for progress. You are somewhat more hesitant to start than the other letters with the one value; however, once your mind is set, you show strong leadership, innovative thinking, and orderly skills for achievement. If cautious and prudent, your abilities can bring considerable gain and reward—particularly if the J is the first letter in your name. The J adds sparkle and dash to the personality, which helps in your dealings with the public. There is a strong moral and ethical fiber running through your personal and business dealings. When J is the last letter, you may miss the point of business or conversation, and be embarrassed later. Trust is important to you, and much suffering can come through affections. Your buoyant optimism and good nature usually allow you to rebound from adversity and enjoy life.

PROGRESSED CHART—brings added responsibility and opportunity to increase earnings, new direction in business or personal affairs, change in residence, brings strain and alterations in personal relations, avoid shortcuts and irresponsible projects, increases initiative, establishes foundation for expanding awareness.

K (11 or 2)—The arms of the letter K move to and from the higher and lower plains through the mental-emotional. As the eleventh letter, the K has higher potency and potential. You are one with a highly kinetic imagination and exciting personality. You are powerful and forceful once your mind is set, but you must understand others' needs and attain your position through cooperation and diplomacy rather than domination. Your extreme nature and immediate sense of values can get you into tight situations. No problem, you resolve them with an easy flair. You flourish emotionally in an environment of harmony and tenderness. When K is the first letter, it gives dramatic coloration to your expression, a gay and cheerful disposition, and a tendency to want to help others with any problems. As the last letter, you can be resentful when others fail to carry out their role in a cooperative manner. Those with K have a keen eye for detail and work to bring peace over each little area of disagreement.

PROGRESSED CHART—do not get caught in trivia and miss the greater opportunity, brings unusual and strange experiences, misleads through strong emotions, time to deal with self-doubt and lack of self-image, brings psychic and spiritual breakthroughs, can bring financial gains, watch for dishonesty and exaggeration.

L (12 or 3)—L receives a direct thrust from the higher consciousness and softly expresses itself in the material form of word or expression. You have a comfortable but colorful style when presenting yourself and your ideas. Your understanding of what motivates others is quite perceptive and useful. Your inquisitive nature is constantly in search of greater learning and self-expression. You are prone to excessive worry when friends and acquaintances disagree with you or each other. If L is the first letter, it

helps with public recognition, social popularity, and creative use of words and ideas, often placing you in a leadership role. When L is the last letter, you can waste much
time and energy pursuing a less than worthy course of
action. The L vibration is romantic, intuitive, and uplifting
in nature. Your sensitivity enables you to size up people
quickly and accurately when in harmony.

  PROGRESSED CHART—good time for meeting new
friends and love, stimulates arts and entertainment, travels
can bring happiness and popularity, favorable for marriage
and home, relaxation and study bring spiritual gain, can
lose friends or resources through thoughtless or careless
action.

  M (13 or 4)—M grasps concepts on the mental-emotional
level and then secures them to a firm sense of reality. You
are a natural builder, and seek solid ground upon which to
build your life and principles. You have a natural technical
and organizational ability which serves you well in the practical world. Your controlled emotional nature makes you appear aloof and difficult to know completely. You keep yourself under strict discipline; personal control is always an
issue to you. When M is the first letter in the name, it gives
qualities of integrity, concentration, and service to man.
Many M's can indicate hard-headedness and narrow attitudes. When M is the last letter in the name, there is resistance to building a proper foundation and credentials for
one's efforts. M in the name stresses reasoning capability,
but there can be difficulty expressing ideas clearly to
others. Your work is to build higher ideals into form.

  PROGRESSED CHART—financial aspects can be tight,
watch for strain on health, give serious thought and planning to the future, deal with added demands from work and
career, travel, secret affairs, time to review spiritual values
and goals, be careful with contracts and business, try to
avoid needless quarrels, overcome opposition by facing
solutions squarely.

N (14 or 5)—The flow of the letter N is one of rapid inspiration from above, tempered with evaluation of experience below. The N seeks experience and knowledge of the world and then places the lessons before the higher self for appraisal prior to new growth. You are energetic, adventurous, and constantly turning over new stones in your quest. A constant search for new knowledge can make your belief structure inconsistent; yet, your restless pursuit of knowledge tends to a deep faith and optimism toward life. Your need for change and excitement gives you an openness and appeal which summons other intriguing personalities. You enjoy luxury, sensual comfort, and are prone to indulgence. When N is the first letter, it enhances social contact and recognition. If N is the last letter in the name, there is a tendency to perform services of giving as a means to get something in return at a later date. You are at your best in positions dealing with people on a daily basis.

PROGRESSED CHART—exercise talents and expand horizons, fluctuations in career and finances, brings sensual intrigue, confusion deciphering proper spiritual path, unique and adventurous experiences, brings new friends and important social contacts, work on underlying friction in family, restless search for love and fulfillment, physical exercise important.

O (15 or 6)—The O is our ring-pass-not and can embrace universal wisdom. Or it can become woefully restricted and egocentric. The nature of the O is to embrace the world's problems openly, and those with O must guard against taking on more burdens and responsibilities than they can handle. Your embracing attitude places you in roles of service in the home and public market. You respond to the demands of domestic responsibility and find deep satisfaction in that role. You collect experience, both trivia and necessary. You must learn when to turn loose those people or concepts with which you have lived too long. O as a first

letter or as the first vowel makes one vulnerable to deple-
tion of energy—as the result of openness to other's problems. Beware of being used by others. O as the last letter
causes prolonged worry and concern over previous relationships or actions which did not work well.

PROGRESSED CHART—activates financial matters in
the home and business, opportunity to assume responsibility and leadership, emphasizes marriage—its problems and
joys, deepens need to understand one's own motives, activates interest in the occult or religious studies, discord
upsets health, a time to resolve conflicts in home and family
relations.

P (16 or 7)—The preponderance of the P's influence is
intuitive and intellectual. Its nature is to store wisdom and
disperse it prudently upon need. The P provides impetus
to the study of deeper philosophies and spiritual sciences.
You are aloof and distant, with your head in unknown
spheres. Do some people consider you difficult to know?
You are a lovely person with a great sense of drive and purpose once your sights are set. Your drive should best be
balanced with a humanitarian consideration, or your personal ambition can become unchecked. You want very much
to establish yourself to leave an impression despite unfavor-
able circumstances and a lack of recognition. When P is the
first letter, it suggests an intensity of drive with clarity
of mind. When it is the last letter, there is frustrated ambition for control and power. The power will either come late
or remain elusive. Higher wisdom should be sought to direct
this energy to more fruitful use.

PROGRESSED CHART—disappointment through love
and affection, study mental sciences and deeper metaphysical studies, confuses sexual need and love, emotional repression and confusion, avoid prolonged withdrawal and
depression, make it a point to open up and enjoy others,

use inward wisdom wisely in outer world, brings recognition for specific skills, use discretion in major decisions.

Q (17 or 8)—The Q is like an O with a way out, and it is a dynamic shot of energy into one's life endeavors and aspiration. The qualities of the awakened Q are a volitile additive to your success quotient. This vibration can create some eccentricities, so many will find you undefinable. When greed is overcome, this can be a strong indicator of financial accumulation. You have the vision to dream and the potential leadership to put your dreams into action, directing and inspiring others. You repeatedly defy social restriction and opposition from those you consider inferior, while taking a fiercely independent position in your self-expression. When Q is the first letter, it is highly inspired (or can become purely eccentric), depending upon the consciousness. You do not like to become dependent upon others and enjoy people who are equally creative, artistic, and progressive.

PROGRESSED CHART—carefully seek application for unusual ideas, brings unusual traits and conflicts into home and marriage, attracts eccentric and colorful acquaintances, significant change in work and finances, activities upset emotional equilibrium, need for recognition and power, can fall for get-rich-quick schemes. Do not let individuality destroy possible alliances.

R (18 or 9)—The R has the stored-up potential of the P, but R goes through emotional anguish to bring wisdom into earth plane expression. The R has tremendous potential, but it brings many trials and tribulations of emotional growth. Your artistic and poetic temperament finds it difficult to deal with harsh realities. You are a natural leader when inspired and are responsive to advanced concepts of social thinking and action. You set idealistic, yet sometimes impractical, goals which can lead to disappointment and cause you to become cynical and mistrusting. The power of R can be used many ways; however, it usually is best expressed when channeled into selfless humanitarian aspiration rather than pure selfish ambition. This is true especially when R is the first letter. When R is the last letter, unaccountable diversions can prevent completion of desired goals. Many R's in the name can stimulate nervous excesses and concern which can deplete the health factor if not corrected.

PROGRESSED CHART—time to exercise caution in all major decisions, brings delays and disappointment, plan and do not plunge, emotional trials, consider motives for marriage carefully, great spiritual growth through trials and tribulations, expand in compassion and broadened understanding of others' viewpoints, use creative mind, deeds without work may collapse, time for self-growth.

S (19 or 1)—The S is symbolic of the progress of the soul on earth and in heaven. Much like the divider of the universal symbol (☯), the S weaves its tapestry of consciousness . . . bringing unity and breakthrough. The S in the name gives an intense creative drive and brings flashes of insight and innovation. You are drawn to religious and philosophical research, but usually follow your own brand of unorthodox and individual belief. A distinct need for self-expression and individuality pervades your nature. You desire to make a favorable impression and to be recognized for your unique personality. When out of balance, you attract needless accidents and minor setbacks. When S is the first letter, you are quick to spot a deal and handle opportunities shrewdly. However, when it is the last letter, there is a likelihood of seeing through situations clearly only after it is too late to cover up misjudgments. The presence of S helps to stimulate the noblest spiritual aspirations.

PROGRESSED CHART—sudden changes in family, job, and/or consciousness, may bring change of location, unexpected events, have beneficial results in the end, can bring unnecessary arguments and emotional bickering, spiritual and mystical revelation, enhances urges for creative thinking, can bring extraordinary events in love affairs, confrontation with strong-willed adversaries.

T (20 to 2)—The T seeks out wisdom on the higher plane and brings it down in flashes of intuitive inspiration. The possessor of a T is very exacting in expectation of others, yet can be very patient. A natural warmth is denoted, and this enhances the maternal domestic qualities, as well as skills in tact, diplomacy, and cooperation. You seek congenial interaction with others and become anxious when relationships deteriorate and cooperation is impeded. You are at a point where it is time to release old ideas and negative traits; let them be hung upon the cross. Now you are free to pursue nobler service. When T is the first letter, the tendency is to carry out others' ideas well and instruct rather than take bold initiative. When T is the last letter, you can easily get yourself into confused states. Then you lack certainty and will not take advice. You should guard against the tendency to become critical and trite.

PROGRESSED CHART—emphasis on partnerships and business, desire to travel and see the world, enhance earnings, brings important lessons in growth through trials, need for security, brings significant relationships, correct impulsiveness and overemotionalism for better health, stress self-discipline, others may interfere in your work, will benefit from periods of solitude and meditation.

U (21 or 3)—The U represents the fully receptive nature of the soul along with a multitude of gifts possessed by the Inner Self. The soul expresses itself through feelings, making them central to your make up. You experience a wide range of emotional reactions to life. Usually you rise from depression and despair to turn your nurturing qualities into assistance for others. Your natural dignity brings traits of charm, effervescence, and persuading confidence into expression when you are in harmony with self. On the negative side, you can be enraptured with so many issues or projects that you scatter your talents, preventing goal attainment. U in the name enhances writing, academic studies, and artistic potential. There is a curious fluctuation between optimistic aspirations for achievement and periodic pessimism. When U is the first letter or vowel in the name, it emphasizes travel and communication. In fact, it can bring an almost divine aura of protection. As the last letter, it scatters native abilities and brings more risks than benefits to unplanned endeavors.

PROGRESSED CHART—mixed time of opportunity and inner fears, may have to force self in order to awaken creative talents, evaluate situation thoroughly before making major moves, unconventional and broken love affairs, brings out underlying emotional troubles, relatives and family can become difficult, be careful to take advantage of good opportunities in business and work, a time to release emotional blocks in order to awaken inner qualities of the soul.

V (22 or 4)—V is the 22nd letter (keep this in mind when working with V), and its symbolical pattern is to draw directly from spiritual sources and plant the inspiration with firm direction into the material life stream. When awakened, this gives qualities for enlightened business savvy along with inspired leadership for interjecting higher wisdom into established social patterns of human endeavor. You are quite capable, determined. Once dedicated to a person or cause, your loyalty is the greatest. You will have to work hard for success, but an unlimited opportunity exists for those who live by the higher precepts working in the new laws of manifestation. You can envision a project, inspire others, and bring things into fruition. When V is the first letter, you will take on difficult plans and bring together the people necessary for most efficient execution. When V is the last letter, you are likely to talk more about

dreams that might have been . . . or perhaps plunge care-
lessly into something without full knowledge of the consequences. You should work to awaken the latent potential of
this master number.

PROGRESSED CHART—discipline yourself and get
the project at hand under control, apply religious or metaphysical principles to your daily endeavors for rapid progress of the soul, wise investment can bring prosperous
returns, compatible relationships bring special personal
satisfaction, celestial ideas bear fruit, a favorable period to
terminate old debts, productive hard work will have great
rewards.

W (23 or 5)—The W draws inspiration from spirit, vali-
dates it on the material plane, consults the higher self for
confirmation, and then lifts human experience to a higher
realm. W seeks life and growth with relish. Its desire is to
get life completed and move on to new levels of existence.
You avidly pursue life; very little can keep you in the doldrums for long. You push aside obstacles, following hunches
in complete defiance of the natural odds. This quest brings
you into every imaginable unique and bizarre experience.
You are adaptable, with a pointed knack for taking old concepts and reworking them into updated ideas. You will find
it hard to stay long in one place. This vibration is favorable for speaking and writing. You are able to dash up your
presentations with a touch of real life drawn from your
wide-ranging experiences. When W is the first letter, it
enhances the likelihood of service and working with diverse
classes of people. As the last letter, there is an initial
hesitation in dealing with people; however, this is generally
overcome as you learn about yourself and others.

PROGRESSED CHART—brings fluctuation and instability which usually works out well in the end, emotional
relationships are varied and can be confusing, spiritual
growth results from intensified life events, sudden changes,

let go of the past and move ahead, travel emphasized, may bring legal settlements, be careful not to overdo and strain physical health.

X (24 or 6) — The X forms an "as above, so below" ($\mathbb{X}$) meeting of downward flow of light and upward reach in consciousness. The two triangular motions meet on the mental-emotional level where misunderstanding and false wisdom should be cancelled out and eliminated. When this letter appears, one is at a crossroad in consciousness where progression can occur or the temptation may bring on repetitive cycles. The need is to let go of personality so you may move more dedicatedly toward aspiration of the soul. Your life is best suited to one of service and improving the human condition. You may feel too much is demanded from you by the world, and you seek recognition for your solution to others' problems. You possess a flair for theatrics and enjoy prestigious company. As the first letter, X very often brings the possessor into public limelight. When X is the last letter, you hesitate to take on the responsibility of working to serve others.

PROGRESSED CHART — can bring public attention and gains in finance, travel is accentuated, secret liaisons, various activities can place strain upon nerves; quick, decisive moves will be required, unusual family strains, may bring need of sacrifice for others, uplift thinking, time for purge and purification, seek soul guidance.

Y (25 or 7) — The Y has a highly intuitive receptivity to higher insight. You are naturally psychic and intuitive and should learn to trust your strongest impressions. The Y gives a secretive tendency and inclination to probe deeply into the mysteries of man and universe. You accumulate wisdom in great force until you are ready to make a decision or evaluation. This reserve makes you appear detached and unfeeling; yet, your true feelings run deep. Do not underestimate your abilities. Now may be the time to let

the world benefit from your abounding skills. You can become critical of circumstances where disorganization and
confusion exist and seek solutions which clarify and establish order. When Y is the first letter, your mental and intuitive acumen is pronounced. As the last letter, you will
likely fail to take advantage of first impressions. You will
derive much benefit from times in meditation and positive
introspection.

PROGRESSED CHART—do not neglect physical realities in pursuit of knowledge, minor health problems may
occur, a deeper sense of spiritual reality slowly emerges,
may bring new circle of friends and professional compa-
triots, psychic occurrences, be cautious toward stimulants,
great insight now from self-examination, meditation, and
soul evaluation.

Z (26 or 8)—The Z transfers information between levels
like a bolt of lightning. The influence of Z is very potent,
and its presence has a marked effect on consciousness. You
have abundant self-confidence, drive, and a great deal of
energy. The Z is like pure energy and as such can be used
constructively or with devious motive. When positively directed, it brings leadership, success with money, and organizational efficiency. You should avoid exaggeration and excesses in personal habits. Misuse of material goods will
chain the soul and bind growth. You have a magnetic influence with the masses and must guard how you use influence.
When Z is the first letter in the name, it can bring prophetic abilities, enhance public recognition, and often put
one into unconventional professions. As the last letter, it
warns of the pitfall associated with misuse of wealth and
personal power. "Regeneration" is an important word for Z
people.

PROGRESSED CHART—wise judgment can bring
gains in wealth and/or prestige, overcome limitations, take
tremendous strides, put universal law into practice, misguided emotions can be a strain on health, avoid schemes

and earn your way honestly, brings unusual mate and
friends, seek efficiency with occult and divine studies,
stresses investigation and truth.

The reader might want to consider, when interpreting
the significance of the letter symbolism in the progressed
chart, the vibrational influence of each specific year the
letter covers. See the next chapter for more details regarding procedure for arranging the chart. For example, let us
use the letter G. The first year in the letter G's influence
will have a slightly different shade than the second, third,
fourth, fifth, sixth, and seventh year of its periodicity. The
accomplished student will eventually want to blend the
numerical value of each year with the vibrational quality of
the number. And it is nowhere near as difficult in practice
as it looks in this brief reading. By developing this awareness, you will add considerable subtlety and insight to your
art of interpretation.

For instance, in the fourth year of the G's influence, the
individual will feel the need to discipline the self to best
attune to accumulate wisdom within. In the fifth year, there
will be expansion and more conscious expression of the innate capacities of mind and soul. With time and practice,
you will be able to establish insights for more thorough
personal evaluations.

IX

A NEW AND REVISED PROGRESSED CHART

The traditional manner of arranging the progressed chart starts with the first letter of the first name. In the progressed chart that letter will influence life for the number of years corresponding to the numerical value of the letter. This procedure is followed for the whole first name, the middle name, and then the last. The sum, or essence, of the letters is then evaluated along with the yearly influence of the letters involved.

Campbell and Jordan have clearly demonstrated the manner of arranging the chart. They have also provided further information for delineating the progressed chart. Other numerology books have given yet more insight concerning progressions. Over the years, this writer has found the system both applicable and quite useful. I urge you to study and employ such a chart if you have not yet learned to do so.

More recently, I have been given insight into a method of progression which I have developed to map the progress of consciousness and inner unfoldment. This method is more suited to counseling than focusing upon outer events. The older method traditionally worked from an outward-looking stance. One system does not displace the other; rather, they balance and compare inner and outer events.

Following is an example of the new, revised progressed chart using James Earl Carter Junior as the referenced name. After the chart, there will be descriptive clarification, detailing how to set up this chart for interpretation.

241

Name: James Earl Carter Junior

Age	0	1	2	3	4	5	6	7	8	9	10
Personality		J	M	M	M	M	S	R	R	R	R
Soul		A	E	E	E	E	E	E	E	E
Personal Year	9	1	2	3	4	5	6	7	8	9	1
Essence		3	11	3	4	5	3	3	22	5	6
Calendar Yr.	24	25	26	27	28	29	30	31	32	33	34

Age	11	12	13	14	15	16	17	18	19	20	21
Personality	R	R	R	R	R	L	L	L	C	C	C
Soul	E	A	A	E	E	E	E	E	U	U	U
Personal Year	2	3	4	5	6	7	8	9	1	2	3
Essence	7	4	5	1	2	6	7	8	7	8	9
Calendar Yr.	35	36	37	38	39	40	41	42	43	44	45

From the illustration above, you see that to set up the progressed charts, you begin by using the consonants of the name on the personality line. Start with the first consonant and project it ahead through the years according to its numerical value. In this case, James starts with J and the value is 1. Therefore, J covers the year number 1. Next comes M, which governs the next four years up to age five. The pattern is repeated with the consonants in all three or more names: first, middle, and last names (adding Junior, in this case).

The same procedure is applied next to the vowels along the soul line. Start with the first vowel, give it the numerical value appropriate; then proceed through the remaining vowels in each name: first, middle, and last.

Next compute the life number (the personal year of birth). Then extend the line for the personal years.

Finally, the essence value is attained by adding the numerical values of the letter of the personality, soul, and personal year together. Do this for each year on the chart. Once you have completed each line, the chart is ready for evaluation.

INTERPRETING THE PROGRESSED CHART

Now you are ready to read each year's full meaning. Usually, it is easiest to start with the qualities of the letter in the personality line, delineating one year at a time. Some reference to the letters' meanings in the progressed chart are in the chapter, Symbology of Letters. You will want to establish your own shades of meaning, adding personal life experience and your private accumulation of numerical knowledge. The descriptions given are guidelines. They are by no means complete or inflexible.

Next, evaluate the individual meaning for the letter in the soul line.

You will then want to take into consideration the influence of the personal year.

Perhaps the single most important indicator is the essence number. The essence number reflects the total influences for the year and sheds considerable light upon its meaning for growth and unfoldment. How one responds to the essence number will have considerable bearing—as an indicator—to his or her growth pattern.

Campbell and Jordan have given some attention to the interpretation of the essence number. This approach hopefully updates the best of both. Competence in working the essence numbers take individual practice and much time; develop your own style and meanings. Therefore, it could be more of an interference than a benefit to describe the essence completely. Your own background (both personal and professional) will provide this personal perspective.

Practical experience plus the development of intuitive confidence should be complementary tools.

As a beginner you may prefer to use the concepts of this writer exclusively. Just review the various sections pertaining to the number desired, and you will find your own understanding emerging clearly.

This book includes much specific psychological theory and material. The more clinical concepts have been written to avoid complex professional language.

As an adjunct to interpretation, you can see that essence numbers are strong indicators. When the essence number is 1, the lesson and challenge relates to tests of will and individuality; when 2, the tests will be related to co-operation, self, and social criticism; when 3, creativity and sexuality; when 4, work, discipline, and determination, when 5, sensual temptation, prejudice, ability to expand; when 6, responsibility, marriage, service; when 7, withdrawal, arrogance, denial of higher self; when 8, power, money, authority; when 9, altruism, release, completion.

The progressed chart is particularly useful when reviewing the formative years of childhood. A trained observer easily recognizes the traumatic years in the chart. And, using his innate or professional abilities, he or she works with the client to bring into conscious acceptance memories and experience which may have been repressed, forgotten, or denied. Needless to say, "caution" should be the code word when digging into subconscious territories. Specific clues as to the origin of trauma can often be ascertained by looking for numerical patterns in early childhood. Are there patterns similar to one occurring during a particularly powerful, difficult, or challenging year in adulthood?

If Carter's chart is progressed on out to the election year of 1976, you will notice the personality letter is R, the soul letter is E, and the personal year is 7. The essence adds up to 21, which becomes 3. This exact pattern had previously occurred at age seven. A detailed investigation of events in his life (conscious and unconscious) at that age would very likely yield definitive keys in understanding his motive for Presidency and the formation of attitudes that influence his decision making in office.

When the essence number is 6 or 9 in particular, there is a probability of emotional trauma in your childhood. This may not always be true, but in almost every instance in my work, a deeper probe revealed experiences that were still very much hidden. If professionally trained or intuitively guided, you will discover many more facets of human understanding.

THE REGRESSED CHART

Many times throughout this book, effort has been made to uncover and assess subconscious tendencies and the origins of subconscious conflicts. An early question from beginners is: How can one more effectively locate these undercurrents using numerology?

In answer, came a whole new phase of interpretation that has proven to be quite rewarding in its effectiveness in reaching prenatal influences. This device should be of invaluable assistance to psychiatrists, clinical psychologists, and other professional counselors—people already knowledgeable of subconscious processes and wanting a tool which quickly yields probable patterns of conflict.

The regressed chart is, simply, the opposite of the progressed chart. By using the date of birth as a starting point, you calculate back nine months to determine the numerical climate at the time of conception. With short term or premature pregnancies, the month of conception is still usually determinable when the length of pregnancy is known.

From this regressed chart, a determination can be made of the personal year and personal month of conception. This tells the climate into which consciousness originated on this plane. Very powerful keys to likely undercurrents within self appear in this chart.

You may ask: why the moment of conception? A general theory in reincarnation philosophy is that the soul enters the mother's aura at the moment of conception. The author subscribes to this based upon reports from his subjects resulting from years of conducting non-hypnotic prenatal and past life regressions.

The incoming child has very acute awareness of the physical, emotional, and mental framework of the parents-to-be. The soul records these hopes, fears, wishes, anxieties, and expectations immediately. An indelible mark upon subconscious patterns is made.

By knowing the numerical climate of conception, one can in most cases, determine possible undercurrents which will develop as the child ages. This is especially true when a comparison is made of parents' charts, taking into account the interpersonal stress patterns for their personal years and personal months. Also, between their personality and soul numbers.

Because this number deals almost completely with subconscious currents, the utmost tact and intuitive guidance should be employed so as to handle this material competently and humanely. If doubt exists, perhaps you should best not work with another's chart quite yet. Use your own chart to see the meaning and how this works. Then try it with your own family and children. If you are to use this for counseling purposes, you will be shown from within when and how best to understand this technique.

Let me illustrate by example how beneficial this regressed chart *can* be. This chart is of a child whose parents are known by me. Obviously, this is an important factor in finding the true guidelines in the regressed chart.

The child was conceived in an 8 personal month of a 4 personal year. In the progressed chart one parent was in a 9 vibration on the personality level, a 9 on the soul level, a 3 personal year, and essence of 3. The other parent was in an 8 vibration of the personality, 1 soul, 7 personal year, and an essence of 7. The personal months were 7 and 2. The interpersonal stress pattern numbers for the year are as follows: Personality 9-8 *(1)*, Soul 9-1 *(8)*, Personal Year 3-7 *(4)*, Essence 3-7 *(4)*, and *personal months* 7-2 *(5)*.

At the time the child was conceived, the mother was working at a job in which she was beginning to become disenchanted and weary. The father's work at the time was unsteady, which placed a strain upon both parents, when thinking of the coming child to support. The child was conceived in its 4 personal year and has a 4 soul number. The child has come to fulfill an important work of the soul and could face strong resistance in finding that goal because of sensitivity, possibly guilt, for feeling like a burden and putting pressure upon the parents' already tentative work situations. Interestingly, the father's work kept him away often and for long periods of time; so the child's early memories could include resentment of the father's work.

The difference between the parents' soul number at the time was 8, which pinpoints the disagreement over spiritual beliefs and their attitudes toward higher authority. The schism likely created confusion in the child toward authority; this will likely create chaos in early adulthood, but should sharpen his discernment with maturity.

The 1 interpersonal stress number on the personality level that year describes the strong clash of wills between partners. The child shows an uncharacteristically strong will. Obviously there will be much to learn before channeling it constructively. The stress number, from comparing the parents' personal months, was 5. The desire at the time was freedom; the birth made freedom less likely even if the marriage did improve. This leaves an impression on the soul and could create an insecurity and lack of identity which may very well manifest near puberty and in early adult years.

By knowing these conditions, the parents now have an opportunity to work out their own conflicts more easily.

More importantly, by having conscious knowledge of the child's inclinations, they can work to reduce the likelihood of severe problems developing in the child's personality.

Hopefully, this example benefits your understanding of the regressed chart. It should be evident that this source of interpretation can be invaluable when used with positive motivation and altruistic resolve in dealing with self-conflicts, not to mention helping others to recognize their own. At base, the example I have given is the message of the entire book: "Know what to expect, and work that knowledge for advancement".

X

CHANGES IN YOUR NAME

Many questions arise concerning the effect of name changes during life. Hopefully, yours will be answered in this chapter. Nicknames, marriage names, and professional or stage names all activate new qualities in our experiential interplay.

The name at birth is analogous to the natal chart in astrology; its influence extends throughout the life. We may put on different outer garments, but at the core is still oneself. This does not mean that the significance of a new name is nil. Rather, the new name reveals specific qualities. When choosing a new name, give consideration to the natal chart or birth name. Does the new name overload or overlook qualities that need to be experienced? . . . Does it help balance out your growth patterns? The numbers for soul, personality, and integrated self remain in effect even when the name is changed. These are foundations from which the new qualities emerge. Following are some terms and delineative methods of use when working with names other than those given at birth.

THE OUTER YOU

To establish the number of the outer-you, just add the consonants together and reduce to a single digit, excepting higher octave numbers. This applies to any names used other than the full name at birth.

The outer-you number signifies the face you present to the public at large. Consider this the garment of your self—

the garment by which friends and strangers alike will identify you.

To get a better idea of qualities associated with the outer-you, reread appropriate personality numbers in Chapter Five. The personality number and outer self are not the same. There is, however, enough similarity for purposes of describing behavior. The outer-you tells what you're projecting currently, as an extension of the personality.

THE INNER YOU

The number of the inner-you is obtained by adding the sum of the vowels together and reducing it to a single digit, excepting master numbers. This applies to any name used, other than the full name at birth.

The number of the inner-you reveals how you incorporate experience into the soul. It reveals how you see yourself (not always accurately), and how you would like to be seen by others. To get a better feel for this number, use the interpretations for karmic accumulation numbers from Chapter Six. They are not exactly the same in meaning, but the karmic accumulation comes close to capturing the behavorial aspects of this number. This is the internal and introspective side of your behavior.

THE ACCOMPLISHED YOU

By now you have probably figured out that the number for the accomplished-you is computed by adding up all letters in the name being used. Reduce them to a single digit (except for master numbers).

This number is indicative of your name-nurtured accomplishments at the time. It defines, gives dimension to, your goals and aspirations. Get a better idea of the effect of this number by reading the descriptions for the same soul number in Chapter Five. The drive is not quite the same as the soul's; yet, the idealism of the desire to achieve approximates soul dynamics. For example, suppose a woman's birth

name was "Jane Smith." Then she married and used the
name Jane S. Jones. The accomplished number becomes 4.
Perhaps she married for material security. With this number, the suggestion is that she has chosen a marriage which
will somehow put her back into a situation of working on
her own to develop personal stamina and perseverance.
Not necessarily divorce, but something is lying quiet which
will one day make her more nearly self-sufficient. Let us
say, for another example, that a woman's married name
comes out an 8 accomplished-self number. This suggests
she will encounter considerable challenge dealing with
authority. This could be because of a dogmatic and critical
husband who constantly belittles her every mental effort;
undermining her beliefs and self-confidence. Having chosen
this number she will attract a husband or marital situation
which will put pressure upon her need to be herself and
stand confidently upon her own self-established belief system of authority.

In the name "Jimmy Carter", we see some noteworthy
perspectives in comparison to his natal chart name at birth.

```
J I M M Y     C A R T E R
1 9 4 4 7     3 1 9 2 5 9
    25 = 7        29 = 11     Accomplished You = 18 = 9
    16 = 7         6 =  6     Outer You        = 13 = 4
     9 = 9        23 =  5     Inner You        = 14 = 5
```

A quick glance shows that this name brings an aspiration to fulfill his deepest dreams, or perhaps great disappointment. Specifically, an idealism is suggested in his
hopes which sometimes may not be lived fully. His inner
self wants to be universally accepted, and he sees himself
as "all things to all people." The outer man will work very
hard and tenaciously (sometimes obstinately) for what he
feels to be right. He should be careful about overworking
himself.

In my work I have many times been asked to select new names for entertainers, professional groups, businesses, and the like. My approach has been to first determine the real motives and goals of the client. I need next to know the client's own perspective on the new name-image. Then the name is mutually developed, so its vocal rhythms and numerological components harmonize. The knack is to help the client recognize and express that true intent.

Recent university research has demonstrated that people form certain opinions about others according to names; for example, people respond differently to Jimmy than to James. Or they expect different behavior from a Jane rather than Sara Lou. It will be fascinating to see if the numerology of names is someday accepted.

XI

YIN-YANG, SEXUALITY, MALE-FEMALE POLARITY

Throughout this volume there has been constant reference to three primal forces: activity, receptivity, and equilibrium or balance. The yang energy, also called assertive or activity energy, has been characterized as masculine. The receptive, intuitive, or yin is feminine in nature. The interplay of these two rhythms throughout all levels of cosmos and universe creates the basis of all life.

Humanity today is once again awakening to the fact that we all individually possess male and female qualities. A female has a dormant male side; a male has a dormant female side. Carl Jung worked toward understanding of this dichotomy through his concept of the anima in men and the animus in women. Part of our preparation for the New Age should be establishment of conscious harmony with these two life forces. And the signs of awakening multiply daily. Women are becoming more assertive and demanding their rights; at the same time, men can choose the length of hair, brighter ranges of colors, and more varieties of grooming aids. They are also more able to express feelings and emotions. These are just minor outer indicators of role change and balance.

As a general descriptive guideline, the qualities of the male polarity expressed in our society today are assertive, aggressive, intellectual, logical, self-reliant. And man traditionally serves as provider.

The qualities of the female polarity as they are expressed in our society today are creative, intuitive, emotional, and supportive. And the woman traditionally provides the nurturing role: wife and mother.

Women's liberation has made it—in some respects—easier today for a woman to comfortably express her male characteristics. Society has not made it as easy for men to demonstrate their femininity. There has been a locker room stigma of equating effeminate leanings in males as being indicative of homosexuality causing a primary reason for male uneasiness in the role evolution. Now that attitudes are changing and homosexuality is out in the open, there is a better climate for men to accept the female (anima) within. In many instances, women have pushed the male side so far that they are in essence repolarizing, denying their femininity. At the other extreme, a man who denies the female aspect diminishes his effectiveness as a male—not protects it. It is important that opposite polarity expression be understood as a natural evolutionary pattern. Too often people equate this with homosexual tendencies. The two are not related. In some instances misunderstanding of the two patterns relates to one's sexual preference for the same sex. The male-female synthesis and expression is perhaps an area of study which will become most important in psychological studies in the near future. It is a must if the field of psychology is going to assist mankind in the transition to the New Age.

Contrary to some popular thinking, men and women are *not* equal. Each complements the other, and both are necessary for life on all planes in all worlds. Well, you might ask; what does all this have to do with numbers?

Plenty. The numbers at birth can be quite revealing of potential for evaluating how the client deals with the male-female polarities.

In application to human dynamics in our current culture, the numbers 1, 4, 7, and 8 are more masculine in their expression. The numbers 2, 3, 6, and 9 are basically more feminine in their expression through current human behavior. The number 5 is universal to life, and at its best can go unequivocally both ways.

Women with the male numbers 1, 4, 7, and 8 prominent in the chart will often subconsciously (or even obviously) identify with their fathers and/or male qualities. Many times when this occurs the male identification is held to subconscious (or conscious) denial of self and that is — being a woman. Let me give a very specific example from my work. In approximately 70% of the cases when counseling a woman with an eight life number, the client was the second or third child, preceded by an older sister(s). The parents (usually the father more intensely) in most cases were wishing for a boy (subconsciously or very obviously). The daughter, therefore, at the moment of conception, felt rejected for being female. She then attempts (consciously or probably subconsciously) to become that boy (in many outer male patterns,) and win Daddy's approval and love. She may possess tremendous drive and executive ability which enables her to become quite accomplished . . . a very positive expression. She is also, in many ways, ahead of her female peers who have not developed self-sufficiency.

But, there is the need to work at accepting the female qualities of intuition, emotion, etc. Most important is the need to accept herself on all levels for what she is — a woman! One polarity does not displace the other; both are needed to work harmoniously.

Men with the female numbers (2, 3, 6, 9) prominent often show a strong maternal identification — and creative, intuitive, and emotional temperaments. A man becomes more masculine by using intuition and sensitivity along with his intellect and drive. Intuition can be a lifesaver when quick decisions are needed and little analytical or factual material exists. As these two polarities become rebalanced, eons of time down the line, we shall once again be complete units within the self — androgynous, hermaphroditic, angelic-like, divine beings.

XII

SETTING UP A CHART

```
R I C H A R D     M I L H O U S     N I X O N
9 9 3 8 1 9 4     4 9 3 8 6 3 1     5 9 6 6 5

    43  =  7          34  =  7          31  =  4

    33  =  33(6)      16  =  7          16  =  7

    10  =  1          18  =  9          15  =  6
```

Integrated Self (IS) = 18 = 9

Personality (P) = 20 = 2

Soul (S) = 16 = 7

```
    1          9          1913

    1          9          5
```

Life Number (LN) = 15 = 6

```
                    3rd
                     ⑤
                    △6
                    4th
                    △6
                    3rd
  ①    △1      △5    ⑨
        1st    2nd
 1st            2nd
```

○ = Triune Cycles

△ = Pinnacles

Karmic Lessons = -2, -7

Karmic Accumulation Number = 9 (2 + 7)

Planes of Expression

P	D	M		2
E	RIR	IOS	IXO	9
M	HA	LH	NN	6
I	C	U		2

19 (Letters)

INTRAPERSONAL STRESS NUMBERS

2 - 9 (7)	2 - 6 (4)
2 - 7 (5)	6 - 7 (1)
7 - 9 (2)	6 - 9 (3)

PROGRESSED CHART

Age	0	1	2	3	4	5	6	7	8	9	
Personality		R	R	R	R	R	R	R	R	R	
Soul		I	I	I	I	I	I	I	I		
Personal Yr.	6	7	8	9	1	2	3	4	5	6	
Essence		7	8	9	1	2	3	22	5	6	
Calendar Yr.	13	14	15	16	17	18	19	20	21	22	

Age	10	11	12	13	14	15	16	17	18	19	20
Personality	C	C	C	H	H	H	H	H	H	H	H
Soul	A	I	I	I	I	I	I	I	I	I	O
Personal Yr.	7	8	9	1	2	3	4	5	6	7	8
Essence	11	2	3	9	1	2	3	4	5	6	22
Calendar Yr.	23	24	25	26	27	28	29	30	31	32	33

PUBLIC NAME

R I C H A R D   N I X O N
9 9 3 8 1 9 4   5 9 6 6 5

    43 = 7   31 = 4

    33 = 33 (6)   16 = 7

    10 = 1   15 = 6

Accomplished You   = 11 = 11

Outer You   = 13 = 4

Inner You   =   7 = 7

Now refer to the appropriate interpretations in the book to determine if the descriptions seem fitting to you.

EPILOGUE

I started this book with the intention of delivering a few specific and personal insights on the subject of numbers. Like any writer, I was confident that my words would both enlighten and entertain the reading audience. Now it is time for you to gauge the success of my aspirations.

Before I was even half finished with the manuscript you hold, I discovered that there was much more to be said than I had preplanned. The writing stopped; I returned to research the avenues which were newly visible. It took time, but I have gloried in the new learning. And I have every hope that my efforts benefit you as keenly. Much of the specifics herein are from my twelve career years in numerological study, teaching, and personal counseling. Portions of the interpretations are — as you know by having read this far — more nearly channeled or inspired.

I have supported the interpretations as fully as possible with data from accumulated charts, files, and investigations in the field. But no study is complete; there *can* be no last word in a field dealing with evolving intuitive mentality. Sincere seekers will research beyond this moment and beyond this book. I would not have it otherwise.

Even at the moment of completion I can look back at parts that I would not write the same way today. To give in to the temptation to revise would trap me into a project ever cyclical, no end possible. Therefore, you must judge only what you hold. What shortcomings you see, I trust, will be offset by the strengths. Some critics will say it is too brief; others will deride my longwindedness. Again, you

259

are the judge. No one has the resources to be completely encyclopedic on numerology. I have tried simply to write what research has proven and intuition has revealed. Interestingly enough, since the material in this book was completed, I have reentered graduate school to complete work beyond my Masters Degree in Psychology. In a recent course on psychological testing I have done some initial work correlating numerological evaluation with those compiled from profiles using psychological tests, particularly personality tests such as the 16-PF and Omnibus Personality Inventory (OPI). So far the results have been very encouraging and the correlation quite favorable which may open a new field of evaluation and counseling possibilities for professionals and laymen alike.

The interpretative descriptions are possessed of highly emotional impact; some are at first discouraging or depressing. These psychological facets of subconscious patterns are not meant to be upsetting, much like one feels after reading a text on abnormal psychology and finding all of the descriptions applying to you. Or the effect can be likened to the plight of the medical student who puts down his first text on internal medicine . . . he suddenly realizes he has been dying of at least nine major diseases for all his life. Rather than have you moan over suspected symptoms, I would have you use these descriptions to define consciousness and work through the inhibiting qualities by transmuting them into growth patterns.

This text is written in hopes you come to recognize qualities within which can be transformed or eliminated. You have chosen the moment to see your inevitable evolution. It is now.

I mentioned in the Preface two books which are excellent texts on the subject of numerology. Florence Campbell brought much soul insight to the field, as well as her clues to karmic trends in the chart. Juno Jordan's lengthy research and detailed study of numbers has also been an influence on my work. I have moved from the site of their attentions to new ground, so the serious reader may want to look back to their work. I have spent little time on areas covered by these authors, so you can benefit by giving these and other texts your attention. My primary intent has been to bring the cosmological, metaphysical, and psychological attributes of numbers to the consciousness of this New Age. Particularly, I hope to show *you* newly-lit avenues into the soul.

Some people hold grave and logical doubts about the notion of linear reincarnation, one life following another. I have used it primarily to illustrate the cause-effect implication of reincarnation rather than to perpetuate the linear concept itself. The karmic attributes given here are also in accord with the notions of coexistent reality.

How can you truly know when a chart is well-balanced? A well-balanced chart has a relatively even distribution of numbers. Or it is a chart whose numbers, though missing from the name, appear in the primary areas of personality, soul, and life number. The balanced chart may simply consist of compatible numbers which focus the skills or personality. Or, finally, it may contain master numbers with elements to support and focus them. With some practice you will see charts that simply glow with unity and direction.

A word of warning: Segmented or selective reading is of little value until it is put into the perspective of a complete chart. Just as in astrology, you must look at all parts in relation to the whole. *Be wary* of overreaction to isolated segments.

It can be mystifying to study the move from personality to soul, and then soul to integrated self. Those of you who study in theosophy or teachings dealing with the seven major initiations may find a relation herein to those seven stages. I feel that the complete transition from personality to soul-centered consciousness approximates the phases of entering and culminating the third initiation (see *The Initiation of the World* by Vera Stanley Alder). The later phases — dealing purely from the Integrated Self — approximate preparation for the fourth initiation. If you already know the initiation schools, you know also how few of us have so far progressed. You know also that now is the time for a mass evolution to qualify many more and pass them through their higher rites.

By having read this far, I hope that you are at peace with the book; can you now lay your hand across its open pages, content that these words have given meaning to you? Using numerology in daily life, we see all the more clearly lessons and applications. We awaken from personality to cycles of the soul, and then we begin to function on a higher level of symbolic guidance and wisdom. Inevitably, at that point, we attune to cosmic and universal cycles and rhythms adding to awareness of the divine spark within our being.

The next step is to consciously work with cosmic evolution; eventually you become a co-creator, working in your corner of the cosmos. Will you take this as a guidebook? Let it guide you through this part of your earthly sojourn toward divine destiny. The planetary, universal, and cosmic spirals lie ahead. May the Light be your companion along the Path. May cosmic attainment one day be yours.

KNOW YE NOT THAT YE ARE GODS?!!